Allen Upward

The Queen Against Owen

Allen Upward

The Queen Against Owen

ISBN/EAN: 9783337321918

Printed in Europe, USA, Canada, Australia, Japan

Cover: Foto ©ninafisch / pixelio.de

More available books at **www.hansebooks.com**

THE QUEEN AGAINST OWEN

BY
ALLEN UPWARD
AUTHOR OF 'THE PRINCE OF BALKISTAN'

A NEW EDITION

London
CHATTO & WINDUS, PICCADILLY
1895

To
CLEMENT HARLEY DOWNS
ESQUIRE

THIS SLIGHT ACKNOWLEDGMENT OF HIS KIND SERVICES
IS TENDERED BY THE AUTHOR

NOTE
TO THE SECOND EDITION.

I TAKE the opportunity of a second edition of this little sketch to point out a rather curious fact in connection with the numerous comments which were made in the press on the evidence presented against the heroine. My object in writing the story was, naturally, to so balance the evidence as to leave it open to my jury to return either verdict, and thus keep the reader in a state of mild suspense during the progress of the trial. How far I succeeded may be gathered from the following extracts:

'*A jury that required to deliberate at all in such a case ought to have been hanged.*'—BRIEF.

'*The way in which the feeblest of cases is worked up to a verdict of guilty is a trifle ridiculous, and a slander on judge, bar, and even jury.*'—LEEDS MERCURY.

'*It is absurd to suppose that upon such evidence any judge and jury could have convicted her of murder.*'—VANITY FAIR.

'*A tangle of circumstantial evidence which is supposed to be conclusive, but on which we feel confident that no English jury would convict.*'—NEW ZEALAND MAIL.

NOTE TO THE SECOND EDITION

'*The prisoner is found guilty on what seems to us most insufficient evidence.*'—DAILY CHRONICLE.

'*It is difficult to believe that the jury on the evidence could have brought in a verdict of guilty.*'—DAILY NEWS.

'*The evidence being purely circumstantial, as well as flimsy.*' —ACADEMY.

[N.B.—Several of the above reviewers were friendly to the book on other points.]

'*In Scotland the verdict would certainly have been "Not Proven."*'—GLASGOW HERALD.

'*Though the evidence is purely circumstantial, it seems at first sight so strong that no magistrate could fail to commit.*' —SATURDAY REVIEW.

'*The evidence of guilt is very strong.*'—MONMOUTHSHIRE BEACON.

'*Certainly the evidence, purely circumstantial, is very strong.*' —PUBLISHER'S CIRCULAR.

'*A case of circumstantial evidence which all seemed to point one way, and to fix a horrible crime upon a young girl.*'— WEEKLY SUN.

'*The evidence against her is damning, though purely circumstantial.*'—LITERARY WORLD.

These extracts, taken together, seem to me to throw a most interesting light upon the subject of trial by jury—the object of a sneer in one of the above quotations. When it is possible for a number of educated minds, engaged in highly intellectual pursuits, to take such opposite views of the same set of facts, it may surely be urged that, if miscarriages of justice occasionally take place, they are due, not so much to any defects in our judicial system, as to those native diversities of the human mind which no legislation can remove. A change is fast coming over our legal procedure in the direction of dispensing with juries, and leaving everything to the decision of a single trained lawyer. Whether this change is certain to ensure greater correctness of decision is, perhaps, more open to argument than is generally supposed.

In conclusion, I have only to express my thanks for the many cordial notices—some of them, I fear, hardly deserved—which this rather slight work received on its first appearance. The kindness of his reviewers has at all events encouraged the author to strive that his future work may be a little better worth their attention.

A. U.

May, 1895.

CONTENTS

CHAPTER		PAGE
I.	THE INDICTMENT	1
II.	THE BRIEF FOR THE PROSECUTION	2
III.	COUNSEL FOR THE DEFENCE	23
IV.	THE ASSIZES	44
V.	THE CASE FOR THE CROWN	68
VI.	THE WITNESSES	85
VII.	HALF AN HOUR	113
VIII.	THE DEFENCE	127
IX.	THE JUDGE	154
X.	THE VERDICT	175
XI.	THE PRISONER'S STATEMENT	192
XII.	THE C.C.R.	212
XIII.	UNDER THE GREAT SEAL	229

THE
QUEEN AGAINST OWEN

CHAPTER I.

THE INDICTMENT.

'MYNYDDSHIRE TO WIT.—The jurors for our lady the Queen upon their oath present that Eleanor Margaret Owen, upon the first day of June in the year of our Lord eighteen hundred and eighty-nine, feloniously, wilfully, and of her malice aforethought did kill and murder one Ann Elizabeth Lewis against the peace of our lady the Queen, her crown and dignity.'

CHAPTER II.

THE BRIEF FOR THE PROSECUTION.

'A BRIEF for you, sir, for the assizes at Abertaff. The great murder case.'

Mr. Prescott looked up as his clerk entered, and heard these words. Then he silently put out his hand and took the brief, while the clerk retired into the outer room of the chambers to make a note of the fee.

Everyone had heard of the great Porthstone murder. Mr. Prescott had followed the papers pretty closely in their accounts of it—the discovery, the proceedings at the inquest, before the magistrates, and so on. The brief did not take him altogether by surprise. He had been entrusted with several important prosecutions before this, and the solicitor representing the Crown in the present case was a personal friend of his own. He had, therefore, all along had expectations of appearing in the case, and his only doubt had been whether, on account of its unusual importance, a Queen's Counsel would be engaged along with him, or whether he would have the charge of the case himself.

It need hardly be added that Mr. Prescott was still a member of the 'Junior Bar,' that is to say, he had not arrived at the dignity of a Queen's Counsel. But he had been some ten years in the practice of his profession, and occupied a foremost position among the members of the Southern Circuit. Tall, thin, and auburn-haired, with a ruddy complexion, his appearance was rather remarkable among the brethren of the long robe. But he had a pattern lawyer's face, with the firm decided chin, the pronounced nose and strongly-marked eyebrows characteristic of the race.

Before opening the document in his hand, he took a hasty glance at the outside. It bore the usual endorsement. At the head were the words 'MYNYDDSHIRE SUMMER ASSIZES, *Holden at* ABERTAFF, 29th July, 1889.'

Then followed the name of the case: 'REGINA, *on the Prosecution of Sergeant Evans*, against ELEANOR MARGARET OWEN,' and the description of the offence: '*For Wilful Murder*.'

Next came the word 'Brief' in very large letters. '*For the Prosecution:* Mr. Chas. Prescott, 20 guineas.'

And a little below, on one side, 'With you, Mr. F. J. Pollard.' This was a younger man, who was to act as junior to Prescott.

Last of all came the solicitors' name at the foot, 'Pollard and Pollard, Abertaff.' They were, as may be surmised, relations of the young gentleman who had been favoured with the junior brief.

Mr. Prescott smiled pleasantly at the number of guineas, and sardonically at the name of the counsel whose assistance he was to receive. Then, pulling off the tape, he unfolded the document, and settled down to a study of its contents.

It was headed inside by the same words as appeared in the endorsement, down to 'wilful murder.' After that it went on to give a copy of the indictment.

Then came the narrative itself:

'CASE FOR THE PROSECUTION.

'In this case the prisoner, Eleanor Margaret Owen, is charged with the wilful murder of Ann Elizabeth Lewis.

'The facts of the case are as follows:

'The deceased, Miss Ann Lewis, was a maiden lady, living at Porthstone, in Mynyddshire, a quiet little seaside place about twenty miles from the county town, Abertaff.

'Her only surviving relative was a nephew, John Lewis, who had been for a considerable time in Australia, but, having made some money, returned to England, and arrived at Porthstone on the evening of the first of June.

'The accused, Eleanor Margaret Owen, is an orphan, her father, the late Rector of Porthstone having died two years ago.'

('Poor old Owen! I remember him well,' murmured the barrister. 'It's well for the poor old chap that he is gone.')

'Immediately on her father's death she went to reside with Miss Lewis, with whom her father and herself had been on friendly terms, in the capacity of a paid companion.

'She was paid £24 a year, and had no other means of support; but Rebecca, a servant in the house, will say that she has heard Miss Lewis promise to remember the accused in her will.

'Deceased was rather eccentric in money matters, and invested a large portion of her savings in valuable jewels. No one ever saw the collection; but William Williams, a jeweller, of Abertaff, will swear that he supplied deceased with something like a thousand pounds' worth of jewels annually for several years past.

'It will be seen below that these jewels have entirely disappeared since the night of the murder.

'Counsel will observe that a motive is here suggested for the crime.

'On the night of the first of June last Mr. Lewis, deceased's nephew, left the house about 10 o'clock and did not return that night.

'Shortly after he was gone deceased was heard to retire by the servants. These are four in number, and consist of a butler or general man, cook, housemaid, and parlourmaid.

'The three women servants went to rest at a quarter past ten, and the butler at half-past.

'All this time prisoner was downstairs in the drawing-room, where she had spent the evening with deceased and Mr. Lewis.

'About eleven the butler thinks he heard her come upstairs to her bedroom, which adjoined deceased's, with a door of communication between. This door was never locked or bolted.

'An hour afterwards Rebecca, the parlourmaid, woke from sleep, and heard a stifled groan somewhere below. Apparently it proceeded from Miss Lewis's room. She did not waken the housemaid, who sleeps in the same room. She attributed the sound at the time to troubled sleep.

'Shortly afterwards she heard a subdued sound, as if of footsteps going downstairs. She was not alarmed, as she thought she recognised Miss Owen's tread. She therefore roused no one, but, inspired by curiosity, got up herself, put on some things, and crept downstairs.

'All the doors were closed as she passed. She listened outside Miss Owen's room, but heard nothing. Just then she thought she heard the front door pulled gently to. She went cautiously down, and discovered that all the bolts had been undone, and the door was fastened simply by the latch.

'Three persons carried a latch-key—Miss Lewis, the butler, and Miss Owen. One of the three had, therefore, gone out. Having ascertained this, she retired to her room.'

('Now we're coming to something like evidence,' remarked Mr. Prescott, as he made copious interlineations with a blue pencil. 'That's the worst of Pollard; he always will write in this florid style. His brother's speeches are just the same.')

'She did not go to sleep, however. She lay awake listening for some time, and then she heard footsteps ascending and going into one of the bedrooms below. Her room was immediately above that of deceased.

'In about ten minutes more, to employ the witness's own expression, the footsteps came out again and descended to the hall for the second time. The parlourmaid now awaked the housemaid, Lucy, who slept in the room with her, and they both sat up and listened.

'The footsteps sounded heavier this time; the witnesses describe them as "thumpy." Counsel will see that this would be the natural result of someone carrying a heavy load.

'This time neither of the servants made any attempt to follow or observe what was taking place. They say they heard the hall door softly pulled to, but nothing more.

'Shortly afterwards they both fell asleep.

'The same night, about 12 o'clock, a fisherman of the place, named Evan Thomas, was coming up from the beach. He had been doing some night fishing.

'As he got on to the esplanade he observed the figure of a woman walking swiftly away from him in the direction of Newton Bay. He knows prisoner well, and believes it was she he saw.

'There is no further evidence as to what occurred that night.

'In the morning the housemaid Lucy was the first down, as was usually the case. *She found the hall door locked and bolted, as the butler left it at half-past ten the night before.*

'One of the household, therefore, must have

been out, and returned after the witness Rebecca had gone back to her room.

'Putting these facts together, it is clear that the only possible authors of the crime subsequently discovered must have been the butler, who had a latch-key, and prisoner.

'At eight o'clock the witness Rebecca came down and took two jugs of hot water to the ladies' doors. She knocked at each. She heard a faint reply from prisoner, but none from deceased's room.

'At half-past eight prisoner usually came down, and deceased was generally seen a few minutes after.

'On this morning, the second of June, neither of them had appeared by nine o'clock.

'The witness Rebecca then remembered that Miss Lewis had not answered when called, and feared that she had failed to waken her. She therefore went upstairs and knocked again.

'There was no answer. Becoming alarmed, because her mistress was old and had once suffered from some seizure, she went to Miss Owen's door and knocked impatiently.

'Prisoner at once came and opened it. She was

completely dressed, and apparently ready to come down.

'The following conversation, or something near it, then took place:

'The witness Rebecca began by saying that she had knocked at Miss Lewis's door, but could get no answer. "Do you know if anything's the matter?" she said.

'Prisoner heard her without any appearance of surprise, and merely answered:

'"No; we had better call to her, and if she doesn't answer, I'll go in."

'They then went together to the door on the landing, and prisoner called out loudly: "Miss Lewis! May I come in?"

'There was again no answer. Prisoner then put her hand to the door and turned the handle. The door, however, would not open. It was locked, and the key was inside.

'The only possible access, therefore, was through prisoner's own room.

'It is unnecessary to draw counsel's attention to the gravity of this circumstance.'

('Quite unnecessary,' said Prescott sarcastically

to himself. 'Bless my soul, how he piles on the agony!')

'By this time the other servants in the house had taken the alarm. The butler, John Simons, came on the scene, followed by the cook and housemaid. It was he who now addressed prisoner:

'"We must get in through your room, miss," he said.

'It may be well to state here that Simons had lived with the deceased for fifteen years, and was greatly trusted.

'He now went straight into prisoner's bedroom. Prisoner now seemed thoroughly alarmed, and ran in after him, the three women coming next.

'As he was about to take hold of the handle of the door opening into Miss Lewis's room, he suddenly beheld a sight that made him reel back. This was a smear of blood on the china handle. The witness Rebecca caught sight of it at the same time, and uttered a loud scream.

'No one noticed the demeanour of the prisoner at the moment of this discovery. But when they had recovered sufficiently to take notice, she was leaning against a chest of drawers, deathly pale.'

('Confound the man!' exclaimed the reader, as he came to this sentence. 'How he does go on against her! It's enough to make me think her innocent. Poor little Eleanor! It's five years since I saw her. She was a pretty little thing of fifteen then. I wonder what sort of woman she has turned out. Well, well, I must stick to business.')

'Simons quickly recovered his presence of mind. Taking hold of the handle so as to avoid touching the smear, he burst open the door, and rushed in towards the bed.

'The bed was empty.

'It seemed to have been slept in the night before, and the clothes were not much disarranged; but on the lower sheet, close to the bolster, was a large stain of blood.

'The stain was about the size of a cheese-plate, dark in the centre, and fainter round the edge. There was no other trace of violence.

'The room was then searched. All present took part in the search except prisoner, who sat in a chair looking on.

'Deceased's clothes, worn by her the day before,

were found in their proper places, thus negativing the idea that she could have gone away herself. Her nightdress, on the other hand, was missing. This would point to the prisoner's having killed her in her sleep and disposed of the body as it was.

'No further trace of violence was discovered in the room. The butler then got them all out, and locked both doors on the outside. He then went for the police.

'This was about half-past nine. On his way to the police-station he met Mr. Lewis, deceased's nephew. He stopped him and related the circumstances.

'Mr. Lewis was greatly upset. As soon as he was able to speak he pointed out that the only possible author of the crime was Miss Owen. He turned and accompanied Simons to the police-station.

'At the police-station they found Sergeant James Evans. To him Simons detailed the incidents already described. Mr. Lewis then stepped forward and said:

'"I charge Eleanor Owen with the murder of my aunt, Ann Elizabeth Lewis. I have made some money, and, please God, I'll spend every penny of it rather than my poor aunt shall remain unavenged."'

('All this is not evidence,' muttered the barrister, impatiently scoring out the paragraph with his pencil. 'Why does Pollard put in things like this? Perhaps it supplies a clue, though, to his enthusiasm,' added Mr. Prescott thoughtfully. 'I dare say he's got this Lewis behind him, and is bleeding him pretty freely. That accounts for the figures on my brief, so I oughtn't to complain. But I wish to goodness it were anybody but old Owen's daughter. Why, I can remember kissing her when she was only six years old.')

'Sergeant Evans, who will be called as a witness, now proceeded to the house and made a thorough search. Two important facts were now discovered.

'The butler had left the house by the back door, but on returning with Mr. Lewis the party entered by the front. Simons stepped forward with his latch-key to open the door, but found the latch already lifted, and stuck fast in its raised position.

'This was a thing which always occurred if the latch was lifted too high. The keyhole is shaped like an inverted T, and the members of the household who carried keys were generally careful not to push them too far upward, lest this result should occur.

'Counsel will probably be inclined to see a sufficient explanation of the incident in the agitation and haste by which a criminal would naturally be overcome just after the commission of such a crime.'

('Yes; I suppose so.' The barrister paused for some time, knitted his brows, and tried to think the matter out. 'Yes, it would be a natural result,' he admitted at length, and resumed his reading.)

'The next discovery was equally important.

'Miss Lewis's bedroom window looked over the front garden. Immediately below it, under the dining-room window, was a grating over a window, which gave light to an underground scullery. This grating was surrounded by a bed of shrubs, which concealed it from the eye of visitors.

'Sergeant Evans's first move was to proceed to this spot. He was rewarded by finding blood-stains on the grating. The nearest shrubs had been roughly handled, and some of their leaves lay scattered about.

'The inference which counsel is asked to draw is that the body—or a portion of it—was lowered down through the window, and thence carried away.

'This would evidently be much easier for a young woman like the prisoner to do than to carry it downstairs.

'Her second journey down, when she appears to have been bearing a load of some kind, may be accounted for by supposing that she returned for the jewels. These, as already stated, have disappeared.

'During deceased's lifetime she maintained great secrecy about these jewels. No one, not even the servants who had been with her longest, seems to have known anything as to their whereabouts.

'It is suggested, therefore, that they were kept by deceased in a secret hiding-place. This secret must have been disclosed to prisoner, or found out by her.

'Probably, had deceased's nephew been home longer, he would have learnt something about the matter.

'Counsel will doubtless have noticed the

coincidence of the crime being committed on the very night of Mr. Lewis's return. Probably this was to anticipate any communications between aunt and nephew which might have resulted in his obtaining access to the treasure hoard.'

('Coincidence, indeed! Some people might think it a d—— suspicious circumstance,' said the reader. Then, shrugging his shoulders, he added: 'Of course, she's guilty, and it's my duty to get a conviction; but, upon my word, I never had a job to do that I liked less. It's all Pollard's fault for writing up the brief so desperately. He and his Lewis!')

'Sergeant Evans now proceeded to arrest the prisoner. When he charged her with the crime she turned pale, and cried out that it was impossible. But she shed no tears, and showed but little emotion after the first surprise.'

('Pooh! What difference does that make? This sort of thing simply depends on the person's character, not on whether he is guilty or not.' And the blue pencil did some more scoring out.)

'The only remaining circumstance of the case is the disposal of the body.

'In the afternoon of the same day, the second of June, a visitor staying in Porthstone, named Wilfrid Meredith, was walking out to Newton Bay. Just as he rounded the corner and came into the bay he discovered on the edge of the waves a human hand.

'Although somewhat bruised and discoloured, this hand has been identified as the deceased's by her nephew and the servants.

'On the fingers were several valuable rings, which deceased constantly wore. About the identity, therefore, there can be no reasonable doubt.

'No other portion of the body has yet been found. For this reason the Treasury have declined to take up the case, which is in the nature of a private prosecution on the part of Mr. Lewis.

'*Call John Lewis.*'

At this point Mr. Prescott laid down his brief and leant back in his chair. The remainder of the document consisted of the proofs or statements of the evidence which each witness was prepared to give. Much of it would, of course, be merely a repetition of the narrative contained in the first part. It could therefore be looked at some other time.

He laid down his brief and began to think over its contents. It was a case of circumstantial evidence, evidence which all seemed to point one way, and to fix a horrible crime upon a young girl whom he remembered as a pretty child.

Though not a native of Mynyddshire, Charles Prescott was familiar with the district. He had, in fact, been educated at a grammar school in the next county, and it was while he was there that he had made the acquaintance of the Owens.

His favourite schoolfellow, a boy a few years younger than himself, came from the little watering-place, and a summer seldom passed without Prescott spending some part of his holiday at his friend's home. There it was that he had seen old Owen, the parish rector, and had caught a few passing glimpses of the little Eleanor.

Hence his interest in the present case, and the unusual feeling of reluctance with which he approached his task. He had not been to Porthstone for five years now. The schoolfellows were still friendly—in fact, they saw a good deal of each other still, having taken up the same profession and joined the same circuit. But Prescott had got on much better than his friend. He had had five years' start to begin with, and his was that firm, persevering temperament which ensures success to the lawyer. He had therefore risen steadily, and was already making an income of twelve or fifteen hundred a year, while his younger and erratic friend had but gained a precarious foothold in the profession by dint of a few brilliant speeches, which covered a very superficial acquaintance with the law.

'I wonder who will have the defence!' meditated Prescott. 'It will surely run to something more than a docker!'

A docker, it should be explained, is the name for a retainer which is handed direct from a prisoner in the dock to a counsel, without the intervention of a solicitor. It is the resource of the poorer class of offenders, who can scrape together that single guinea, but no more.

'I have it. I'll go and see Tressamer about

this. He goes there still, and ought to know all about it.'

Tressamer was the name of his old friend. His chambers were in an adjoining court of the Temple. Prescott put on his hat, told his clerk where he was to be found, and strolled forth.

CHAPTER III.

COUNSEL FOR THE DEFENCE.

'MR. TRESSAMER is inside, sir. Will you walk in?'

Thus said the clerk at Mr. Tressamer's chambers as soon as he saw Mr. Prescott. Then, stepping to the door, he rapped and opened it, saying the visitor's name.

'Well, Tressamer, where have you been this age?'

The speaker stopped, startled at the sight that presented itself, for there, lying on his face on the hearthrug, with his hands clutching at his thick black curls, lay George Tressamer, the very picture of one in mortal despair.

He sprang to his feet as his friend entered, and made an awkward attempt to behave as if he had not been seen.

'Why, Prescott, where do you come from, pray? More excursions to the County Court, with the solicitors on opposite sides racing to you to see which can get his brief into your hands first?'

Prescott thought it best to take the hint, and not remark on his friend's trouble. He quietly answered:

'No; I've not been anywhere. Been in town, preparing for the assizes. By-the-bye——' He paused to look for a chair, and was surprised to find every one in the room littered with books. He proceeded to clear the nearest to him, lifting the books on to the floor. 'I've just had a brief to prosecute—Hullo! "Hawkins' Pleas of the Crown"! I had no idea you were such a student—in that Porthstone case—the murder——'

Again he stopped short. A look of anguish had come into his friend's face.

'What is it, old man? I can see something's gone wrong.'

'Charlie,' was the reply, spoken in a tone hardly above a whisper, 'are you prosecuting Eleanor Owen?'

Prescott nodded.

'And have you read your brief?'

'I've just come from it.'

'Then you can understand how I feel. I am defending her—and I love her!'

He threw all the energy of his passionate nature into the last sentence, and then sank down upon the window seat and hid his face with his hands.

For several minutes neither spoke. Prescott hardly knew what course to take. To offer to resign his brief might be to let it pass into the hands of one who would share Mr. Pollard's prejudice against the accused. On the other hand, to retain it, unless he were prepared to bring the case fully home to the prisoner, would be alike a breach of professional honour and an act of dishonesty. He resolved at last to leave the choice to his friend.

'George,' he said.

The other slowly lifted his head. Looking upon that face, his friend could see the marks of the terrible experience he was passing through. Tressamer had always been a youth of wild and stormy emotions; no man less calm and steadfast than Prescott could have maintained a friendship so long with such a nature. But now he was struggling with passions compared with which the emotions of schoolboys were as nothing.

'George, what shall I do ? I want you to decide. You know me too well to think I care about the little benefit to myself when it's a case of life and death with a friend like you. Shall I chuck up the case ?'

Tressamer gazed at him gratefully at first, and then with a hesitating, pondering look. Finally he said:

'You have read your brief, and, of course, you know the worst. Tell me, what do you think, honestly ?'

'Honestly, George, I see no defence. There is no doubt the old woman has been murdered. I don't see how it could have been done by anyone outside the house; and then there is the blood on the door-handle. I may tell you that, even before I knew how you stood, in reading the brief I felt a sort of hesitation—that is, I couldn't get that feeling of confidence that one generally has in one's case when the evidence is clear. I felt as if I shouldn't put much heart into the prosecution. But, still, I don't see what defence there is.'

Tressamer listened in silence, and let a moment or two go by before he gave his decision.

'I would rather you kept your brief. I would rather you did it. After all, you have merely a mechanical part to perform; it is only routine. Suppose I were to have a limb amputated, I should like it to be done by a man I know. And this is something of the same sort. The evidence is there, and you will not make it any worse—or better.'

The other was shocked at the gloomy, resigned way in which he spoke.

'Good heavens! you don't mean that you too believe——'

'No, Charles. I believe she is innocent. But I do not expect her innocence will ever be proved in this world.'

'Oh, come, you mustn't give up now! All sorts of things may happen. The trial may go differently to what you expect. Half the time these witnesses don't swear up to their proofs.'

'They have given their evidence twice already—at the inquest and before the magistrates.'

'Yes; but then they weren't cross-examined. It is very different when they have a man like you to turn them inside out. You're not nervous about it, are you?'

'Nervous!' He smiled grimly. 'No; it was at my own request I received this brief. A breach of etiquette, you see'—with another heavy smile. 'If she can be saved, I shall save her. Shall I tell you my defence?'

'No, don't; I would rather be taken by surprise. I don't want to shine in this case, Heaven knows! Take every advantage I can fairly give you. I know you don't expect more.'

'Thank you,' was the answer.

There was a little pause, during which neither spoke. At last, returning to the only topic in either mind, Tressamer observed:

'I have been deep in this ever since it occurred. I have been running up and down to Porthstone. I was at the inquest and in the police-court, but I thought it best to do nothing, and let the public think she was undefended. It may soften their feeling towards her. All these little things have to be thought of.'

'Yes; don't you remember that famous Shepherdsbury case? The man who acted for the prisoner—the solicitor, I think it was—made such a brilliant fight in the police-court that the magistrates hesitated to commit; but the result was that the Crown knew all about the defence, and when the real trial came, the man hadn't a chance. Always reserve your defence.'

'Yes; but you forget, the solicitor has got a splendid practice through it,' was the bitter answer. 'Few men in the West of England are doing better in that class of business. Did you know—but of course you didn't—that I was down at Porthstone only two days before the thing happened?'

'No; were you?'

'Yes; and I was staying in Abertaff that very night. I intended coming up to town the first thing in the morning, but something detained me, and in a few hours the news arrived. So I went down at once, saw Eleanor at the police-station, and advised her what to do before any of those meddling Pollards got at her.'

'Pollards? Why, they are briefing me for the prosecution!'

'Yes, I know. Pollard conducted it in the police-court. At the inquest he represented that man Lewis, the nephew, and very bitter he was, too. But I made Eleanor choke him off before that. Wouldn't have him at any price. I have got a quiet old chap in Abertaff now who won't interfere—old Morgan.'

'Do you know, I thought he was trying to press the case rather in my brief. This accounts for it. But what sort of a man is this Lewis?'

'Oh, a big, coarse-looking fellow. Came back from Australia just before it happened. A brute! He's egging on the Crown. She left him all her money—about twenty thousand—but the jewels are supposed to be worth nearly as much more, and he's lost them, and so he's savage.'

'I say, George, I don't know that I ought to say it, but has it occurred to you as at all curious that he should have returned the very night it was done?'

A gleam of furtive joy crossed the other's face, and instantly vanished again.

'Has that struck *you*?' he said, and seemed about to add something more. But he restrained himself, and merely added: 'The less you and I talk about it the better, perhaps. Coming out?'

And they left the chambers together.

But though Tressamer ceased to discuss the subject with his friend, he could not dismiss it from his mind. The sparkling wit, the wild, extravagant humour, for which he had been famous, seemed to have withered up in the furnace of his terrible grief. He lunched with Prescott in almost dead silence, and as soon as it was over got up hurriedly and disappeared.

He had truthfully described himself as having been deep in the case from its commencement. When the news of what had happened at Porthstone reached the town of Abertaff he was walking in the High Street alone. He saw the unusual excitement, and meeting an acquaintance, learned from him that Miss Lewis had been murdered.

'And they say it was done by her companion, a girl named Owen,' added the man.

Tressamer turned white, gasped for breath, and cried out loudly:

'It's a lie! I swear she is innocent!'

In another moment he had darted off to a cab-stand, and was on his way to the station.

There he had one of those sickening waits for a train which are inevitable on such occasions. Twice he was on the point of ordering a special, but each time he restrained himself by the thought that by the time it was ready the ordinary train would be nearly due. He shunned the gloomy waiting-room, and strode up and down the narrow platform with swift, excited strides.

The porters and newspaper-boys stared as he rushed to and fro, hardly heeding the piles of luggage with which railway servants seek to break the dull monotony of a platform promenade. There was French blood in Tressamer: short, dark, thick-necked, yet far from stout in figure, he possessed the strain of sombre passion which runs through the blood of the Celtic races. He could no more control himself in deference to the officials of Abertaff Station than a madman when his frenzy is on him can conceal it from his keepers.

At last the train drew up. He sprang into a carriage, and impatiently endured the journey down to the seaside. Arrived there, he proceeded instantly to the police-station and demanded an interview with Miss Owen.

At first there was some difficulty, but Tressamer was not to be checked.

'I am her legal adviser,' he announced. 'I am a member of the Bar, and I consider it of vital importance that I should see the prisoner at once. If you refuse, I shall wire straight to the Home Office.'

This threat produced its natural effect. The police, in doubt as to their powers, gave way, and he was taken into the cell where Eleanor had been secured.

If Eleanor had not wept when she was accused of the terrible crime, neither was she weeping now. She was sitting in a dull, stony apathy, from which she was hardly aroused by the sound of the barrister's familiar name. She looked up, it is true, and gazed at him with lack-lustre eyes. But she uttered no word.

He, on his part, waited till the constable had withdrawn. Then he advanced a step from the door, and said:

'Eleanor, you are innocent. Will you let me save you?'

Then at last the light came into her eyes. Then at last the unnatural stiffness faded out of her frame. Then at last the awful coldness loosed its hold of her heart, and answering, 'George, I do not deserve your help,' she gave way to a tempest of tears.

He waited till the storm had spent its first fury. Every shade of anguish passed across his face meanwhile. But he strove to master his feelings, and to put a commonplace expression into his voice, as he said at length:

'I have been in Abertaff the last two days—since I left you.' His voice trembled an instant, but he went on: 'I heard the news this morning, and came down at once. I want to defend you. I want you to accept my services as a token that you still look on me as a friend, in spite of all that has happened.'

'I don't know how to answer you,' she murmured. 'The more generous you are, the more ashamed I feel. I ought not to take your help. And yet you are the only creature in the world who has not forsaken me.'

'Don't say that, Eleanor. No one else knows you as I do. No one else feels to you——but I won't say anything about that. One stipulation I must make. You are not to thank me—not one word.'

And with a stern gesture he waved her off, as she made a movement as if to throw herself at his feet.

'But you must forgive me,' she said. 'Whether I am as wicked as you told me I was when we parted or not, you must tell me that you take me for what I am, that you expect no change in me.' She paused a moment, and then cried out with sudden vehemence: 'Oh, I have done you injustice! I didn't know how noble you could be! But it is too late; I cannot alter now.'

An angry throb convulsed the man during her first words. At the end he ground his teeth and clenched his hands together.

'Silence, Eleanor! If you speak to me like that again, I shall go. There are to be no thanks, no praises. Never refer to the past. I know you and understand. If I cannot tear all hope out of my heart, what is that to you? I ask nothing, and will take nothing unless it is freely given.'

He ceased, and she looked at him with a mixture of gratitude and fear.

Then he referred to her dreadful situation.

'I needn't tell you, Eleanor, that as your counsel you must confide in me fully. I have heard the story so far as it is public, and up to now I may tell you that, as a matter of law, you are in no real danger.'

Eleanor stared at him.

'In no danger? What do you mean? Is the murderer discovered?'

'No, and never may be. But neither is the body.'

'Why, what difference does that make?'

'Don't you know?' answered the barrister. 'I thought most people knew that till the body was discovered no one could be convicted of murder.'

A ray of hope shone out in the prisoner's face.

'Then do you mean that Miss Lewis may be alive still?' she asked quickly.

'No, no. Nobody doubts that she is dead, nor

that someone has killed her. But the point is this, that you cannot be legally tried and convicted. The body has disappeared.'

The heavy shade of despair settled down once more.

'What good is that?' she answered reproachfully. 'If they believe me guilty it makes it worse for me, because I can never be acquitted. I shall be suspected till I die. Oh, I would rather suffer death, I think.'

'Hush, hush!' he exclaimed, shocked and agitated. 'Listen to me, and try to bear it as best you can. The evidence against you is simply overwhelming. Probably I am the only man in the world who believes in your innocence.'

'Except the murderer,' she interrupted.

'Except the murderer, of course. But what I want to say is this—as things stand now no jury that ever breathed would acquit you. Only a miracle can reveal the truth. But what I can do, and mean to do, for you is to save you on the ground I have told you of. You must expect nothing more.'

'George, it will kill me! Alone, hated, abhorred,

what use would my life be to me when the whole world believed me guilty? No, I will pray for a miracle; but if not——' She stopped and panted in anguish of soul.

Her suffering was reflected on the man's face.

'Don't—don't talk like that!' he cried. 'Remember, there will be always one who trusts you, one who reveres you, loves you! I don't mean to ask anything. I would not speak to you like this if I could help it; but remember, if the worst comes to the worst, you have always one friend to turn to, one man who asks no higher joy than to pass his life with you, whether here or in some far-off country, and devote himself to soothing your distress.'

While he was unfolding these views a sudden misgiving entered Eleanor's mind. Rising up, she crossed the cell to where he sat, and, laying her hands on his shoulders, she gazed full into his eyes.

'George,' she uttered in solemn tones, 'I adjure you to tell me the truth. Do you really believe me innocent?'

'Before God, I do!' burst out his answer, as he looked her in the face.

She was satisfied, and returned to her seat.

'And now,' said Tressamer, assuming a more lawyer-like tone, 'tell me all that occurred that night.'

A long conversation followed, of which the barrister took copious notes in his pocket-book. It was late in the afternoon when he came out of the cell and went to secure accommodation in Porthstone for the night.

His step was slow, his head drooping, as he came along the esplanade. Suddenly he saw in front of him a concourse of people following a policeman, who held something in his hand, and a gentleman dressed in the unmistakable garb which proclaims the seaside visitor.

As the crowd came on, Tressamer noticed that this gentleman appeared much agitated. Even the constable's face betrayed an excitement unusual among his kind. But it never occurred to the barrister that this excitement could be connected in any way with the case in which he was so deeply concerned. He took a closer glance at what the policeman was carrying, and then, to his horror, perceived that it was a human hand, the fingers still gay with precious rings. The next moment they all came up to where he was, and he heard someone in the crowd saying:

'That's the hand of the woman that was murdered. A gentleman has just found it in Newton Bay.'

The fearful truth burst on him like a thunderclap. The blood forsook his veins; he staggered helplessly to the nearest seat and sank down upon it, moaning to himself: 'Lost! She is lost!'

The firm ground on which he had been standing had crumbled all at once. The law point on which he had relied to save Eleanor's life, in spite of the crushing weight of evidence against her, was robbed by this accidental discovery of more than half its strength. Who could any longer pretend to doubt whether a murder had been committed? Hence Tressamer's despair. Coupled with what Eleanor had said to him in their interview, however, it drove him to seek more earnestly than he would otherwise have done for some theory of defence upon the facts, some means whereby, if possible, to force a doubt into the minds of the jury, and wring from them a verdict of acquittal.

To this task he now devoted himself. He assumed the part of a detective rather than a barrister. In the case of an ordinary client conduct such as this would not have been tolerated for a moment by the rigid etiquette of the Bar; but where a case is of such a nature that the barrister is personally concerned, and where he acts as a private individual pursuing his own interests, etiquette has nothing to say. In joining the Bar a man does not cease to be a citizen and to enjoy the rights and privileges of ordinary mortals. It is only in his professional character that his acts come under that rigid supervision which is at once the dread and envy of inferior professions.

But, in any event, George Tressamer's present mood would not have let him give much weight to considerations of such a character. Too much was at stake. He had to keep in constant communication with Eleanor, to encourage her in face of the ordeals of the coroner and the magistrates, and to protect her from the zeal of the various graduates of the Incorporated Law Society who were thirsting to win glory in her defence.

As a blind to the public, he caused the rumour to be spread that she was without professional advice. This idea was confirmed when it got to be known that she had refused the services of Messrs. Pollard and other gentlemen of the neighbourhood.

Meanwhile Tressamer was enabled to go about with less publicity and to pursue his inquiries. Eleanor was disposed to wonder at him for not employing a detective. But he soon explained that.

'I know detectives,' he said to her. 'I have seen them in the witness-box and out of it. They are admirable men in their own groove. Give them an ordinary crime—a robbery or a forgery— and they can grapple with it. They will track the defaulting cashier to America for you, or run down the absconding broker in the depths of the Australian Bush. But there their usefulness ends. They are no good in the face of a real mystery like this. This is not a question of clever detection; it is a case of reading the human heart and penetrating its motives. A genius could help us, but I know of no genius in Scotland Yard. No, I will do what I can; and if I come to anything in the way of ordinary detective work I will send for Sergeant Wright.'

So he continued to work alone. He had by this time seen and talked with every witness whose name appeared in the brief for the Crown. He had been present, with the air of a casual spectator, at the inquest, and afterwards at the inquiry before the magistrates, which ended in the committal of Eleanor to the assizes to take her trial for wilful murder.

He did not tell Eleanor much as to the results of his inquiries. He would simply mention that he had been talking to Simons, or that he had had a game of billiards with John Lewis, and she had to form her own idea of what had passed between them.

Finally, he went up to London and plunged into that minute study of Hale and Hawkins which had awakened the surprise of his friend Prescott. He was thus kept occupied till both he and his friend were summoned down from town by the approach of the assizes.

CHAPTER IV.

THE ASSIZES.

On a certain day in the month of July our lady the Queen, probably clad in ermine, and wearing on her head that gorgeous specimen of the jeweller's art which, when not in use, may be viewed at the Tower of London for the absurdly moderate sum of sixpence—our lady the Queen, I say, was reminded by her faithful Chancellor that various prisoners were awaiting trial in different parts of England and Wales, and among other places in Mynyddshire.

Whereupon her Majesty, with that constant attention to the welfare of her people which befits a sovereign, at once sat down and wrote, or possibly only signed, a stately document requiring and empowering Sir Daniel Buller, Knight, one of the judges of her High Court; Sir John Wiseman, Knight, another of the aforesaid judges; Walter Reynold Davies, Esquire, one of her counsel learned in the law; Joseph Robert Pollington, Esquire, another of her counsel learned in the law; and Henry Jones, Esquire, yet a further specimen of her counsel learned in the law, to proceed to Mynyddshire, and there and then open the gaols and try such prisoners as were inside them.

In a similar and not less elaborate document she thoughtfully went on to provide for their hearing and deciding, at the same time, any disputes over civil matters which might possibly have arisen among the population of that remote locality since it was last honoured by the presence of such bright visitants. This considerate act on her Majesty's part was, of course, intended to save her emissaries a second journey. Even a monarch, in the administration of justice, need not be above killing two birds with one stone.

In proceeding to Mynyddshire, however, a very invidious distinction was drawn between the gentlemen named in the Royal Commission. The two first named, simply because they were knights and judges, went down in state, were met at the station by the high-sheriff of the county, and escorted by twenty javelin-men in gay attire to the comfortable lodgings prepared for them. The other three, for no other earthly reason than because their position was less exalted, had to get down as best they might, scramble into cabs with their portmanteaus, and put up at a common hotel. How true is the venerable saying, 'To him that hath shall be given, and from him that hath not shall be taken away even that which he hath'!

Having thus got an unfair start, the two judges preserved it to the end. They tried all the cases themselves, and their unfortunate colleagues had to be content with what crumbs they could pick up by appearing in court as common advocates

The Southern Circuit has long been popular with judges. There is a great difference in circuits. The two northern ones, with their vast populations and immense amount of work, are the bugbear of the puisne judge. The scenery of some of the other circuits is flat, and there is not much amusement going on in the assize towns. But the Southern combines several advantages. It is far from heavy as regards work, the country in many parts is beautiful, and the train-service between the county towns is fairly good.

For these reasons the old stagers on the Bench are in the habit of trying to get the Southern Circuit. On the present occasion they had been successful. Sir Daniel Buller and Sir John Wiseman may not have been extremely popular with the Bar, but they were very popular with each other. They came down to Abertaff feeling in good form, Sir John to preside over the civil court, and Sir Daniel to mete out justice to the inmates of the county gaol.

Not for many years had there been such excitement at assize time in the city. This excitement was due to two causes—the javelin-men and the society murder.

Javelin-men are dying out. In former times, when the office of sheriff was a mark of high social dignity, and before the new-fangled post of lord-lieutenant had usurped so much of its splendour, the shrievalty was an epoch in a county gentleman's career. It was considered almost worth being ruined for. A heavy mortgage was not grudged as a consequence of the lavish splendour with which the office was surrounded. In those days javelin-men were a reality. Clad in semi-military uniforms modelled on the master's family livery, and armed with weapons of an extinct fashion, they simulated the state of vice-royalty. Many a German princelet has enjoyed a less imposing body-guard than an English sheriff of the olden time.

But the railways have killed all that. Everyone now seeks distinction in the Metropolis. County society has become a byword for the old-fashioned and the humdrum, for bad living, bad manners, and bad taste. No one would now dream of embarrassing his estate to secure a merely local renown. Hence the decay of the shrievalty. The modern high-sheriff looks upon his obligatory office as a duty rather than an honour. He contents himself with the cheap services of the county police force for his retinue, and foregoes the expensive luxury of the javelin-men.

There are a few brilliant exceptions, however. The present sheriff of Mynyddshire was one. In the first place, he was master of what in the country is regarded as a colossal fortune. In the second place, he was the founder of his family. Money, therefore, was not an object to Mr. Simon Reynolds. Glory was. His office gave him just the chance he wanted, and he revived its mediæval honours with a willing hand.

Two-and-twenty men, counting the buglers, in gorgeous clothing of pink and yellow hue, accordingly gladdened the eyes of the Abertaffians as they paraded the streets and hung about the court-house. Each man of the rank and file carried a weapon the like of which had not often been looked upon. It resembled an axe with an exaggerated handle, only the back of the blade was prolonged into a formidable spike, while the handle extended beyond into a species of spear-point. Armed with these truly terrific weapons, Mr. Reynolds's faithful henchmen might well strike awe into the heart of the boldest boy in Abertaff. It was felt that they were the principal feature of the assize. The judges, by common consent, took a secondary place. Their robes were fine, no doubt, but their rather ill-fitting wigs formed a poor substitute for the gleaming steel of their rivals. The sober charms of justice cannot successfully compete with the dazzling splendour of arms.

As for the high-sheriff himself, in his black velvet coat and frilled shirt-front, he was a very inferior attraction, while his chaplain was simply nowhere. He had his innings for one brief hour in the cathedral, where the judges were compelled to sit as meekly as so many jurymen under a lengthy summing-up; but after that one bright flash he sank into insignificance, and dragged out the remainder of the assize like the stick of a burnt-out rocket, unpitied by all.

Yet even the javelin-men were cast into the shade by the other great feature of the assize week. The crime of murder remains, after all is said and done, the one thing which most fascinates the public mind. And when to murder is added mystery, and when that mystery centres round the figure of a woman, and when that woman is young and beautiful, and in a social position which does away with the presence of squalid details or coarse motives, the public may be pardoned if they take the very fullest interest in her fate.

Indeed, the case of 'The Queen against Owen,' to

give it its legal designation, was of more than local interest. The whole kingdom was excited about the position of the unhappy girl who lay in one of the cells of Abertaff Gaol. Every eye was watching eagerly for the unfolding of the tragic drama in which she was about to play the leading part. All the great London dailies had their representatives down at the assize town to gather every detail of the forthcoming trial. Already the names of the counsel on both sides were being wired from one end of the country to the other, while in Mynyddshire and in the county town itself the excitement was so great that not the smallest attention was bestowed on any other case that was to come before the courts.

Even the judges themselves were infected with the excitement all around them. Mr. Justice Buller had read the depositions taken before the magistrates prior to leaving town. He had discussed little else with his brother Wiseman in the train. In all their experience, they agreed, they had never met with a case so clear upon the evidence, and yet so unsatisfactory to the mind.

In the presence of the sheriff, of course, the

subject was dropped. Nor could it be resumed after dinner. Later on the judge of the criminal court sat down to make notes for his charge to the grand jury on the morrow. In this he dealt with several other serious cases that appeared in the calendar. But his gravest attention was devoted to the one that dwarfed all the others. This disposed of, he soon retired to rest.

The formal business of opening the assizes had been gone through on the afternoon the judges arrived. Sir Daniel Buller had been trumpeted off to the Court-house, and had sat with as much patience as he could command—and that was not a great deal—while a rather short-sighted and very fidgety clerk of arraigns, afflicted, moreover, with a severe cough, stumbled his way through the important documents already described. This proceeding was necessary in order to inform the loyal inhabitants of Mynyddshire, chiefly represented by errand-boys and loafers from the neighbouring taps, who their red-robed visitors really were, and what they had come to do.

On the following morning, therefore, the judges were free to proceed to work. They drove down to the court at half-past ten, accompanied by the swelling Reynolds and the visibly crestfallen chaplain, and escorted by the inevitable javelin-men, who swarmed about the place all day under the pretext of keeping order.

Sir John Wiseman went quietly off to his own court, and began at once at the unexciting work of trying whether the drippings from a wholesale piano warehouseman's spout had or had not damaged the hats in a neighbouring hat store, and, if so, whether the wholesale piano warehouseman was to blame, and if to blame, how much he ought to pay to the aggrieved hatter. Two of the gentlemen so unfairly deprived of seats upon the bench were engaged in this important case, and it occupied more than half the day.

But it had a rather poor audience. The crowd had rushed into the other court, where the gentlemen of the grand jury were answering to their names as often as the infirmities of the clerk of arraigns would allow them to discover whom he was calling. As soon as the necessary twenty-three were sworn, Mr. Justice Buller began his charge.

After a few civil remarks on the state of the county as regarded crime generally, and brief references to some of the other cases, he came to the all-absorbing topic. And now the reporters, who had sat listlessly under the infliction of the previous remarks, woke to sudden life, and every word of his lordship was caught and taken down as eagerly as if it had dropped from the lips of Shakespeare.

And this is what he said:

'And now I come to what is by far the gravest case in the calendar—one of the gravest cases that has ever come before me in my judicial experience. The prisoner, Eleanor Owen, is accused of the most serious crime, short of treason, known to our law. Gentlemen, it is not for you to try whether she is guilty. You have to hear the witnesses who will be sent in before you on behalf of the Crown, and if you are satisfied that they are speaking the truth, and the effect of their evidence on your minds is such as, if uncontradicted, to raise a fair presumption of the prisoner's guilt, then it is your duty to find a true bill against her. From the depositions taken by the magistrates, which have been put before me, I do not anticipate that you will have much hesitation in coming to your decision. The case is entirely one of what is called circumstantial evidence, as such cases most generally are, and must be from the nature of things. Doubtless there are difficulties in the case—many and grave difficulties—with which it will be the duty of this tribunal to deal when the prisoner comes, if she does come, before us. The fact that the prisoner is charged with the deliberate murder of her friend—I may almost say her benefactress—with whom she had been living on terms of intimacy for a considerable time, and for no motive that has yet been suggested except a low and mercenary one, is calculated to arouse a natural repulsion in the mind, and to indispose it to believe that the charge is well-founded. But, gentlemen, these things, as they come before you, are matters of evidence. If the witnesses you are about to hear satisfy you that there is a *primâ facie* case made out against Eleanor Owen, that there are grounds for suspicion which she ought fairly to be called upon to answer and explain away if she can, then it is your duty

not to hesitate, but to bring in a true bill for
murder. And I must tell you, gentlemen, that so
far as my reading of the depositions has guided
me, this is not a case in which the crime admits
of being reduced to any lesser charge. There are
none of the elements present which may, and often
do, justify a jury in reducing the charge of murder
to that of manslaughter. There is no question, so
far as I have been able to discover, of sudden
provocation, of accident, or anything of that sort.
Whoever committed this crime must, if you believe
the evidence, have done so knowingly, designedly,
and with premeditation, and therefore your finding, if you find against the prisoner must be one
of wilful murder. Gentlemen, I leave you to your
deliberations.'

With these words his Lordship dismissed the
grand jury; and the barristers, in their wigs and
gowns, some of them with briefs and a good many
with none, came streaming into the well of the
court, filling up the seats specially reserved for
them, and overflowing into those occupied by their
colleagues of the 'lower branch.' It seems rather
hard on the Bar that some mysterious rule of

etiquette, which they themselves probably do not understand, should forbid them to enter the assize court till this particular stage in the proceedings. Or can it be that this rule had its origin in the wisdom of their remote predecessors, devising artful means to escape the infliction of a tedious charge without appearing disrespectful to the Bench?

A lull followed. The judge, accustomed to have the eyes of men upon him, calmly betook himself to letter-writing. The high-sheriff, not so accustomed, fidgeted in his seat, looked round and counted the javelin men in court, wondered how long the grand jury would be, and remembered, let us hope with remorse, the time when he was a grand juryman himself and wasted the time of the county by unnecessary questions to the witnesses. The fact is that the grand jury is played out. Everything for which they originally existed is now done by somebody else. Every case that comes before them now has already been investigated once by the committing magistrates. Their duty is simply to accuse the prisoner, nothing more; and it would be quite sufficient if they would just read the depositions and sign the indictment. But man, brief man, placed on a grand jury, and shut into a room without the interference of a legal authority, delights to show himself off by vain and superfluous inquiry. And hence it was that more than half an hour elapsed before the foreman was seen returning into the court with a trumpery indictment for larceny.

The interval had been usefully employed by the clerk of arraigns in compiling a petty jury, something in this fashion:

The Clerk of Arraigns (*taking up a ticket, rather larger than a visiting-card, from a heap before him*): 'John Henry Mullerall!' (*To his clerk, a humble person in plebeian attire, who is popularly believed to know a great deal more about the procedure than the judge and the whole court put together*): 'Did he answer?' (*The clerk hasn't heard him.*) 'John — Henry' (*very loudly*) 'Mull—— Oh! I see it's Muggle'—(*at the top of his voice*) 'Mugglewrath!' (*testily*) 'Are you there?'

John Henry Mugglewrath (*from a seat close by*): 'Here!'

The Clerk of Arraigns: 'Oh! there you are.

Why *don't* you gentlemen answer when you hear your names ? Go into the box, please.'

After about ten minutes of this sort of thing, twelve respectable inhabitants of Mynyddshire were collected in the jury-box. Then they all had to stand up while their names were read over a second time. Then the clerk of arraigns counted his tickets to make sure he had used up twelve, while his clerk counted the jurymen to see that they came to the same number. Then all was ready to begin.

Meanwhile, those gentlemen at the counsel's table who rejoiced in the possession of briefs made a great show of reading them, and making copious notes and interlineations with pencils of different colours—red, blue, and black. The public were greatly impressed as they watched these young giants of intellect at their work. There they were, mastering the most knotty points with ease, and constructing ingenious arguments, doubtless, as they went along. One gentleman excited the greatest interest, and quite threw his brethren into the shade, by pushing aside his brief and drawing towards him one of the loose sheets of foolscap which the kind forethought of the authorities had provided, and beginning to write on it in an abstracted manner. The onlookers deemed him to be wrestling with an opinion on some weighty question bristling with legal difficulties. They little guessed that he was addressing congratulations to a maiden aunt on the occasion of her approaching birthday.

But what really occupied the minds of the spectators, and kept their lips moving in subdued conversation, was the ending of the judge's charge.

'He has made up his mind that she is guilty,' whispered Mr. Jenkins, the stationer from Queen Street, who had come to the court in the capacity of a common juryman, but had not been among the names first selected.

'And I don't wonder at it,' replied his neighbour, a farmer from near Porthstone, who had been summoned in the same way. 'A bad lot, I'll be bound. Wouldn't say nothing when her was before the magistrates. That looks bad, don't it?'

'Silence!' bawled a javelin-man just behind them, a rebuke which the worthy farmer at first thought was meant for himself. But the word was repeated instantly by other javelin-men, and then he perceived that the grand jury had at last achieved a stroke of work, and that the satellites of justice were merely drawing attention to that fact in their usual impressive manner.

The clerk of arraigns now received the document, and proceeded to expound its contents in this manner:

'Gentlemen of the Grand Jury, you find a'— here he stopped and turned it over to read what was on the back, a task which occupied several seconds; but he completed the sentence as if no break had occurred—'true bill against'—another pause, he was looking for the name concealed amid the mazes of technical phraseology. This time the foreman rashly attempted to help him out by murmuring, 'Joseph Hall.' The clerk of arraigns turned round and glared at him, then resumed his investigation, and finally brought out the name in a tone of triumph, as of one who gloried in overcoming obstacles, and was not to be baffled by any indictment in the power of man to draw—'Joseph Hall, for stealing a coat of the value of thirty shillings; also for receiving the same, knowing it to be stolen.'

He then turned again, and bestowed an impatient nod on the waiting foreman, who withdrew, a crushed and miserable man.

'Put up Joseph Hall,' was the next command.

The governor of the gaol leant forward and repeated the order to a warder, who had already heard it perfectly and dived below, apparently through the solid floor of the court. The next moment Mr. Hall appeared, with easy nonchalance, and leant forward in a graceful attitude on the bar of the dock, while the clerk of arraigns proceeded to acquaint him with the crime of which he was accused.

Exhibiting no surprise at this piece of information, which, considering he had been lying under the accusation for two months, was perhaps hardly to be wondered at, Mr. Hall in emphatic tones pronounced himself innocent.

'What?' said the clerk of arraigns, stretching anxiously forward.

Mr. Hall repeated his sentiments.

'What does he say?' exclaimed the clerk of

arraigns, appealing to the court generally for assistance.

The response was a loud but confused roar of voices from the junior Bar, out of which the only clear sound that penetrated to the unfortunate man's brain was the word 'guilty.'

'He says he's guilty!' he remarked to his clerk, in what he intended for an aside, but which was perfectly audible over the whole building.

At this point the judge, becoming impatient, leant over and tapped the clerk of arraigns on the shoulder. He turned round.

'He pleads guilty, my lord,' he said, thinking that the judge wished for information.

'No, he doesn't, Mr. Hughes. He said "Not guilty,"' answered the judge.

Mr. Hughes was nearly beside himself by this time. Leaning forward in the direction of the prisoner, he shouted fiercely:

'What *do* you say? Are you guilty or not?'

'No,' came in tones loud enough for him to hear at last.

'Then *why* can't you speak distinctly? The names you are about to hear called are those of the jurors who are to try you if you have any objection to them or any of them you shall make it as they come to the book to be sworn and before they are sworn and you shall be heard. John Henry Mugglewrath, stand up.'

And, leaving this overwhelming communication to gradually make itself clear to the prisoner's mind, the clerk of arraigns went on swearing in the jury as hard as he could go, with the assistance of the judge's clerk (who recited the oath) and his own clerk (who handed the Testament, as it is called, though really containing only the works of the four Evangelists). It need scarcely be observed that the jurors never came to the book at all. The book came to them.

A rather flighty young counsel, who seemed to consider the whole thing somewhat in the light of a joke, or a species of amateur theatricals on a large scale, having presented the case for the prosecution, Mr. Hall was called upon for his defence.

It then came out that the poor man, than whom no more honest creature ever walked the earth, had been made the victim of a truly diabolical hoax.

He was sitting reading the newspaper in a public-house, the Three Hens — he had not even been drinking, mind, simply reading the newspaper — when a perfect stranger, whom he had never seen before nor since, but whom he should know anywhere, came in, with an overcoat (the one produced in court) over his arm. The stranger, with a craft for which an innocent being like Mr. Hall was no match, began by offering refreshments. These consumed, he asked Mr. Hall to do him the favour of pawning his overcoat for him. Mr. Hall naturally put the question, Why didn't he pawn it himself? The stranger replied that he was unfamiliar with pawnshops, that he doubted his ability to make a good bargain, and that he was willing to pay his new acquaintance a commission on the proceeds. This last offer Mr. Hall had magnanimously refused, but out of mere good-nature he went forth to do the stranger's bidding. The pawnbroker, however, with a distrust in human nature which stamped him as having an evil mind, called in a passing policeman, and gave this victim of his own kindly disposition into custody. The sequel was inevitable. The constable was led by the unsuspicious Hall to the bar of the Three Hens, but the mysterious stranger had gone and left no trace. Poor, humble, with nothing but his good character to rely on, Mr. Hall now cast himself with confidence on the discernment of the gentlemen before him.

The gentlemen had made up their minds already. But they could not give their verdict till the judge had had his turn. Mr. Justice Buller set to and occupied exactly fourteen minutes in telling the jury that there was not much evidence of stealing, but there was strong evidence of the receiving. The jury then occupied exactly fourteen seconds in deciding that the prisoner was guilty of stealing.

It then transpired that this was not the first time Mr. Hall had been the victim of appearances. His trusting nature had led him on six previous occasions to incur the censure of the law. He was, therefore, now bidden to take up his abode where no such temptations could assail him for the next five years.

By this time several other bills had come in from the grand jury, and it had become apparent that the all-absorbing murder would not be tried that day. The audience gradually drifted off, and the remainder of the day's performance took place before a half-empty house.

CHAPTER V.

THE CASE FOR THE CROWN.

MAY it please your Lordship,

'Gentlemen of the jury, I am merely repeating a commonplace when I say that I rise to address you under a very heavy sense of responsibility. As you have heard, the prisoner at the bar is charged with the crime of wilful murder. It is now my duty, acting on behalf of the Crown, to tell you how that crime was committed, according to the view which I have to ask you to take; and to bring before you the witnesses whose evidence, if you believe it, goes to establish the guilt of the accused.'

Thus Mr. Prescott. It was the third day of the assizes. On the Tuesday afternoon, after a true bill had been found, Mr. Justice Buller had announced that he should set apart this day for the trial of the great case. The court had opened at ten o'clock. It was crammed to suffocation. The intensest excitement, whetted by the interval of delay, reigned supreme. All eyes were strained towards the dock as the words were uttered:

'Put up Eleanor Margaret Owen.'

Another moment and she stood before them. Clothed in black from head to foot, pale as a lily, and trembling in every limb, she sank upon the chair behind her, and covered her face with her hands.

A great throb of sympathy shook the court. Sobs were heard. The most prejudiced of those who had bandied her name about for the past few weeks felt a dim sense of shame. Only a few out of all those present were unmoved: the judge, schooled to conceal all trace of emotion, nay, schooled to stifle it as it rose; the jury, too overcome by the duty thrust upon them to be just then alive to what was happening; the counsel on both sides, who, for different reasons, forbore as long as they could from looking at the dock.

She was beautiful. All the suffering she had

gone through had not been able to affect that,
unless to render her beauty more spiritual and
delicate. Her hair of that light glistening brown
which is best known as golden; her drooping eyes
of deepest blue; her wide, square forehead, un-
shaded by that device of ugliness, the artificial
fringe of hair; the full, open lips; the rounded
chin—every mark of a certain order of loveliness
was there.

And she wore no veil. Some of the women
present condemned her for that. The matron of
the prison had besought her to use one. Her
answer was decisive. She had never put a veil on
since childhood, and she would not wear one now.
She would not shrink beneath a false charge. She
would show her face to them all.

She spoke bravely; but she had not realized all
that was before her. And when she came up the
dark winding stairs from the underground cells,
and found herself in that—great God! was it some
crowded theatre, or a solemn court of justice?—her
physical strength gave way, and she scarce knew
what happened for some moments.

Then her will asserted itself again. She stood

up. She faced the judge, the jury, the crowded bar, the fashionable dames in the gallery, and showed no more signs of fear. Her name was called, the hideous accusation was made. She answered it out loud. Her counsel, dreading another scene like that already recorded, had bent across the table and warned the clerk of arraigns beforehand of what the plea would be. The jury were sworn, including in their number the two onlookers whose remarks on the previous day had been so suddenly cut short. The last formula had been recited by the clerk.

'Gentlemen of the jury, the prisoner at the bar stands indicted for that she did wilfully murder one Ann Elizabeth Owen. To that she has pleaded that she is not guilty. Now, you are to try the issue, and to say whether she is guilty or not.'

And now the counsel for the prosecution had begun his speech.

'Two years ago the prisoner was left an orphan by the death of her father, the Rector of Porthstone. She went to live in the house of a lady who had known her from a child, and who lived in the same place. With that lady she remained down to the first of last June, and it is that lady with whose murder she now stands charged.

'Miss Lewis, the deceased, may be described as eccentric. She was in the habit for some years before her death of making very large purchases of jewels——'

'I beg your pardon.' It was the counsel for the prisoner who rose to his feet and interrupted. 'My lord, I am sorry to interrupt my learned friend at this early stage, but may I ask him if he has any evidence that the prisoner knew of the existence of these jewels. If not, my lord, I submit he is not entitled to refer to them at all.'

The Judge: 'What do you say, Mr. Prescott?'

'My lord, I am entirely in your lordship's hands. This is the first time it has been suggested to me that the fact of the deceased's having this jewellery was not a matter of common knowledge in the household. I therefore can't say at this stage whether I shall be able to distinctly fix the prisoner with such knowledge.'

The Judge: 'Of course you mean to bring this in as motive?'

Mr. Prescott: 'Yes, my lord.'

The Judge: 'It is a very important matter. If the jury were satisfied that the prisoner did not know of these purchases, and if there were no other motive suggested, it might have a very great effect on their minds.' [At this point the jury tried to look as if something were having a great effect on their minds, and did not altogether succeed.] 'Perhaps you had better not say anything about the jewels now. You will have another opportunity after you see what your evidence is.'

Mr. Prescott: 'If your lordship pleases. Well, then, gentlemen, I will come at once to the night when this crime was committed.'

Here Mr. Pollard was observed to write something on a slip of paper and hand it to his leader. Mr. Prescott stopped to glance at it, and then went on:

'I may, however, mention one thing before leaving the question of motive, and it is this. I shall be able to prove to you that the deceased on one occasion, in the presence of a witness, made some promise or offer to the prisoner as to remembering her in her will. It is, of course, for you to say what weight you will attach to that circumstance.'

Here the jury tried to look as if they knew what weight to attach to it, and again utterly failed.

'On the first of June a nephew of Miss Lewis's, and her only surviving relative, as I am instructed, and who will be called before you, arrived at Porthstone. He had just returned from Australia, and went to see his relative. He dined there, and spent the evening. At 10 o'clock he came away to his hotel and at once retired to bed.

'The deceased lady had also retired to her room, and from the evidence there can be no doubt that she undressed and got into bed. She was last seen alive a few minutes after ten. The murder was discovered the next morning at nine. Between those hours the crime must have been committed.

'The female servants followed their mistress. At half-past ten the butler fastened the front-door. He will describe the fastenings to you, and he will also tell you of a peculiarity in the latch, about which I shall have something to say presently.'

The counsel then went on to detail the events narrated in his brief, only throwing in an observation now and then as he went along. When he had described the evidence of the removal of the body by the window, he said:

'And now we come to one of the difficulties in the case. If the prisoner lowered the body out of the window in the first instance, why did she afterwards return to the house, and take a second journey, carrying a burden of some kind? I am hardly at liberty, after what has fallen from his lordship, to suggest to you that this second exit was in order to remove something which the murderer wanted to steal, something with the object of stealing which she committed the graver crime. But, gentlemen, there is another explanation, a terrible way of accounting for that second journey, so terrible and horrible that I wish it were not my bounden duty to put it before you. And it is this:

'Only a portion of the victim's body has been recovered. That portion is a hand. Now, in the absence of anything to make us think that the cutting off of the hand was a solitary mutilation, we are forced to the probable conclusion that whoever killed this poor woman mutilated her in a very dreadful manner. It is possible, therefore, that after lowering one portion of her victim's remains through the bedroom window, she returned upstairs to bring down some other part or parts of the body.'

As the counsel with evident reluctance brought out these horrid points, a shudder ran through the court. The prisoner had borne it all with tolerable firmness up to now, but she was completely overcome by this part of the speech, and cowered down into her chair, again concealing her emotions by putting her hands before her face.

If Mr. Prescott had any idea of making the jury revolt at the thought of associating such shocking brutalities with the prisoner, his speech produced the very opposite effect to what he intended. The jury saw in it nothing but the natural reluctance of a man at making such a charge, overborne by the counsel's conviction of the prisoner's guilt. Their faces assumed an aspect of stony horror as they turned their eyes upon the shrinking girl. A slight frown crossed Tressamer's countenance, followed by a look of contempt.

'The second difficulty in the case,' resumed Prescott, 'is as to the latchkey. As I have explained, there were only three keys in existence so far as the prosecution have been able to discover. These will all be produced before you. One was found in the pocket of the deceased's dress, the other was never out of the possession of the witness Simons, the third was on the prisoner's person when she was arrested. One of these keys, therefore, must have been used in the latch that night, and must have been used with such carelessness or ignorance—it is for you to say which '— [again the jury tried to look as if they were prepared to say which, and again they broke down]— 'that the latch was raised too high, and stuck. Now, here I must draw your attention to a very important circumstance. The person who entered the house last, whether the prisoner or anyone else, and who fastened up the front-door as it was found by the witness Lucy Jones the following morning, that person must, for some reason or other, have failed to notice the condition of the latch. She, if we assume it was the prisoner, must be supposed to have been so agitated from some cause that she failed to notice what she was doing when she raised the latch with her key, and failed again to notice how the latch was caught when she proceeded to fasten the door inside.

'Gentlemen, it is for you to ask yourselves whether a reasonable explanation, an explanation that will justify you in coming to an adverse verdict in this case, is furnished by the suggestion that the prisoner's mind was excited by the crime she had just committed to such an extent as to deprive her of the power of observing these things.'

At this point Mr. F. J. Pollard began to be aware that his leader was not pressing the case very vigorously. He looked round at his brother in the solicitors' seat behind. That gentleman looked extremely angry. He had noticed something curious in his counsel's manner from the first. He now leant over and whispered to his brother:

'What's the matter with Prescott? I can't make him out. He talks as if he were the judge summing up, instead of the counsel for the prosecution.'

Mr. Pollard, the barrister, shrugged his shoulders and bit his lip. He could do nothing. It was not for him to offer advice to his leader. A man of Mr. Prescott's standing was not likely to tolerate any interference from a young fellow just called.

But the offender proceeded to cap his misdeeds by a new suggestion, which had never occurred to either of the Pollards. It had been noted down long ago by Tressamer, though.

'The third difficulty in this case, gentlemen, is one which has doubtless been present to your minds all the time I have been speaking.'

This time the jury made a desperate effort to conceal their astonishment, and to look as if they perfectly well knew what was coming. But no one was deceived.

'I refer to the disposal of the body. On this point we have exactly two pieces of evidence. A young woman like the prisoner was seen walking in the direction of Newton Bay, about midnight, by the witness Evan Thomas. On the following afternoon the severed hand was discovered on the beach of Newton Bay by a visitor.

'How did it get there? It is for you to say. On behalf of the Crown, it is my duty to suggest to you that the prisoner in the dock may have carried the result of her crime to that distant spot, in several journeys, one of which happened to be seen. I must put it to you that piece by piece she accomplished her revolting task, and that she sought to hide the traces of her guilt in the sea. If you think that a rational and likely course of circumstances, no doubt you will say so.

'Gentlemen, I have done. I trust I have not detained you at undue length over this case, which must strike you as one of the most grave and difficult that could well come before a court of justice. I shall now, with the assistance of my learned friend, put the evidence before you. If you are left in any doubt after hearing it, and, after hearing the prisoner's defence, if you feel that there are mysteries in the case which have not been properly explained, and difficulties which have not been fully met, then you will, I feel sure, be only too glad to acquit the prisoner of this dreadful charge. But if, on the other hand, you are fully and entirely satisfied, if you feel no doubt whatever—of course, I mean no reasonable doubt— you will, I am equally sure, do your painful duty by returning a verdict of guilty.'

The barrister sat down, and his junior, who had listened impatiently to the close of the speech, at once started up, and called out:

'John Lewis!'

And now, for the first time, Charles Prescott ventured to look towards the dock. After the first involuntary glance at Eleanor's entrance, he had steadily kept his eyes averted. During the whole of his address, which took up nearly an hour, he never once looked round. He was afraid to trust himself. That one brief glance had revived the memories of old with an added force which almost overwhelmed him.

Yet he was not what would be called an emotional man. His was one of those natures which maintain a seeming coldness under all circumstances, but which often conceal in their depths a strength of passion and devotion compared to which the fiery outbreaks of others are mere 'sound and fury, signifying nothing.' And now this hidden force was stirred. It held him in its grasp, and his whole being shook and quivered to its centre.

Not love at first sight, for he had seen her before. Yet love, awakening suddenly as he looked upon her in the full bloom of opening womanhood, surrounded by a halo of suffering, and peril, and mystery, the fated victim of an accusation which he would not believe and could not disprove. This it was that overpowered him; this it was that led to that feeble, halting advocacy which surprised all who heard it. They could not recognise the keen, trenchant Prescott who had made such a name for himself on the circuit. The Pollards were the only ones there who resented it, but they were by no means the only ones to be puzzled at the change.

But Prescott did not easily give way to his feelings. The sense of duty was sufficiently strong in him to keep him from absolute abandonment of his cause. He had gone faithfully through the case, and he was now preparing to take his part in examining the witnesses. Pride and professional training asserted themselves, and he stood firm.

At this moment, however, and when he was suffering most acutely, one of those happy accidents which men call good fortune or Providence, according to their dispositions, came to his aid. A solicitor's clerk hurriedly came into the court and made his way to the barrister's side. An unforeseen event had occurred. A case in the other court which had been expected to last all day had suddenly come to a settlement by agreement between the parties. The next case on the list was one in which Mr. Prescott was engaged, and engaged by himself, and his immediate presence was called for. Breathing an ejaculation of thankfulness, he got up, and quickly withdrew, leaving young Pollard to manage the witnesses as best he could.

The judge looked annoyed, and the solicitor Pollard somewhat dismayed, at this sudden disappearance of the leader for the Crown. But young Pollard himself was only too pleased. At last he was to have his chance. He was left captain of the ship. If all went well he might hope to get through the evidence, and have the concluding speech in Prescott's absence. And his satisfaction was shared by Tressamer. Tressamer knew his man. For the first time that morning a look of satisfaction crossed his face, and he settled his wig firmly on his head as he prepared to encounter the moving spirit of the prosecution.

And Eleanor? She did not altogether understand what had happened. But she saw that the man who had put the case against her so mildly had now gone out of it altogether, and her heart gave a great beat of joy for the first time since she had parted with George Tressamer two days before the memorable first of June.

CHAPTER VI.

THE WITNESSES.

'John Lewis!'

A dark, big man stepped into the box, frowning heavily around him. The oath was administered, and then Mr. Pollard commenced in the approved style.

'Your name is John Lewis, and you are now living at The Shrubbery, Porthstone?'

'Yes.'

'That's where the murder was committed?' interrupted the judge.

'Yes, my lord. The witness inherited it under Miss Lewis's will.'

The Judge: 'Have you lived there ever since?'

Witness: 'Yes, my lord.'

The Judge (after a pause, during which Mr.

Pollard waits impatiently) : 'Go on, Mr. Pollard. What are you keeping us for ?'

Mr. Pollard : ' I beg your lordship's pardon.' To witness : ' You are the nephew of the deceased, and have just returned from Australia ?'

' Yes ; I came back to my aunt.'

' After making some money out there, I believe ?'

'*I object !*'

This interruption, it need not be said, came from Tressamer. He had risen to his feet, and put on that scowl of scornful indignation with which an experienced counsel knows how to daunt a young beginner and make him feel he has committed himself.

' My lord, my friend cannot prove that, and if he could it cannot possibly be evidence against the prisoner. It is a most improper question.'

The Judge looked a little puzzled.

' It is irrelevant,' he said, ' and I won't allow it if you object. In a case like this we can't be too strict, of course.'

Mr. Pollard began to realize that greatness has its snares as well as its triumphs. He tried to get back on to the track.

'You went to see the deceased on the first of June?'

'I did.'

'And you came away——'

Here the barrister's brother leant over and handed him a slip of paper. He took it and read it, turned red, and, trying to appear as if he had not been prompted, put the question contained in the slip of paper:

'Was anything said about the jewels?'

The judge stared. Tressamer started to his feet in a transport of fury.

'My lord, my friend is deliberately leading the witness. In a case of murder it is disgraceful!'

'I agree with you, Mr. Tressamer. Don't answer that question, sir.'

Thus the judge. Poor young Pollard turned as red as the judge's robe, and stammered out some apology. His brother mentally swore at him, and every solicitor in court resolved never to give him another brief.

'Go on, Mr. Pollard; you mustn't keep us waiting.'

The wretched young man gave a last look at his brief, and closed the examination.

'And you left about ten o'clock?'

('Leading again!' ejaculated his opponent.)

'Yes. My lord, may I say——'

'No!' snapped the judge. 'Say nothing unless you're asked.'

The witness looked angry, and frowned savagely at his counsel. But the latter had now sat down, and the cross-examination was about to begin.

Tressamer had been studying the witness, with a view of ascertaining his weak point. This was evidently his temper. Accordingly he avoided irritating him till he had obtained as much as he could from him. He began:

'Had you any other relatives living besides Miss Lewis?'

The witness was thoroughly thrown out. He could not see what was coming. In a sullen voice he responded:

'Yes, I've a sister in the North.'

'Did you go to see her before your aunt?'

'No.—My lord, may I explain?'

The Judge: 'You had better confine yourself to the questions now. You will have an opportunity of explaining afterwards.'

'You went straight to your aunt. Was she pleased to see you?'

'Yes, she seemed very pleased.'

'And yet she let you stay at a hotel?'

'That was only the first night. It was arranged that I was to occupy a bedroom in her house afterwards.'

'Oh!'

Type cannot do justice to the peculiar intonation with which the barrister uttered this exclamation. The whole court was aroused to suspect something beneath the surface. Then he turned round to the jury with a mysterious expression, and slowly repeated the answer:

'It was arranged that you were to occupy a room in her house after that night?'

The jury roused themselves for a grand effort, and succeeded in imparting a distinct air of suspicion to their countenances.

At last Mr. Lewis's temper came into play. He cried out:

'Yes; and if I had been there the first night, I might have prevented this murder.'

'Silence, sir!' said the Judge.

And now Tressamer brought out the question for which he had been preparing the way all along:

'When this arrangement was made about your living in the house, did your aunt (remember you are on your oath, sir!)—*did she happen—to—furnish—you—with—a—*LATCHKEY?'

The effect was electrical. He had brought out the last words of the question slowly one by one, and then he suddenly hurled the final word at the witness like a weapon.

John Lewis instantly realized the situation. The question was tantamount to an accusation. The whole court took it in that sense, and gazed at him in deadly earnestness. He turned livid. For a moment he could hardly bring his lips to frame a syllable. At length he recovered his self-command, and thundered out:

'No, sir. May God strike me dead if she did!'

The fierce earnestness of his denial produced a revulsion of feeling in the court. The jury felt that the counsel had been guilty of unfairness in making such a charge so suddenly, and, as it seemed, with such absence of grounds. The Judge was annoyed, too. Sir Daniel Buller hated sensationalism. In fact, he did not like anything which threw his own dignity into the shade. He liked to feel that he was in the star part, and that everybody else in court was merely playing up to his grand effects. He therefore refrained from rebuking the witness, and from this stage he showed himself less favourable to the counsel for the defence.

But Tressamer had anticipated something of this sort, and he had a card in reserve. He went on with his cross-examination as if nothing had happened.

'You gave the prisoner into custody, I think?'

'I did.'

'You made up your mind that she was guilty, I suppose, without much thinking?'

'I thought there was absolute proof of it.'

'That's what I mean. You were anxious that she should be convicted, were you not?'

'I was anxious that she should be tried. I thought it my duty to see that this crime was punished.'

'By the conviction of the prisoner?'

'If she was guilty.'

'But you felt sure she was guilty? You were the one to accuse her, you know.'

Mr. Lewis was getting irritated again. He made no answer to this suggestion, and the barrister forbore to press it, contenting himself with a meaning glance at the jury.

'You were represented at the inquest, were you not, by Messrs. Pollard?'

'Yes.'

'The gentlemen who are now conducting this prosecution—nominally on behalf of the Crown?' And with this parting shot he resumed his seat.

Young Pollard instantly rose.

'My lord, the witness was anxious to explain one of his answers to my learned friend. Would your lordship allow him to do so now?'

'Yes, yes,' was his lordship's answer.

The witness instantly took advantage of the permission.

'I wished to say, my lord, that the reason why I went first to see my aunt, instead of going to my sister's, was because she had befriended me when I was young. She furnished the money to start me with in Australia, and I felt it only right, in common gratitude, to come straight and thank her on my return.'

Another revulsion of feeling swept over the court. The effect of Tressamer's last suggestion was obliterated. Lewis was once more in favour.

Pollard had scored. His brother twitched him by the gown from behind as a hint to sit down. But the unfortunate young man must needs try and improve on his lucky shot. He summoned up a very tragic demeanour, and put the fatal question:

'And is there the smallest ground for suggesting that you were near the house or out of your hotel after ten that night?'

The witness showed confusion. Instead of answering in the prompt, decided style he had hitherto shown, he hesitated for some seconds, and then said with visible embarrassment:

'No, there is none.'

Pollard hastily sat down. The rules which govern the production of evidence did not permit Tressamer to put a further question to the witness, but he was skilful enough to do what accomplished the same result. He called across the barristers' table, in a perfectly audible voice:

'Is anyone from the hotel here, Mr. Pollard?'

'Not that I know of,' was the sullen answer.

And now it was the judge's turn, and he proceeded to put to the witness that question which was in the mind of every person in court, but which neither of the counsel had dared to put, each fearing the answer might be unfavourable to himself.

'Tell me, Mr. Lewis, had you any special reasons—don't tell me what your reasons were—but had you any reason apart from what you were told by others for accusing the prisoner of this murder?'

'I had, my lord.'

'Did that reason arise in your mind as a consequence of anything which you saw the prisoner do, or which took place in her presence?'

'Not exactly, my lord. My aunt said to me——'

The judge swiftly raised his hand with a forbidding gesture, and pursed up his lips.

'That will do. You can go.'

Mr. Lewis retired, and the jury were left to wonder what the mysterious reason could be, the result on most of their minds being far more unfavourable to the prisoner than if the rules of evidence had allowed the witness to speak freely.

The next witness was the butler, John Simons, who deposed to having fastened up the door at half-past ten on the night in question, and to having found the latch stuck on the following day. He further described the finding of the blood-stains on the bedroom door-handle. His cross-examination was listened to with interest.

'Has it ever occurred to you yourself to accidentally raise the latch too far in the same way?'

'Oh yes, I've often done it, sir.'

'Were you out on the evening of the first of June?'

The butler, a good-natured-looking man, with a pleasant smile, but whose mind was evidently rather unhinged by the position he found himself in, looked bewildered at this, and rather frightened. The barrister hastened to reassure him.

'What I mean is this. If you had been out some

time during the evening, before half-past ten, would it not have been possible for you to have accidentally left the latch in this position?'

The witness looked relieved, and hastened to answer.

'Yes, of course, I might have.'

Tressamer turned round to the jury to see if they appreciated his point. Then he resumed.

'You have known Miss Owen some time, I think. Tell me, have you ever noticed that she was liable to nervous headaches?'

'I have heard her say she had a headache.'

'What was the last time you heard her say so?'

The witness looked puzzled, and seemed to be trying to remember.

'Perhaps I can help you,' said the barrister. 'About this very time, now; just before this happened?'

'Ah, yes, sir, now you remind me, I remember. When she didn't come down that morning, I said to Rebecca, "Very likely she's had another bad night."'

'*Another* bad night? Then she was liable to insomnia?'

The witness stared.

'I beg your pardon. I mean, she sometimes did suffer from want of sleep?'

'She sometimes had bad nights, sir.'

'Exactly. And you remembered she had been having them just before this?'

'Well, no, sir; I can't say as I do remember that.'

The barrister frowned impatiently.

'Well, tell me this,' he said: 'do you know what she was in the habit of doing on these occasions, when she couldn't get to sleep?'

'No, sir.'

'Did you ever hear of her going out for a walk at night?'

The whole court was eagerly following this cross-examination, as the defence now began to be visible. But the answer of the witness fell like lead:

'No.'

Tressamer looked deeply disappointed. He had been baffled just where he had evidently built upon success.

He only put one more question.

'You had a good many opportunities of seeing your mistress and Miss Owen together. Did they always seem to you to be on friendly, affectionate terms?'

'Yes, sir, always.'

'Thank you.'

This finished the butler's evidence, as Mr. Pollard wisely abstained from any re examination.

He next proceeded to call the parlourmaid, Rebecca Rees.

A pretty, vain, pert-looking girl stepped into the box, and took hold of the Testament.

'Take off your glove,' said the clerk.

She did so with some difficulty, as the thing had about half a dozen buttons to unfasten. Then she was sworn and proceeded to tell her story.

In a shrill voice, which visibly irritated the judge, she went on, and described how she had gone to bed, how she awoke at midnight and heard a sound proceeding from below.

'What was the nature of the sound?' asked the counsel who was examining her.

'It was a groan,' was the reply, 'like as if somebody was being hurt.'

The prisoner's counsel here hurriedly turned over the pages of his brief till he came to a certain place, where he made a note in the margin.

'What did you hear next?'

'I heard the prisoner going downstairs.'

The Judge: 'What do you mean? Could you see her?'

Witness: 'No, sir. I heard her.'

Mr. Pollard: 'She means she recognised the footsteps, my lord.'

The Judge: 'Don't interrupt me, please. (*To witness*) 'Young woman, be careful. That is not the way to give evidence, as you know perfectly well. You mustn't tell us that you heard the prisoner. You heard footsteps; that's all.' (*A pause.*) 'Now, Mr. Pollard, you can go on.'

Mr. Pollard: 'Did you recognise the footsteps?'

His lordship frowned and shrugged his shoulders.

Witness: 'I thought it was Miss Owen.'

Mr. Pollard: 'Well, now tell us what you did.'

The girl proceeded to describe how she had got up and gone down to the front-door.

'How was it fastened?' was the next question.

'It was on the latch. The bolts were drawn back, and it wasn't locked nor yet chained.'

'Did you see whether the latch was up or down?'

'I object!'

Mr. Tressamer had risen in a fresh burst of indignation.

'My lord, my friend has distinctly suggested the answer to the witness. I object to her being allowed to say anything about the latch after such a question as that.'

'I didn't intend to lead her, my lord,' said Pollard.

The judge hesitated for awhile between his natural desire to hear the answer and his fear that the witness was not wholly impartial. Perhaps a slight prejudice against Tressamer's hectoring manner had something to do with his decision.

'You should have asked her whether she noticed anything about the latch,' he said at length. 'Did you?' he added, turning to the witness.

'It was *down*, sir,' she returned, answering Pollard's question rather than the judge's.

The importance of the answer was chiefly in its disposing of Tressamer's suggestion that the butler might have forced the latch up. He turned round to the jury, and assumed the air of one who is being unfairly treated. But of course he could not help their seeing that the prosecution had scored a point.

Rebecca's evidence was continued till she came to where she heard footsteps ascending the stairs.

'How long was this afterwards?' asked Pollard.

'About ten minutes.'

'Did you recognise those footsteps?'

'No, I didn't notice them; but I think they must have been Miss Owen's, or else I should have noticed the difference.'

Tressamer ground his teeth. He was afraid to interrupt again, for fear of the effect on the minds of the jury. They are apt to think a man is losing when he interrupts too often.

'What happened next?'

'She went into the bedroom below.

'What bedroom?'

'Her own, I suppose, or Miss Lewis's.'
'You couldn't tell which?'
'No.'
'Well, and how long was the person, whoever it was, inside?'
'About a quarter of an hour, I should think. I thought she had come in for good, and gone to bed.'

The Judge (*suddenly looking up from his notes*): 'Look here, don't let me have to stop you again, or I shall do something you won't like. It's not for you to tell us what you thought. Confine yourself to answering the questions.'

Mr. Pollard (*thinking the judge has finished*): And then what did you——'

The Judge (*superbly indifferent to Mr. Pollard*): 'Do you realize that you are giving evidence in a court of justice? You must be extremely careful —extremely careful.' (*A long pause; Mr. Pollard afraid to begin again.*) '.Well, do you ask her anything more?'

Mr. Pollard: 'I beg your lordship's pardon. If your lordship pleases.' (*To witness*) 'After the quarter of an hour, did you hear anything more?'

Witness (*now thoroughly frightened*): 'Yes.'

'What did you hear?'

'I heard her come out.'

At this point the judge threw down his pen, and threw himself back in his chair. Mr. Pollard hastened to take off the edge of his lordship's wrath by reprimanding the witness himself.

'You mustn't tell us that. You don't know it was the prisoner. What was it you actually heard?'

The girl now felt and looked ready to resort to tears. She really did not know what answer was safe, and prudently adopted a strictly non-committal form.

'I heard a noise below.'

'What was the noise like?'

'Like someone going downstairs.'

'Well, why didn't you say that? You heard footsteps going down?'

'Yes.'

The judge took up his pen again and took down the answer.

'And did you notice the footsteps this time?'

'Yes; they were——'

'Stop! Not so fast. Answer my questions.'

Mr. Pollard was by this time little less nervous than the witness. He was really utterly at a loss how to frame his next question without incurring Tressamer's wrath or the rebuke of the Bench. At last he blurted out:

'Was there anything different about the footsteps this time?'

Tressamer opened his mouth, but the judge was before him this time:

'Don't answer. Really, Mr. Pollard, you are as bad as the witness. You know you ought not to put a question like that.' Then, seeing that the poor young man was quite unequal to extracting the desired evidence, his lordship quietly took over the examination himself:

'Did you notice the footsteps this time when they were going downstairs?'

'Yes, sir—my lord.'

'Did anything strike you about them?'

'Yes, my lord.'

'What?'

'They were heavier, sir, and thumpy.'

'Had you ever heard anything like it before?

I mean, did they or did they not sound familiar in spite of this heaviness?'

'No, my lord; I don't remember.'

'Did you go downstairs again?'

'No, sir.'

The judge turned round to the jury with complacency, and smiled as if to say, 'You see, gentlemen, how it can be done by one who knows how.' Then he asked the counsel:

'Now, Mr. Pollard, do you want anything more from this witness?'

'No, my lord, thank you.'

He sat down, feeling considerably the worse for his experience, and Tressamer got up.

He looked severely at the young woman for some seconds, and then suddenly asked her:

'Why do you dislike Miss Owen?'

At once the court was all ears. It was one of those strokes of brilliant advocacy which few men care to venture on. It was dangerous, but in the present case it was completely successful. The witness lost countenance, stammered, and with difficulty got out a lame denial.

'I don't dislike her particular.'

'Do you like her?'

'No.'

'Did you ever have any complaint against her when you were her servant?' (He intentionally chose a phrase calculated to irritate.)

'I wasn't her servant,' was the angry reply. 'I should be very sorry to be.'

'I thought so. Tell me, you said to my learned friend that the first sound you heard on this night was like somebody being hurt, didn't you?'

'Yes, sir.'

'When did you discover that?'

'When did I discover that?'

'Yes, woman; don't echo me like that. You know what I mean.'

'I thought so at the time.'

'*What!*' The barrister assumed an expression of amaze.

'I thought so all along.'

'Then why didn't you say so all along? When you were before the magistrates, did you say anything about somebody being hurt?'

'Yes, I think so.'

'You think so! Remember you are on your

oath, please, and that I have a copy before me of what you actually did say before the magistrates. When you were before them, did you say a syllable about a sound as if somebody were being hurt?'

'I don't know whether I did or not.

'I thought so. Did you tell the magistrate that you thought it was the sound of someone in troubled sleep?' Here the barrister read from his brief.

'Yes, sir.'

'And that you thought'—here he turned over the page at which he was looking and glanced at the top of the next, so as to give the impression that he was still reading her exact words—'that the sound came from Miss Owen's room?'

The witness fell into the trap.

'I dare say I did,' she answered.

The judge was equally taken in. He had read the depositions, but had not remembered their contents clearly enough to check the barrister. Tressamer went to another point.

Taking out his watch, he said:

'I want to test your notion of ten minutes. Will you turn round, with your back to the clock, and tell me when one minute has passed, after I have said the word "Now."'

All the jurymen and most of the other persons in court took out their watches to check this experiment. The girl turned round, and Tressamer gave the word, 'Now!'

'Tick—tick—tick—tick—tick——'

'Now!' said the witness, turning quickly round.

A general smile passed over the court.

'Seventeen seconds exactly, my lord,' observed Tressamer. 'The witness's ten minutes may therefore be put down as three. You have told his lordship that the last set of footsteps you heard sounded heavy when they went downstairs. Will you swear that they did not sound equally heavy coming up?'

'I didn't notice.'

'I didn't ask you if you had noticed. Don't try and shirk my question, please. Will you pledge your oath that they weren't equally heavy coming upstairs?'

'No, I won't swear it.'

'Have you any reason, except your dislike of

the prisoner, for suggesting that those footsteps were hers?'

The judge interposed.

'Really, Mr. Tressamer, you mustn't put it like that. She says that she didn't dislike the prisoner, and you must take her answer. I allow great latitude to counsel in your situation, but you must treat the witness fairly.'

'As your lordship pleases.'

Tressamer sat down, rather glad to leave his question unanswered, as the effect thereby produced on the jury's mind would be better than if the witness had had a chance of offering her grounds for suspicion.

'Lucy Griffiths.'

This was the housemaid, and her evidence contained nothing of importance. In cross-examination she admitted that she had detected no likeness between the descending footsteps heard by her and Miss Owen's. In fact, she had at first thought they sounded like a man's.

The next witness was the fisherman, who stated to Mr. Pollard that he had met a female about midnight on the eventful first of June, whom he at the time believed to be the prisoner. He thought so still.

His cross-examination elicited two facts: First, that he had once met Miss Owen at the same late hour before; secondly, that he had met other persons going in the same direction the same night at or about the same time.

Tressamer chose to emphasize this point.

'Could you tell those gentlemen,' he said, indicating the jury, who instantly tried to look as if they had been attending, and had not long ago given up the task in despair, 'what the other people were like whom you saw?'

'Well, one of them was a man.'

'Come, that's something; but it's not much. Can't you tell us what sort of a man? Was he tall?'

The jury instantly looked at Lewis.

'No; I didn't notice as how he was particular tall. Middlin' short, I should say.'

'About my height?'

'Yes; about that. Summat about your size.'

Tressamer laughed, and a smile went round the court at the serious way in which the witness gave his answer.

'Well, who else did you see?'

'I see another man afore then.'

'Ah! Was he tall?'

'Why, yes; I think he was.'

The jury again looked at Lewis. But that gentleman's face revealed no emotion, except a sort of sullen wrath which had overhung it ever since his appearance in the witness-box.

At last, when all the other witnesses had been disposed of, the policeman was called and gave the usual routine evidence.

Mr. Pollard was rash enough to ask him:

'Who came to the station to inform the police?'

But his opponent at once objected, and the judge ruled the question out. Mr. Lewis's indignant declaration, therefore, which Prescott had struck out of his brief with such prompt disdain, fared equally ill in court, and was not allowed to get to the ear of the judge or jury.

At last the evidence was gone through, and then the prosecuting counsel stood up and made the final announcement:

'That is the case for the Crown, my lord.'

'I will adjourn for half an hour,' observed the judge, getting on his feet.

The whole court rose with him, and in a few minutes the entire place was empty.

CHAPTER VII.

HALF AN HOUR.

SCRAMBLING, rushing, hurrying, squeezing, talking, laughing, and sighing, the great throng poured out of the building and dispersed down the streets of Abertaff. One topic was on every tongue. The fate of the prisoner was the sole thing discussed. They weighed the evidence, they repeated it, they distorted it. Some were violently in favour of the prisoner, and considered half the witnesses to be committing perjury. Others were violently against her, and could not see, so they professed, a shadow of doubt in the case from first to last. Others, again, in complete doubt as to how the case would end, wisely declined to commit themselves till they had heard more of the defence.

Then, again, these parties were subdivided into

groups. There was the ignorant group, who knew nothing about the case, and went about asking questions of their wiser neighbours. There was the mysterious group, who suspected many things, but said nothing, contenting themselves with shaking their heads in corners, and suggesting that not half the real motives of the parties to the affair had come out at all. And there was the well-informed group of those who had watched the whole thing from first to last, and knew more, far more, about it than the counsel on either side, or the criminal either, for that matter.

And they were not churlish in bestowing their information, either. There were the Lewisite partisans, who knew exactly the value of the jewels to a halfpenny, and how they were kept in a box under the bed, and how the prisoner had carried them off by stealth, and buried them somewhere in the sands of Newton Bay. Some of these, the more charitably disposed, could go even further than this. They explained how it was that the prisoner had never meant to commit the murder at all, but simply to steal the jewels, but had been interrupted in the act by the unexpected waking of the deceased woman. They grew impressive as they pictured the elder woman suddenly roused from sleep by the midnight robber, and the emotions of that robber detected in the act of guilt. They could tell you how she started back in terror, and then, realizing that ruin was upon her, succumbed to temporary frenzy, and with the weapon which she had brought to open the jewel-chest dealt the fatal blow to her unhappy victim.

Others, less lenient in their views, had obtained quite different details. They could relate numerous previous attempts of the prisoner on the life of her benefactress. They knew how she had sought to introduce poison into her food, from which she was only saved by a miraculous chance, which caused her to be summoned from the table just as she was about to taste the fatal dish. Also how she had on one occasion led her victim along the cliff with the well-formed purpose of pushing her over the edge; only the curate happened to come along and meet them, and accompanied them till the opportunity was gone.

The Owenite section, on the other hand, had

their account, equally authentic, and, if possible, more minute and graphic than the other. They would tell you more about their villain, Lewis, than he himself could possibly have remembered. They took you back to his childhood. They started you with the well-known story of his beating his little sister, the sister in the North whom he had refused to go and see. They explained the causes which led to his expulsion from school after school. They tracked him to Australia, and unearthed dark secrets in his life out there which would have made the bushranger Kelly reject him from his historic gang. Finally, they brought him back to England a ruined desperado, intent on getting at his relative's wealth by fair means or foul. The robbery of her jewels was only part of his scheme. By killing her he obtained the whole of her wealth at once. Then a victim became necessary—a stalking-horse to mislead the minions of justice, and whose punishment would ensure his own safety. He was thus a double murderer.

So the tongues wagged. Meanwhile the object of these rumours had made his way round in a towering passion to the seat from which his solicitor was trying to get away.

'What does this mean?' he cried, as soon as he got near enough to speak without being heard by others. 'Are you playing me false? Where is Mr. Prescott?'

'He was called away into the other court,' said Mr. James Pollard, the barrister's brother, who was a partner with his father in the Porthstone firm.

'He ought not to have gone. Your brother managed the case wretchedly. I wasn't allowed to say the most important thing of all.'

'My brother did the best he could. No one could dream that Prescott would desert us like this. I shall never give him another brief, I promise you.'

By this time they had got outside the door of the court-house. They turned towards a hotel close by, where a general luncheon was put on the table for the convenience of people having business in the assize-courts. The civil court had risen a few minutes before the other, and the place was crowded with solicitors, witnesses, jurymen, and the general public.

'Look here, Mr. Pollard,' Lewis said, as they fought their way into the room, 'I could have proved that about the jewels up to the hilt if I had been allowed. Why, my aunt was speaking to me about them that very night, and she said Miss Owen knew of them.'

'And why on earth didn't you tell me all this before?' retorted the solicitor.

'I thought I had.'

'Thought you had! Goodness me! that's just like you laymen. You keep back the chief points in a case, and then you're angry with us because we don't guess them by instinct. Why didn't you tell the judge this when he was examining you?'

'Because it wasn't said in the prisoner's presence.'

'Pooh! Why, it was evidence of motive. But there, it's no good trying to explain the law of evidence to you. If anything's gone wrong, you have yourself to thank for it—a good deal, that's all. What shall you take?'

And they fell to on the refreshments before them.

Meanwhile the barristers, whose self-imposed

code forbade them to enter a public hotel room in a town where the assizes were being held, had straggled off, some to the County Club, and others to the common-room reserved for their especial use in the chief hotel of the place.

Among the latter was Tressamer, who found Prescott awaiting him anxiously, and trying, with poor success, to get through the wing of a fowl. He (Prescott) looked pale and dejected; but Tressamer rushed into the place in a state of exaggerated buoyancy, and loudly called for a bottle of champagne.

'George, how goes it?' cried his friend.

'All went merry as a marriage-bell,' returned the other. 'Have no fear; keep up your heart, old man. Leave it to me; I'll get her off. Much obliged to you for going away, though. Young Pollard did come some croppers, I can tell you. Buller's against us, of course, on the evidence; but what do I care? I'll get the jury, see if I don't. I'll make a speech this afternoon the like of which hasn't often been heard in this dead-and-alive hole. Lewis, beware! Here's confusion to the guilty, and safety to the innocent!'

He had rattled on in a jerky, excited, nervous manner, and he wound up by drinking off nearly a tumblerful of champagne. Prescott could hardly make him out. He feared the strain of the last few weeks was unhinging his friend's mind.

'Gently,' he said, remonstrating; 'you must keep cool, or you will spoil everything. Beware of old Buller. When he is giving you the most rope, he is getting ready to come down on you most heavily at the end. I think you'll find it a weak jury. They will do pretty well as the judge tells them.'

'Don't you be afraid, Charlie,' retorted the other in the same unnaturally careless strain; 'it's my case, and I know how to manage it. I've sworn to save her, and, by God! I'll do it, if I have to declare I did the thing myself! By Jove, didn't I touch up that scoundrel in the witness-box, though! You saw me, Beltrope?'

He called to another barrister, who had been present in court the whole morning.

'Yes, I know,' answered Beltrope; 'but you'd better be awfully careful, Tressamer. So far as I could see, your line of defence is that Lewis must have done it. Now, unless you're prepared with some very strong evidence against him, you'd far better change that tack before it's too late. You'll have old Buller dead against you, as Prescott says, and, I dare say, the jury too. Whatever you do, don't leave it in such a way that they must convict one or the other.'

'Rubbish! You don't understand,' replied Tressamer. 'Wait till you've heard my speech, that's all. Well, I must be off.' He drank some more champagne. 'I want to have a wash just to cool my head.'

And he darted out of the room to go upstairs. The other barristers looked at each other and exchanged meaning glances. They did not like to say much out loud before Prescott, who was known to be Tressamer's friend; but they whispered together, and the tenor of their whispers was precisely that of Prescott's own reflections. Tressamer, they agreed, had lost his head through over-excitement, and would probably create a scene in court that afternoon.

So anxious did Prescott feel, that he at last resolved to bare his own feelings to his friend in the hope of thereby sobering him. He accordingly went up to his bedroom, where he found him with his head in a basin of water, and addressed him in very grave accents:

'George, you must listen to me. You have told me that you love Eleanor Owen, and I suppose, as she has you to defend her, that she returns your love. Now, I have a confession to make to you. I love her, too.'

'What! You, Charles!' He was certainly sobered for the moment.

'Yes. You know I saw something of her as a child. I was fond of her then, I recollect. But to-day, when I saw her, so beautiful, so innocent, in that dreadful place, I found another feeling overmastering me. Oh, do not be afraid! She shall never know it. I shall not try to take her from you. I am not the sort of man to rob his friend. But, George, let me say this to you: that if anything—oh, the thought is horrible!—if any miscarriage of justice should occur, I shall blame you. I shall never forgive you if she comes to harm through your means. Be careful. Oh, great Heaven, man, do your best, your very best! It is the crisis of our lives—of all our lives. Beware how you fail to prove yourself worthy of your trust.' And without waiting for an answer he turned away, and hastened back to his own work in the Nisi Prius Court.

In spite of the confident opinions expressed by the barristers, the judge's mind was less firmly settled than they supposed. Sir Daniel Buller was in the judges' private room at the court-house, sharing a dish of cutlets with Sir John Wiseman. And, of course, they were discussing the case.

'I tell you what it is, Wiseman,' the first judge was saying, 'there is something in this case that hasn't come out yet. So far, there has been absolutely no real defence. Waiter!'

The waiter darted into the room.

'Look at this cutlet! It's burnt to a cinder. Take it away. And tell your cook, with my compliments, that it's always better to have a thing underdone than overdone, because if it's not cooked enough you can always do it more, but if it's cooked too much you can't do it less. D'you hear?'

The waiter bowed low and retired, deeply

impressed with the profound wisdom displayed in these observations.

'You know, if that man who's defending her—what's his name: Tressamer?—thinks he's going to get her off by attacking Lewis, he makes a mistake. I shall go for him if he tries it on.'

'Most improper—most improper,' assented Sir John. 'I don't know what the Bar's coming to, I don't indeed! These young men are throwing over all the old traditions. The judges will really have to do something.'

'You see, Lewis has acted a perfectly natural and straightforward part. He was bound to do what he did.'

'What sort of a girl is she? because that will make a good deal of difference with the jury.'

'I don't quite agree with you,' answered Sir Daniel. 'My experience is that in a case of this kind the jury are sobered by their sense of responsibility too much to be influenced by a thing like that. It's the outside public afterwards who get up petitions and kick up a row in the press about a pretty woman.'

'Then she is pretty?' said the other.

'You old sinner!' retorted Sir Daniel playfully. 'It's well for the interests of justice that you're not on the jury. Yes, begad! Wiseman, she's one of the loveliest creatures I've ever tried. Waiter! Where are those tomatoes?'

The tomatoes were brought in and hurriedly partaken of, as the time was running out.

I suppose you'll sum up for a conviction, then?' questioned the other judge, as he rose and put on his wig.

'No, I shan't,' said Sir Daniel, helping his brother on with the purple-coloured garment which is worn in presiding over the civil court. 'I shall just leave it to the jury. I don't feel a bit satisfied, and I'm very glad, for once in my life, that I have got a jury to take the decision off my shoulders.'

And with these words he drew his own scarlet gown around him and, grasping a small square piece of silk in his left hand, strode back to his seat in court.

At his entrance the whole assemblage rose, including the prisoner, who had been brought back a minute before. Then a start of horror ran through them, and Eleanor's calmness for a moment gave way in a faint gasp. For the object which the judge had just laid on the desk beside him was—the Black Cap.

CHAPTER VIII.

THE DEFENCE.

'May it please your lordship. Before I go into the case for the prisoner, I have to submit that the Crown has not produced sufficient evidence to warrant a conviction.

'It has been laid down by the authority of Lord Hale, which your lordship will find quoted on page 276 of *Archbold*, that no man should ever be convicted of murder or manslaughter on circumstantial evidence alone, unless the body has been found; and in a comparatively recent case—*Regina v. Hopkins*——'

'Yes, I know that is the law, Mr. Tressamer,' said the judge, interrupting him; 'but how do you say the body has not been found? The prosecution have identified the hand.'

'I submit that is not sufficient, my lord.'

'The coroner's inquest was held upon it,' called out the counsel for the prosecution, who was decidedly taken by surprise at this unusual objection. Tressamer treated the interruption with contempt.

'The coroner is hardly an authority to quote to this court. Your lordship sees my point is this. Of course the finding of the hand is some evidence of some crime. But it is nowise decisive. The deceased, or, rather, the person said to be deceased, might have cut off her own hand. We have no *conclusive* evidence that she is really dead.'

'But what do you want? Do you mean that in every case the entire body should be found?'

'Oh no, my lord. If some vital part were discovered, and sufficiently identified, I should say that was enough to go upon. But what Lord Hale means, I take it, is this: that where you are going upon circumstantial evidence—as in this case—where no one saw the crime committed at all, then you must have conclusive evidence from some other source, namely, the dead body.'

'But that is not conclusive. That might be the result of suicide.'

'Still, it affords a very strong presumption. In any case, there is the rule, laid down by Lord Hale, and acted upon ever since.'

'I know, Mr. Tressamer; I am not disputing the law. The only question in my mind is whether this case is not taken out of it by the production of what is part of the body. Of course, I will leave it to the jury to say whether they are satisfied that this is the deceased's hand, if that is any use to you.'

'No, my lord, I don't know that I can hope to contest that. But this is a case of life and death, and I certainly would strongly urge your lordship to consider my point.'

The judge got up.

'I will just go and ask my brother Wiseman what he thinks,' he said. 'Personally, I am afraid I cannot go with you.'

He went out, and Tressamer sat down in a state of intense agitation. He dared not look round at the dock; but others did, and saw, to their surprise, that the prisoner seemed indifferent to what had just passed.

Eleanor did not want to get off on a law point. Without a real, full acquittal her life, as she had told Tressamer, would be too wretched to be worth preserving. And even an acquittal would not be enough while the mystery of her friend's death was left unexplained. Only the full clearing up of the whole story, only the exposure of the real criminal, could bring peace back into her life.

She showed no disappointment, therefore, when the judge returned, with a grave face, and took his seat, saying:

'The trial must proceed. My brother Wiseman inclines to your view, but I am dead against it. I will, of course, reserve the point for the Court for Crown Cases, if you desire.'

'If your lordship pleases,' said Tressamer.

This was exactly what he had wanted. He now had the chance of getting an acquittal from the jury before him, and, if that failed, of succeeding on the point reserved in the court above.

He rose and said:

'I have one witness to call as to the state of the prisoner's health. I shall, therefore, say nothing now, but call my witness, and address the jury after. Alfred Benjamin James.'

A respectably-dressed man stepped into the witness-box.

'You are a chemist, carrying on business at Porthstone. And you have known the prisoner some time?'

'All her life, sir.'

'Now, have you advised her recently as to the state of her health?'

'I have.'

'Will you just tell us briefly what she has spoken to you about?'

'For some time before the day of the murder she had been unwell. She came to me and asked me to give her something to make her sleep at night. I persuaded her to do without anything, and to take a walk before going to bed instead.'

'Yes, and what else?'

'The last night but one before the murder she came to me complaining of nervous headache. I gave her something for it and advised her to go

for long walks, two or three miles or more, so as
to tire herself out before going to bed. She said
she had mislaid her latchkey lately, but would ask
Miss Lewis to let her have another, as she thought
Miss Lewis had a spare one.'

This statement caused the jury to prick up their
ears. Even they had realized by this time that
something in the case turned upon a latchkey.

No further questions were put to the witness by
Tressamer, and Pollard saw no opening for cross-
examination. The former, therefore, at once began
his speech.

'May it please your lordship: Gentlemen of the
jury——'

The counsel paused a moment, shook his robe
out of his way, clenched his fists upon the table in
front of him, and bent forward towards the jury
with stern and solemn brow.

'I shall not weary you with the platitudes usual
on occasions like this. I shall say nothing to you
about banishing from your minds all you may
have heard or read in the newspapers about this
case, for I am sure it is unnecessary.

'Nor shall I say anything about the weight of

responsibility which rests upon my shoulders, because, after all, what is my responsibility to yours? If I make any mistake, if I fail after doing my best, I shall have the consolation of knowing that I am in no way to blame, I have not to answer for the result.

'But you have! In your hands are life and death! The hangman is your instrument; the judge upon the bench is but your assistant. Seek not to shirk your liability; do not trust to others to shield you. On the way in which you discharge your duty to-day depends the most solemn and awful of all considerations—a human life. If you by any prejudice, by any weakness, by any deference to superstition or authority, give an innocent fellow-creature to the tomb, it had been better for you that you had never been born!'

The twelve men in the box shifted themselves uneasily under this indignant apostrophe. They had expected to be cajoled. They found themselves threatened. The rest of those present looked on amazed, and held their breath to listen. The speaker seemed perfectly indifferent to the impression he was creating around him. He glanced at neither the judge nor the prisoner, but fixed his searching eye upon the dozen men he was addressing.

'You know your duty as well as I do. You know you must not give a verdict upon suspicion, no, not though that suspicion were as dark as Erebus, as heavy as lead. You must have proof. You must have certainty. You must know how this crime was done, and why and wherefore, or you must acquit the prisoner.'

It is only under great provocation that a judge will interrupt the counsel for the defence in a case of life and death, but Sir Daniel Buller frowned and fidgeted as he listened to this extreme view of a jury's duties. However, he reflected that he would have the last word. He could afford to wait till the summing-up. Meanwhile he took up his pen and made a note.

'Now, gentlemen, let me say this to you, and let me enforce it with all the earnestness I can command—the fact that a murder has been committed is no evidence whatever against the prisoner at the bar.

'No one denies that the crime has been committed. To do so were absurd. Elderly ladies do not disappear mysteriously in the night like this unless somebody has an interest in making them disappear. The whole question for you is this—had the prisoner any such interest?

'Something has been said in this case about jewels. A question—a shamefully leading and improper question—was put by the counsel for the prosecution, the junior counsel—who seems to have brought to his work a bitterness and an amount of prejudice against the unhappy prisoner which is fortunately rarely met with in a case of this kind; a demeanour which presents a contrast, indeed, to the moderate and judicious tone adopted by my learned friend Mr. Prescott, whom I was sorry to see summoned elsewhere—a question, as I was saying, was put to the prosecutor Lewis, who was only too ready to take a sinister hint, with a view of making him swear that the prisoner knew something about those jewels, about which so much prejudice had been imported into this case. Gentlemen, you know nothing about jewels. No evidence has been put before you to-day as to anything of the sort. So far as you or I can tell, the prisoner was never aware of the existence of such things. We are bound to assume—you are bound by your oaths to assume—that there was no such motive to operate upon the prisoner's mind. What motive was there, then?

'Gentlemen, from the beginning to the end of this case not one motive has been suggested, not one syllable has been uttered from first to last, to account for the theory which you are asked to accept, that a young, beautiful, well-cared-for, and well-brought-up girl has suddenly, without the smallest provocation, developed the instincts of a cannibal, and committed a shocking and ferocious murder under circumstances which would revolt the most bloodthirsty of savages.'

Every word was emphasized by look and gesture. Every word went home to those who heard it. The crowded Bar stared in astonishment: they had not believed their colleague to possess such force. But he went on with hardly a pause.

'You have been told that this is a prosecution on behalf of the Crown. I deny it. Technically it is so, of course; but who is the real prosecutor? Who has been the moving spirit all along—if not the prosecutor, then the persecutor? Who has lost, or professes to have lost, his wretched jewels? Who, the moment he heard that the crime was discovered, turned round and hurled his brutal accusation at this helpless girl? Who rushed off to lodge his information, so as to be beforehand in case any information were to be lodged against him? Who instructed the solicitors at the inquest? Who gave evidence there and at the police-court? Who has been hand in glove with the prosecuting solicitors all along? Who is sitting by their side at this moment, without a particle of decent shame?'

This furious burst of invective seemed to fairly overwhelm the subject of it. He made a movement to go away, but the solicitor restrained him by a whisper in his ear.

'Gentlemen, I am here to defend the prisoner. I am not here to attack anyone else. I do not wish to do so. Would to God that I could shut my eyes to the fact that a terrible murder has been done! But I cannot, and you cannot. Someone did that deed. Someone who had a motive for his act treacherously murdered and brutally mangled that old, feeble, defenceless woman. I ask you to say it was not the prisoner. I ask no more.

'In the old days it would have been different. It was once the law that when a prisoner was accused of murder by a coroner's inquest, then the jury in this court were not entitled to bring in a verdict of acquittal unless they at the same time, and by the same verdict, indicated the person who was really guilty. If that were still the law—and I am glad it is not—but if it were, I should not hesitate for one moment in pointing out to you at least one person who is more likely to have been guilty of this crime than Eleanor Owen.

'I should ask you, in the famous Ciceronian phrase, *Cui bono?* For whose profit was this murder? You have been told by a spiteful servant-girl, whom you may believe for aught I care, that Miss Lewis once promised to remember the prisoner in her will. But did she? In the will which has been proved—and if there was any other will it has been destroyed by the same criminal hands that dyed themselves in blood—in a will dated two years ago, there is not one stiver, not one half-farthing left to Eleanor Owen. But the whole of the testatrix's property, amounting, I believe, to between twenty and forty thousand pounds, is given unconditionally to her beloved nephew, John Lewis!'

What a depth of sarcasm on the word 'beloved' as the barrister brought it out! The object of this terrible attack fairly writhed in his seat.

'Mind,' resumed the speaker, 'I am not responsible for the suggestion that this crime was committed for the sake of profiting under this poor woman's will. That suggestion came from the other side, prompted, I dare say, by the man Lewis himself. What applies to the prisoner applies to him. As far as motive is concerned—and I am now dealing solely with the question of motive— everything is against the prosecutor, and everything is in favour of his victim.

'And now to examine more closely the evidence, such as it is, of the way in which this crime was brought about. It must have been done after ten that night. So far I agree with the prosecution. Now, where is the evidence as to the prisoner's doings that night?

'We know—we have it from the witnesses for the Crown, and from the respectable chemist, James—that she had been unwell, and had been in the habit of taking midnight walks for some time previously. She took one on this particular night. I do not deny it—I admit it. I demand of you to believe it. She went out at twelve, or rather before, let us say, just as the spiteful servant-girl told you. She went out, leaving the door latched, but not bolted, and she walked in an easterly direction along the shore, where the fisherman met her.

'And I want you to note here for a moment how the evidence for the prosecution has been coloured even in small things. As you have heard, the body, or rather the hand, was found next day at the entrance of Newton Bay. Now, as most of you know, Newton Bay lies to the east of Porthstone, some two miles further along the coast. When the fisherman, Evan Thomas, met the prisoner, she was nowhere near Newton Bay, and she had not the smallest intention, so far as we know, of going there. She was simply strolling up and down the Porthstone Esplanade, and her face happened to be turned towards the east when she was met by him. Yet, how is his evidence put before you? "I met her. She was going in the direction of Newton Bay." Gentlemen, I say that is a poisoned answer. It is a poisonous suggestion to your minds that the prisoner was actually going to Newton Bay—was making for it at the time. Why didn't they say that she was going towards the tennis-ground, or the Grand Hotel, or the bathing-place? All those lay in the same direction, and there is not a tittle of evidence to show, there is not the smallest reason to suppose, that she ever went a yard beyond those places.

'That is how the prosecution has been conducted throughout. That wicked servant, who practically admitted that she nursed a dislike to her young mistress, got into that box, I put it to you, for the deliberate purpose of making the case against her as black as she could. In reality her evidence was strongly in the prisoner's favour, as I shall point out to you. But she, too, was instructed, or was taught by her own evil nature, to so distort the facts as to make them bear an appearance against the unhappy girl who is on trial for her life.

'First, we have the incident of the groan. On that subject I ask you to accept her first story, that it was a mere troubled exclamation in sleep, if it was really heard at all, which I may be permitted to doubt. For when a witness exhibits such recklessness and malice and wilful perversion of the truth in a case of this solemn character, I cannot willingly believe that any jury of Englishmen will consent to take away a human life on such testimony.

'Then we come to the incident of prisoner's going out. Good heavens! what colouring is put into a simple incident like that! The prisoner, as we now know, and as this wretched woman doubtless knew perfectly well, often went out at night. She suffered from some nervous attack, accompanied by insomnia, and the chemist, Mr. James, whom the counsel on the other side, with all his bitterness, dared not cross-examine—Mr. James told you that he had himself advised her to take these walks at night. Do you believe him? Do you think a respectable tradesman—I may almost call him a professional man — would come into the box and perjure himself on such a subject?

Hardly. It would be too much to expect. I do not think that even my learned friend will ask you to say that Mr. James has committed perjury, though I have no doubt at all that Lewis would like to have it suggested.'

There was an intense bitterness in the way in which he brought out Lewis's name. Unconsciously the jury began to be influenced by it, and to look at Lewis each time he was referred to with undisguised aversion.

'Yet how this simple incident is magnified and invested with importance and mystery by the other side—by Lewis and his friends! They tell you how the servant awoke at midnight—you know it is an absurd trifle, but the word "midnight" sounds so much more solemn and dreadful than the words "twelve o'clock p.m."—how she woke at midnight and heard a door open—as if people didn't always open doors when they wanted to go out! How she got up quietly—perhaps you may be inclined to say treacherously—and stole downstairs. How she had recognised the footsteps as those of Miss Owen. How she heard the front-door go, and finally found it unfastened, except for the latch. And all as if something very dreadful had taken place, instead of the ordinary incident of a young lady going out for an hour to walk off a headache!

'And, after all, what does it come to? Why, it sounds ridiculous, but the whole end and result of all this is to prove the very thing which I am most anxious to have proved on behalf of the prisoner—namely, that she was out of the house when this murder was committed. They have tried to incriminate the prisoner, and they have ended in proving an unimpeachable alibi!'

He stopped to let his words sink into the minds of the jury, and everyone in court took advantage of the break to change their positions and breathe more freely. Whispers were exchanged, and the feeling began to prevail that a good point had been made, and the prisoner might very likely get off.

'With what happened after that the prisoner has nothing to do. Mr. Lewis and his friends do not seem to realize, what I hope you will realize, that the fact of footsteps being heard a few minutes after is the strongest point in the prisoner's favour.

Why, if no one else had been heard to enter the house on that night, it would have looked bad for her. But that is just what the prosecution, in their blind mismanagement, have proved. They have shown out of the mouth of their own witness that someone did come in; someone who had been waiting outside ready to come in, and who took advantage of Miss Owen's exit to slip in by means of a latchkey which he had found, or stolen, or borrowed from the deceased.

'Now you have the clue. This girl, who stated that ten minutes had elapsed, when it must have been only three, to judge by her notions of time in other matters, this same girl wanted to insinuate that the footsteps she heard the second time were the prisoner's. Gentlemen, I ask you frankly not to believe it. I ask you to discount her evidence by the evident ill-feeling she manifested. I ask you to believe that the last footsteps were those of the murderer, and that they were heavier because they were a man's.

'What else is there against the prisoner? I ask, what else? She came down late the next morning, forsooth! That is the reason why you are asked to send her in her youth and beauty to a felon's doom. Incredible! Monstrous! As if we all did not constantly get up late, for some reason or another. As if a person who had been out late the night before would not naturally oversleep herself. Why, if she had committed a crime she would have taken particular care to be down early. She would have tried to throw off suspicion by acting in her ordinary way. I am ashamed of answering such arguments.

'The latchkey incident is dead in her favour.'

Here the jury, who had shown signs of weariness after their long sitting, brightened up again. They had made up their minds that this was the real point in the case, and were honestly anxious for light upon it.

'Two things are clear—first, that the person who last came into the house, and did up the fastenings, was the prisoner; second, that the prisoner had a latchkey, whether her own one found again or one which she borrowed from Miss Lewis. Now, if the prisoner had committed this murder, let us see what she would naturally have done in trying to throw suspicion off herself.

'In the first place, I say she would not have fastened up the front-door. To do so was practically saying that the crime was not the work of an outsider. No, she would have left the door wide open, as if the criminal were some common robber who had carried off his booty and run away. In the second place, she would have thrown away her latchkey, so as to make it appear that she had not been outside. These points are so important that, with your permission, I will repeat them again.'

Anyone who has had experience of juries knows how difficult it is to get into their minds a process of logical reasoning. To the trained lawyer such a thing is not so hard, but even to him it is far easier to master reasoning from a book than by word of mouth. Oral teaching has its advantages, doubtless, but few things are harder than to convey ideas of any subtlety by means of speech to an audience.

Tressamer patiently set to work, and for twenty minutes he repeated and explained all that he had been saying. When he thought that the jury really understood him he returned to where he had started from, and re-directed their suspicions on Lewis.

'Before I sit down I think I ought to suggest to you how this crime really was done. You have heard the story of the prosecution. Now let me put to you my story on behalf of the prisoner.

'The deceased woman was wealthy. About her jewels we know nothing, and I do not refer to them, but she had other property to a large extent. The whole of this was to go at her death to a nephew. For two years she lived in this house alone night after night with the prisoner, and nothing happened. At last the nephew who was to inherit her wealth suddenly returned from the other end of the world. That night she met her death.

'At twelve o'clock her companion, who suffered from sleeplessness, went out for a long walk. Hardly had she closed the door behind her than the murderer stole up to it and made his way in. Probably he had a latchkey. We know that Miss Owen had mislaid hers. It may have been that. We also know that Miss Lewis had a spare one, and that her nephew was to take up his residence in the house on the very next morning. So that, mark this, if the murder had been deferred for one more day he would have fallen under the same suspicion as Miss Owen, and probably a good deal more.

'The murderer entered, as I said, by means of his latchkey. But it was the first time he had used it. He did not know the peculiarity of the latch. He raised it too high, and it stuck.

'Not staying to notice this, in his wickedness, he passed into the house and upstairs. He tried the door of his aunt's—I mean the deceased's—room. It was, of course, locked, as it was found the following morning. He went into the next, Miss Owen's, which he knew to be empty, having seen her leave the house. Through this he passed into the adjoining chamber. Beneath the bed, in all probability, lay a chest of valuables. Charity would fain suggest that his first intention was merely to steal these, and that the blacker crime was, in a sense, forced upon him by the awakening of the sleeper. The secrets of that terrible night will never be known. We cannot say what passed in that room between that strong, evil man and that weak old woman. We only know the result. A blow was struck, perhaps blows. A life was taken, and the robber became a murderer as well.

'The next step was to remove the body. For what reason it matters not. It is an impulse with all murderers to conceal the traces of their guilt. They dig holes in the earth and bury it, they carry it into the wilderness and hide it, they sink it in the depths of the sea. But the earth will not contain it, the wilderness betrays the ghastly secret, the waves cast up the horror.'

His voice rang through the crowded court like that of one possessed, and every man trembled.

'He lowered it through the window, where the traces were found next day. Then, clutching up his booty, and forgetting, it may be, that all would be his erelong, or possibly not feeling sufficiently sure of his heirship, he hurried down, with agitated tread, so that even the half-sleeping girl in the room above could discern a something strange about his walk.

'Then he carried off the body, mutilated for

some mysterious and terrible reason which may never be revealed—possibly to lighten his hideous load; but let me spare you these shocking considerations. (All this, remember, Lewis asks you to think was done by a young girl not twenty years of age.)

'You know the rest. You know how the fisherman saw others that night, one of them a tall man, going in the direction of the bay where the remains were washed ashore within twenty-four hours. One only point I have to notice. Whether in carelessness, or whether in hellish malice, that man left a damning stain upon the door-handle in the prisoner's room. I say I know not whether he did this in his haste and guilty dread, or whether he did this with a deliberate and diabolical intention of throwing suspicion upon a hapless, innocent girl, whom he has since pursued through every stage of this history, and under every form of law, with the persistence of a machine, and the passion of a bloodhound!'

The speaker's voice vibrated with the fury which he threw into this denunciation. The jury trembled under his eye, as he rolled it fiercely from face to face. As for the object of these fearful invectives, he turned red and white by turns, and would have interrupted over and over again if he had not been almost forcibly restrained by the solicitor for the prosecution.

Tressamer went on, after a moment's pause to recover from his exhaustion:

'And Eleanor Owen, what of her? What was she doing meanwhile? Pacing the shore, and trying to soothe her throbbing head with the medicine of the sea breezes. At last she returns, tired and abstracted. She puts her key into the latch, the door yields before her; she notices nothing, but comes in, closes and fastens the door behind her, and retires to rest. And there she sleeps the sleep of innocence, knowing nothing, dreaming nothing, of the dark shadow which hangs over her head, nothing of the foul deed which has so recently been perpetrated under that roof, nothing of the frightful stain upon the empty bed next door, nothing of that yet more appalling stain which will meet her eyes when she attempts to pass out of her own room into that.

'The next morning she awakes. Just as she is

dressed, the servants rush up; the whole horror bursts upon her. She is stunned. She does not realise what has happened, or how it concerns her. She finds herself seized and dragged away by this devoted nephew and his creatures. And thus, gentlemen, in that state of darkness and bewilderment, has she rested ever since, and must rest till your just verdict sends her forth once more into the light of day, and the verdict of another jury, not less courageous and righteous than yourselves, sends the real author of this hidden tragedy to the doom he has now doubly deserved.'

He sat down. But there was no applause in court, as happens so often at the end of a speech on the prisoner's behalf. All present felt that they had listened not so much to a plea for Eleanor Owen as to an accusation against John Lewis. The barrister had put it too plainly for any man to be deceived. It was not a mere question of guilt or innocence. The issue now before the jury was —which of these two is guilty?

CHAPTER IX.

THE JUDGE.

WHEN evidence is called on behalf of the prisoner, counsel for the prosecution enjoys the right of reply. This right young Pollard rose to exercise, and, as is often the case with beginners at the Bar, he did much better as a speaker than he had done as an examiner.

As soon as he was fairly on his feet, his leader came into court and took his seat. The other case in which he had been engaged had come to an end shortly before this, but Prescott had purposely lingered outside, so as to avoid the duty of replying, which would have been assigned to him had he returned in time. As he had heard nothing of the case, nor of Tressamer's defence, the course he adopted was the best even for the interests of the prosecution—in fact, it was the course usually followed under parallel circumstances.

The first part of Pollard's reply was simply a recapitulation of the evidence. Afterwards he made an attempt to answer the attack on Lewis.

'Gentlemen,' he said, 'my learned friend has practically charged Mr. Lewis with this murder. On what grounds has he done so? What evidence has he brought against Mr. Lewis? Mr. Lewis is the heir of the deceased, it is true, but then he is her nephew. When he came back from Australia, he went at once to see her. He has told you, in answer to my questions, that this was out of gratitude to her for her kindness to him when he was a young man. There is nothing suspicious, therefore, in his going to her before his sister, who lived in the North of England, moreover, probably a long way off.

'Then my learned friend has laid stress on the fact that this crime occurred the night of his arrival. But I submit, gentlemen, that it would have been more natural if he had abstained from it the first night, and done it some time after, if he did it at all. I might suggest to you that the prisoner did it the night Mr. Lewis arrived on purpose to throw suspicion on him.'

And so on. Finally he closed in a form of words which even the most inexperienced prosecutor has by heart.

'In conclusion, gentlemen, I ask you to banish from your minds every trace of prejudice, and to forget everything which you have read elsewhere about this case, and to determine it solely on what has passed here to-day. If the evidence you have heard leaves a fair and reasonable doubt in your minds as to the prisoner's guilt, no doubt you will acquit her; but if that evidence is so strong and convincing that you are morally satisfied that the deceased woman met her death at the prisoner's hands, then it is your duty to return a verdict of guilty.'

With this he sat down, and his brother leant over and congratulated him, while the other solicitors began to consider whether there might not be something in the young man after all.

And now it was Sir Daniel Buller's turn, and all eyes were directed upon him as he settled himself in his chair, with his face towards the jury, who strove to catch his lordship's eye, and conveyed as much appreciation as possible into their faces.

'Gentlemen of the jury, it now becomes my duty to recall your attention to the facts of this case, and to give you what assistance I can towards finding your verdict. You have been told by counsel on both sides that this is a grave and important case. Gentlemen, every case which comes before a criminal court is grave and important. In this case, it is true, the life of a fellow creature is at stake, but that consideration ought not to affect you one way or the other in bringing to bear upon the evidence before you that impartiality and cautious discrimination which it is the duty of a jury to apply indifferently to every matter that may come before them.'

A slight sensation of relief in the jury-box. Among the audience an impression that his lordship is going against the prisoner.

'The duties of a jury in a case like this are exceedingly simple, but perhaps it may be advisable that I should briefly remind you in what they consist. And, first of all, it is, I am sure, unnecessary for me to insist on the absolute necessity of your resolutely putting out of your minds every particle of knowledge, and every impression of whatever kind, which you may have collected in regard to this case from sources external to the inquiry conducted here to-day. It is, I feel, equally superfluous for me to caution you against attaching the smallest weight to any evidence which I was compelled in the course of this case to exclude. The law of evidence is the accumulated experience of the ablest intellects that have adorned that Bench of which I am so unworthy an occupant.' (Strong impulse on part of jury to murmur 'No,' manfully suppressed.) 'And in applying it I can only say that I have never personally laboured under any hesitation as to its general soundness, though I may occasionally doubt as to its applicability to particular instances.

'You will remember that allusion was made by the prosecution in their opening to the supposed existence of certain valuables, the property of the deceased. It is my duty to tell you, speaking as judge in this case, with all the evidence before me, that there is not sufficient evidence that any such valuables were in the deceased's possession at the time when she came to her unhappy end, and that in any case there is not a particle of evidence that the prisoner had ever heard, or was even remotely aware, of the existence of the articles in question.

'Whether they were there or no is, of course, immaterial to the case. The jeweller, whose name, I believe, was John—Thomas—no——'

'William Williams, my lord,' called out Pollard.

'Ah, thank you, Mr. Pollard! But it is of no consequence, because, as I am explaining to you, gentlemen, his evidence really ought not to affect your minds one way or the other. Even if deceased bought these things, there is no evidence that she kept them by her. She may have disposed of them in some manner of which we know nothing. The fact that they have been missing since her decease affords in itself some ground for supposing that she did so part with the control over this property. But, as I must repeat, what became of it is perfectly immaterial, because there is absolutely nothing in the whole of the evidence before us, and by which we must be guided, to fix the prisoner with knowledge that these valuables existed at all.

'You will observe, gentlemen, how important

this becomes when we come to consider the question of motive. I agree with Mr. Tressamer, about whose general line of defence I shall have something to say presently'—(Tressamer frowned, the rest of the Bar looked nervous)—'in saying that the apparent absence of motive is the most inexplicable feature in the case for the prosecution. You will, of course, have fresh in your minds the evidence of the servant on this point.' (The jury found it quite hopeless to even pretend that they had anything of the sort.) 'I refer to her statement, which I will read to you presently'—(visible depression in the jury-box and throughout the court) —'that deceased promised the prisoner on one occasion to leave her a legacy, or something of that sort. Gentlemen, that is peculiarly and emphatically a matter for you to deal with, and on which it would be out of place for me to offer you any guidance whatever.' (Dismay among several jurymen, stolid pride among others.) 'If you believe that evidence, and I confess I am wholly unable to follow the prisoner's counsel in some of his comments upon the general demeanour of the witnesses, most of whom appeared to me to give their evidence with every appearance of impartiality, and in a manner which showed that they realised their responsibility—but all that, again, is rather a matter for you than for me—if, I say, you believe that evidence as to the legacy, you must consider for yourselves what weight you ought fairly to attach to it, and how far in your opinion it furnishes a motive adequate to inspire the very heinous crime into which we are now inquiring.'

The jury by this time were fairly at sea. They could not for the life of them make out which side his lordship was taking, and, of course, it never once occurred to them that he was trying to avoid taking any side at all.

'And now, gentlemen, to consider the evidence against the prisoner more in detail.' (Suppressed sighs from the gentlemen.) 'This is one of those cases which depend entirely on what is commonly known as circumstantial evidence. Well, gentlemen, the evidence of circumstances is just as good as any other evidence, and very often it is far more reliable and far less subject to be vitiated by improper influences than ocular and oral testimony. In cases of this kind it is seldom that we can get

anything but circumstantial evidence. When a
man is going to do a wicked and criminal act he
does not call witnesses around him. No, he avoids
all human sight, he perpetrates his deed in secrecy,
and all that we can do is to seek to penetrate
the mystery by such means as are at our disposal.'

Impression confirmed that judge is against the
prisoner. Tressamer looking slightly anxious.

'The question for us, therefore, or rather for
you, gentlemen'—(the jury look important)—'is not
whether the evidence is circumstantial or not, but
whether it is sufficient to convict the prisoner.
Sufficient, that is, in your opinion, as men of
intelligence and firmness, bringing to bear on this
case the same qualities of mind which you bring
to bear from day to day upon your ordinary
avocations, whatever those may be. That the
evidence is sufficient in law I am reluctantly
compelled to decide. Whether the court which
deals with points of this description will confirm
my judgment or overrule it I cannot say. In the
meantime, you must take it from me that you
are legally justified in convicting the prisoner.

Whether you are really justified on the facts is, of course, a very different question.'

Impression among many that judge is going for acquittal. Jury still in doubt.

'This is one of those cases which make a judge congratulate himself on the existence of trial by jury. It is one of those peculiarly difficult cases in which the mind is perplexed between its desire to mete out punishment for a singularly atrocious crime, and its inability to disentangle the knotted skein of mystery which shrouds the whole circumstances of the affair. I rejoice unaffectedly that the responsibility of discharging this delicate and dangerous task is thrown not upon my shoulders, but upon yours.'

Undisguised dismay of jury. They cast appealing looks round the court and meet nothing but contempt. The general feeling now is that the judge is in the prisoner's favour. By this time the majority of those present share the same view.

Then Sir Daniel proceeded to go into the evidence at great length, reading passages here and there from his notes. When he came to the evidence of the servant Rees, he threw out a suggestion which struck doubt into many a mind which had till then believed in the prisoner's innocence.

'A very great deal in this case undoubtedly turns on this evidence as to footsteps. You may, I think, take it as admitted on all hands, by the prisoner's counsel as well as by the prosecution, that the witness is correct in saying that she heard the prisoner leave the house. That she recognised her walk correctly that time there can be no manner of doubt. Then we come to the second time, when she heard footsteps ascending the stairs. And I may pause here to remark that I think a quite exaggerated importance has been attached to the discrepancy between the witness's ideas of time and the correct idea. Gentlemen, we should all of us fail if we strove to indicate with accuracy the length of a given interval of time. We use the expressions "five minutes" and "ten minutes" in ordinary conversation, without attaching any very definite meaning to them, and, therefore, I cannot see that the witness is in any way discredited if she mistook a period of three minutes for one of ten, or *vice versâ*.'

The jury nodded approval. Now they were on firm ground.

'But it is her answer to Mr. Pollard, when he asked her as to the second set of footsteps, that I wish to draw your attention to. She said, as I took it, "I did not notice them"—that is, the footsteps—"but I think they must have been Miss Owen's, or else I should have noticed the difference." Now, I think you will see the importance of that.' (The jury try to see it, and, failing in that, try to look as if they saw it, and fail a second time.) 'Remember the state of things is this: the witness is wide awake; she has just been down to the front-door and up again, and ten minutes after, or three minutes only according to Mr. Tressamer, she hears someone come in and walk upstairs. Now, gentlemen, under those circumstances, one would naturally expect the witness to be on the alert to distinguish any difference, if difference there were, between the footsteps. And if the person entering the second time were not the prisoner, to whose tread she was accustomed, and which she was expecting to hear, but if it were someone else—a man, let us say, with an entirely different tread, and a tread to which she was wholly unaccustomed—I say one would naturally expect the witness to note the difference instantly, to wonder who it was that had entered, to feel alarm when she heard the unknown stranger proceeding upstairs and into the bedroom; and, in short, one would expect her to get up and rouse the whole household to discover the robber, as she would naturally assume him to be.'

The jury were much impressed. A feeling of gravity spread all over the court. In the prisoner's mind there was a sensation as if the sun had retired behind a cloud, leaving a leaden atmosphere all round her.

'Leaving you to attach much or little importance, as you please, to that observation' (jury puzzled again), 'I will pass on to the point about which so much has been said—namely, the latch.' (Jury bend forward with straining ears. They have felt this to be the difficulty all along, and are anxiously desiring to be told what it all means, and what bearing it has on the case.) 'This latch, or rather lock, appears to have been of peculiar, though not unusual, construction. As you doubtless know, gentlemen, locks do differ very much from one another, and it is essential to their usefulness that they should do so. If all the locks on our doors were of the same pattern, one key would open them all, and consequently the locks would be rendered useless for the purpose for which they were designed. In ancient times, before such articles had come into common use, it was no doubt the custom to have a rude species of door-fastening, calculated rather to keep the door fixed in its place as against the violence of the weather, than to furnish any obstacle against the ingress of undesired visitors. But, gentlemen, we are not living in those times, but in our own; and we are here to administer justice, not with regard to the ideas prevalent among our remote ancestors, but with regard to the ordinary and reasonable practices of everyday life around us.'

This last part appeals to the jury. They nod their heads in approval, and wait for further enlightenment.

'Law, gentlemen, it has often been said, is common-sense; and though there may be a sense in which that maxim is not strictly verifiable, yet in a broad and general way its applicability has never been and cannot be disputed. And, therefore, gentlemen, your common-sense will agree with me when I say that it is a lawful presumption—a presumption which the law warrants you in drawing and in holding till you have some satisfactory evidence to rebut it—that the person who obtains access to a house or any other building secured by a lock of this description must have in his or her possession a key which is capable of opening that lock.'

Continued approval of the jury. They find his lordship a little tedious perhaps, but sound. At last there seems a fair prospect of light being thrown upon the case.

'Now, that there were in existence keys which fitted this particular lock cannot, I think, be seriously doubted by anyone who has listened carefully to the evidence which has been put forward both by the prosecution and by the defence in this case.' (Gratification of jury. How simple it all seems when a master-mind is at work upon the apparent mystery!) 'The only question left for you to decide, so far as I can discover, and if I am wrong it is not for want of careful consideration, is this: whether on that night into which we are inquiring the prisoner had or had not a latchkey, and, if so, whether she used it, and in either case, whether any other person had a similar key, which he also employed in opening the door of this house.' (Jury getting slightly fogged again. But they no longer sorrow as one who hath no hope. They rely on his lordship to pull them through.)

'It is perhaps a circumstance worth noting, though the explanation may be very simple, that neither side has produced a latchkey purporting to be one of those belonging to the latch in question.' (The explanation *was* simple. Neither side had thought of it.) 'But in the absence of any ocular demonstration one way or the other, we are, I think, justified in assuming that the keys in question were small, portable articles, such as could conveniently be carried in the pocket. In saying this I merely appeal to your own experience as men of business and householders, who are most of you probably in the constant habit of carrying articles of this kind yourselves.' (Jury in smooth water again. How could they ever have thought this matter presented difficulties ?) 'There, gentlemen, I must leave you. I can throw no farther light upon the hidden circumstances of that night, and must leave you to decide for yourselves on a calm and deliberate review of the evidence whether, in your opinion, such a key as I have indicated was, or was not, in the possession of the prisoner at the bar, or of any other individual whose name has or has not transpired in the course of this trial, and if so, whether the prisoner, or that other person, or both of them, did or did not obtain access to the house by means of that nature.'

Collapse of jury. Dashed in a moment from their height of fancied security, they lie helpless at the bottom of the abyss.

The summing-up was nearly over. Tressamer had begun to hope the judge had forgotten him. But Sir Daniel had reserved his melodramatic effects to the last, as all orators know they ought to do.

'And now a few words as to the unusual, I may say, I hope, the extraordinary, though unhappily not quite unprecedented, line of defence which has been adopted in this case. The prisoner's counsel has not contented himself with merely defending the prisoner; he has gone far beyond that, far beyond the necessities, so far as they present themselves to my mind, of his position, and has distinctly and deliberately brought an accusation against one who is not on trial before you, and has, therefore, no means of rebutting the attack. For such a course there is, in my opinion, not a shadow of excuse. I have listened with great patience to the evidence in this case from the beginning to the end, and I have not detected anywhere anything that casts one particle of suspicion upon Mr. Lewis.

'He was attacked for having come so promptly to visit his relative on his return. But his explanation was straightforward, and such as to commend itself to everyone who heard him. I shall not trouble you with any defence of Mr. Lewis, however'—(gratitude of the whole court)— 'but I must condemn in the gravest and strongest manner the way in which Mr. Tressamer has abused his privilege as an advocate to spring a charge of this deadly character upon one who is, so far as we can see, a perfectly innocent man. If this sort of thing is to be indulged in, the honour of the Bar—that noble profession to which it is my glory to have belonged—will be dragged in the dust, and its formidable immunities will have to be sharply and summarily curtailed. It has been well said that no assassin is so terrible to the community as the assassin of reputations, and in my opinion the man who is capable of taking advantage of a technical immunity from punishment to lie in wait for and destroy in cold blood the whole character and career of another, reveals a blackness of disposition which fits him for the commission of any crime, aye, though it were as heinous as that of which he has accused his victim.'

It was a crushing rebuke. The crowded bar turned and looked at their comrade as though they expected him to sink through the floor. But he sat pale and rigid, tearing off the feather of a quill with his teeth, but showing no other sign that he had heard the judge.

'It is the prisoner who must suffer most by such a line of defence.' (Here Eleanor looked up suddenly, as if she had only just begun to pay attention to what was going on.) 'Its natural effect on your minds must be to induce you to ask yourselves not the real question before you, namely, is Eleanor Owen guilty or not? but this other question: which is guilty, Eleanor Owen or John Lewis? And to that you could, as conscientious men, give only one answer.

'But that is what I want, if possible, to avoid. My principal reason for making the remarks I have made about Mr. Tressamer's speech is that I do not want you to confuse the issues, as he has confused them, but to return your verdict freely and impartially, having regard solely to the bearing of the evidence which has been given upon the guilt or innocence of the prisoner.'

Here his lordship abruptly came to an end, just when the long-suffering jury were expecting that he was at last going to give them a hint as to his own leaning in the case.

It was now the part of the clerk of arraigns to rise and request the jury to consider their verdict. But that functionary had taken advantage of the charge to fall into a light and pleasant slumber, from which it became necessary to rouse him. One of the Bar, therefore, put out his hand and pulled the clerk of arraigns by the sleeve. He started awake, and, hastily stumbling on to his feet, looked wildly round for information.

The day before this incident would have provoked mirth. To-day it caused nothing but impatient annoyance, except to a few junior barristers, who thought it professional to show callous indifference to what was going on. At last, however, the clerk of arraigns was made to realise what stage had been reached, and he called the bailiff of the court and gave the jury over to his charge, with the following form of words :

'You shall take this jury to some convenient place, where you shall lock them up without meat, fire, or light; you shall suffer no man to speak to them, neither shall you speak to them yourself, except to ask them if they have agreed upon their verdict; so help you God.'

The oath was taken, and the twelve men filed slowly out.

CHAPTER X.

THE VERDICT.

The secrets of the jury-room are little understood. Doubtless this is because all the more intellectual classes are exempted, by a beautiful provision of our law, from serving on juries, and the remainder have not yet produced a man competent to chronicle his experiences.

The Mynyddshire jurymen were very much like their brethren all over the country. They had sworn a solemn oath to well and truly try, and true deliverance make, between our sovereign lady the Queen and the prisoner at the bar, and they honestly tried to act up to their obligation.

Mr. Jenkins, the Queen Street stationer, was among them, and his first words, after the door was closed on them, were:

'Well, I don't know what you think, sir, but I couldn't make out whether he was for her or against her.'

The person addressed was the foreman, a rich building contractor from a large seaport at the end of the county. He was a man of judicial mind, a model foreman, and wisely abstained from committing himself at this early stage. He turned round and asked his next neighbour, who happened to be the farmer from near Porthstone, whose remarks to Mr. Jenkins were given in the fourth chapter:

'How did it strike you, sir?'

'I thought he was against her,' was the answer. 'Didn't you hear him say, "The prisoner must suffer by that line of defence"? And then he didn't say nothing about reasonable doubts.'

'No; but the young barrister did—the one that prosecuted,' observed a tall, thin man, a tailor by trade.

'He's got nothing to do with it,' said the farmer. 'I thought him a fool all along. I know his whole family, and they're all alike.'

'What a terrible speech Mr. Tressamer made!'

ventured a fifth juryman, a short, stumpy watchmaker from Porthstone itself. 'I believe he's her lover.'

'What!' cried the foreman, losing his calm demeanour in the presence of this interesting revelation. 'How d'ye know that?'

'Oh, it was common talk in Porthstone,' was the answer. 'They knew each other ever since they was children, and he used to come down every summer and go about with her. That's what made him so fierce against Mr. Lewis, you may depend.'

'And did you know her?' 'What was she like, really?' 'What do you think of her?' broke from several voices as the whole jury clustered round the little man.

But he drew in his horns at once.

'Don't ask me anything,' he said. 'I've mended her watch, and I always thought she was all right up to this, but the Lord only knows whether she did it.' He paused, and then, as if there were some vague connection in his mind between this charge and a general disposition towards acts of dishonesty, he added: 'She always paid me regular.'

Perhaps the jury scented an underlying distrust in this. At any rate, one of them said:

'I watched the judge carefully all through, and I saw him frown at her several times. To my mind he meant us to say guilty.'

The word came with a little shock to the men. They instinctively realized its terrible gravity as falling from their lips. The tall, thin tailor put in his word again:

'Anyhow, he said there was no evidence of motive.'

'Except they jewels,' corrected the farmer.

'Ah, but there was nothing came out about them.'

'Phoo! that there was. Didn't you see how her counsel was fighting to keep it back? You may depend she knew all about them, and could tell us where they are now if she liked.'

'You seem to have made up your mind,' said another man, who had been talking aside to a little knot of three; 'but for the life of me I couldn't make it out one way or the other.

What did you think he meant about that latch-key?'

This was offensive. It was reminding them of their weak point. It threw the whole room into confusion. Eight or nine of the jury all began to speak at once, and four or five could find no listeners.

When the hubbub had a little subsided, the foreman said:

'Gentlemen, it's no use talking it over in this way. We must argue it out one at a time. I propose that we all sit round the table, and the one that has anything to say stands up and says it properly.'

This suggestion was well received, but it had a fatal effect on three of the jury, who were wholly unable to attempt anything so much like a set speech as this course involved.

As soon as all were seated the foreman commenced:

'Gentlemen, this is a doubtful case, a very doubtful case. Talk of reasonable doubts, there's nothing but reasonable doubts, so far as I can see, from beginning to end. Now, it would have been a great help to us if the judge had showed us which way he thought we ought to go, but I must confess I couldn't tell which side he meant to lean. If any other gentleman thinks otherwise, we shall be glad to hear him.'

But no other gentleman thought otherwise. The man who had thrown out the suggestion about the latchkey, and who was a fishing-boat proprietor from a seaside suburb of Abertaff, murmured from his seat:

'I call it a shame. I should like to know what a judge is for. We might as well try the case ourselves as this.'

'So we are trying it, aren't we?' rebuked the man who had been the first to blurt out the fatal word, and who was a farmer from near the same place.

'You may be, Mr. Rees,' returned the boat proprietor, with what was intended for biting sarcasm.

'Come, gentlemen, gentlemen,' said the foreman impressively, 'let us remember that we are engaged on a case of life and death. We have got to come at the truth somehow, and we must do what we can by ourselves.'

'They should have give us more evidence,' objected Mr. Jenkins. 'What did they want to make so much fuss about those jewels for ?'

'Aye, and there was another thing,' said the Porthstone farmer; 'did you notice that when Mr. Lewis wanted to say why he suspected her, the judge wouldn't let un ?'

'Well, she's an orphan,' said the tailor, 'and her father was Rector of Porthstone for thirty years, and I say we ought to let her off.'

'For shame, John,' said the watchmaker, who happened to be his next-door neighbour; 'don't you know we've got to decide according to the evidence ?'

The tailor hung his head.

Then the foreman interposed again.

'Really, gentlemen, I think it will save time if we go round the table, and let each man express his opinion in turn. Of course, I don't say his final opinion, but just any remarks that strike him on the evidence. Will you begin, sir ?'

Mr. Jenkins rose from his seat on the foreman's right and cleared his throat.

'Mr. Foreman and gentlemen, I think this is,

as our foreman has told us, a case of very great doubt. At the same time, it is our duty to punish the guilty, and not let the prisoner off simply because she is a woman and good-looking, and that sort of thing.' (Subdued applause. The foreman raises his hand for silence.) 'Now, what I look at in this case is the motive, and that is, I take it, the jewels. I don't believe she would have done it simply on the chance of getting something under the will. I don't know whether you remember, but the judge said Miss Lewis might have parted with the jewels, because they weren't found after her death. Now, it seems to me that that points just the other way. I mean, it looks as if she had been murdered for the sake of them. It seems to me the only question is, Who murdered her? Was it Mr. Lewis or was it Miss Owen? That's my difficulty.'

He sat down. The farmer, who sat next him, stood up in turn.

'I say what the judge said; let us decide according to the evidence. Now, what evidence is there against Mr. Lewis? Why, you say the judge didn't speak out clearly, but he did say there wasn't any evidence against him. All the evidence is against her, and we ought to act upon it.'

The next speaker was a rather young man, who occupied a position of superintendence in a large millinery establishment, exclusively patronised by ladies. With such associations he was naturally disposed to be chivalrous. He said:

'I know a lady when I see her. Miss Owen's a lady; anyone can see that with half an eye. As for Lewis, I didn't like the looks of him at all. You know they're a wild lot out in Australia. I heard that he came back for good reasons, if the truth was known. Then look how he lost his temper in the witness-box! And then, as Mr. Tressamer said, the very night he got there the murder happened. That looks as if he did it. He said she didn't give him a latchkey, but I believe she very likely did, else why did the barrister ask him? And then look at the hand being cut off. No young lady would go and do such a thing as that, surely!'

The jury were impressed. The next man was of a shy and gentle disposition. He did not venture to get on his feet, but threw out a suggestion as he sat: 'I suppose it must have been one of the two. There couldn't have been somebody else, could there?'

A withering look from eleven faces rewarded this disconcerting query. The foreman expressed the general feeling:

'Really, sir, I can't think what ground you have for suggesting such a thing. The case is difficult enough as it is, without having fresh doubts raised.'

'Ah, there should ought to have been a London detective brought down,' muttered another juryman, who had taken little part hitherto. 'One of them would have puzzled it out, you may depend.'

'Well, I don't see what more you would have,' said the other farmer, Rees, rising in his turn. 'Here is this young woman, sleeping in the next room, going out at night secretly, under some pretence of headaches—why didn't she tell other people about them beside that chemist?—and here you have her mistress murdered, and the blood found on the door of her own room the next morning. What more do you want?'

He sat down. It was now the tailor's turn.

'And how do you know Lewis didn't put the

blood there?' he asked. 'I believe it's Lewis myself. Anyway, one of them must have done it, that's clear.'

But this was felt to be a weak defence, and the next two jurymen shook their heads, and professed themselves unable to throw any light upon the question. Then it was the turn of the boat proprietor.

'Look here,' he said, ' what's the good of our trying to come to a verdict when we're none of us sure which of them did it? Better give it up, and tell the judge we can't agree.'

But the foreman would not hear of this.

'No, sir,' he said, 'we are here sworn to do justice between man and man and mete out punishment to the guilty, and we must not shrink from our task. We have heard the case through, and if we are not competent to give a verdict on it, who is?'

This was felt to be unanswerable. Not only were the foreman's words worthy of attention in themselves, but he was a great man, the reputed possessor of twelve thousand a year; he wore a frock coat and a white waistcoat as well, and his word was, therefore, practically equivalent to law.

There remained only the watchmaker. He felt a friendly feeling towards the prisoner, but he was troubled by real misgivings as to her innocence.

'The judge said we oughtn't to go against Mr. Lewis,' he said, 'and I stand by what the judge says. Besides, I look at what he said when he gave her in charge.'

'What was that?' said the foreman eagerly.

'I'll tell you, sir. It was in the paper at the time, and I happened to keep it by me, and so when I was summoned as a juror, thinks I to myself, "This may come in useful if I should happen to be on the jury that's to try her," so I just cuts it out and brings it in my pocket.'

The other men looked on keenly, as he slowly drew out his pocket-book and extracted a newspaper cutting, embracing some two and a half columns of the *Southern Daily News*. Everyone hoped that something of a decisive character would now be forthcoming.

The watchmaker ran his finger down the columns.

'Here it is!' he exclaimed, and read it aloud.

'"On reaching the police-station, of which Constable Smithies was then in charge, Mr. Lewis said: 'I charge Eleanor Owen with the murder of my aunt, Ann Elizabeth Lewis. I have made some money, and, please God, I'll spend every penny of it rather than my poor aunt shall remain unavenged.'

'"Constable Smithies at once summoned Sergeant—" that's it,' concluded the watchmaker, looking up from his extract.

A murmur and shaking of heads followed, and the foreman again felicitously voiced the general feeling:

'*That* doesn't sound like guilt,' he said, with emphasis. 'May I see that paper? Perhaps it has some other things which we have forgotten.'

'Certainly, sir. But I don't know whether we ought to be reading this,' hazarded its owner, handing the slip across.

'Why not? We're only doing it to refresh our memory.'

This reply was again felt to be worthy of its author. It had a fine flavour of legality about it too, which gave confidence to the other jurymen. They realized that they were fortunate in their foreman.

That gentleman meanwhile proceeded to glance down the document before him. Presently he stopped, frowned, pursed up his lips, and breathed a stern sigh. The others watched with anxiety. He proceeded to enlighten them.

'Gentlemen, listen to this, and tell me what effect it has on your minds. Sergeant Evans said, "I arrested the prisoner on the morning of the second. I told her she was charged with the wilful murder of Ann Elizabeth Lewis. She turned pale and said, 'It is impossible.' I cautioned her. She said nothing more, and *shed no tears*." Gentlemen, is that like innocence?'

He laid down the paper. The prisoner's doom was sealed. The waverers among the jury went over at once, and even the friends of the prisoner no longer dared to hold out. The tailor would have resisted if he had dared, but his sense of social inferiority was too much for him. What was he, a humble little tradesman, to set himself against eleven men, headed by a wealthy contractor who wore three spade guineas on his watch-chain?

Then a solemn awe settled down over the faces of the twelve men. They did not hesitate in doing what they believed was their duty, but they felt some natural horror of the result. At last the foreman said:

'Gentlemen, are we all agreed?'

And, as there was no reply, he led them back into court.

They had not been out quite an hour, but the interval seemed terribly long to those they left behind.

When they came in one by one, with drooping heads and set faces, the verdict was read before it was heard. Only the prisoner still held out, with that obstinate unbelief in the worst which is a part of strong natures. Only the prisoner and the prisoner's counsel. He manifested no sorrow and no surprise. Prescott put his stoical calmness down to over-exhaustion, others of the Bar attributed it to his confidence in the point reserved. The public hardly noticed him. Their eyes were fixed upon the dock.

The clerk of arraigns stood up, and went as best he could through the tedious process of calling each juryman by name. Then followed the routine question, followed by the awful word, heavy with issues of death, pealing forth through the hushed, agitated hall:

'*Guilty!*'

The prisoner neither moved nor answered, as the clerk formally summoned her to declare if there were any reasons why sentence should not be passed upon her. Some of the women whispered that she had gone mad, or that she was going to faint. The judge covered his wig with the sombre square of silk.

Suddenly she looked up, cast her eyes rapidly round the court, and fixing them full on Prescott, who was attentively watching her, she exclaimed:

'I am *not* guilty.'

'Eleanor Margaret Owen, the jury, after a long and patient hearing, and after taking time for careful deliberation, have found you guilty of the crime of wilful murder. What motive inspired you to commit such a crime I cannot say, and it may, perhaps, never be known. It only remains for me to discharge my very painful duty, which I do by declaring that the sentence of the court upon you is——'

The details followed. The words are too familiar to need setting forth. They sounded in unconscious ears. Eleanor Owen had fainted at last, and was carried helpless and lifeless away from the scene of her long martyrdom.

CHAPTER XI.

THE PRISONER'S STATEMENT.

THE day after the trial Tressamer went with confident mien to the prison for the purpose of having an interview with Eleanor as to the appeal of which he had given notice.

The governor at first hesitated about permitting this. The prison regulations forbid intercourse with a convict, except under certain rigorous limitations. But the name and function of counsel prevailed, and a warder was sent to fetch the prisoner.

Presently he returned alone, with the startling message that Eleanor positively refused to hold any communication whatever with her late advocate. Tressamer left the gaol with the air of a beaten man.

In his dismay he bethought himself of Prescott, and hurried to the court-house to find him and get his advice. He was there, but he was busy in a case then before the Nisi Prius Court, and it was not till late in the afternoon that Tressamer could get a word with him.

The case had been decided in favour of Prescott's client, and he strode into the robing-room with a little natural elation. But no sooner did he catch sight of his friend, who was waiting for him there, than his whole manner changed, and a stern expression settled round the corners of his mouth.

It was their first meeting since the result of Eleanor's trial. They were alone in the room, and Prescott at once addressed the other: .

'Tressamer, what have you to say for yourself? I told you yesterday that I should hold you responsible. You disobeyed my advice, and that of everybody else. You set the judge and jury against you, and the result is what you were told it would be. I gave you fair warning, and I tell you now that, unless you have some reason for your conduct of which I know nothing, I cannot look upon you as a friend.'

Tressamer pinched in his lips hard as he listened to this.

'I might have expected it,' he said. 'We all know that love is stronger than friendship. The first woman that likes can break up the strongest attachments of some men.'

'Silence!' cried Prescott. 'I am not going to bandy retorts with you. Ever since we were boys I have liked you and befriended you, and borne with your waywardness. You have outraged all your other friends long ago, but I bore with everything till now. But this is too much. Where a life is at stake, to indulge in your freaks of eccentricity! It is murder morally. What are you better than the man who killed that wretched woman?'

Tressamer shook with anger.

'Be careful, Prescott! I will stand a great deal from you, but you are going too far now. You know as well as I do that her life is in no danger. What is old Buller's opinion worth on a criminal case? Wiseman is worth ten of him, and he is in our favour. The C.C.R. will save her.'

'Wretched man! Have you no heart, no moral

sense, that you talk like that ? As if a mere escape on a technical point could give any comfort to a woman like her! One would think you were wanting in some ingredient of human nature. What does Eleanor herself say ?'

'I haven't seen her,' was the muttered reply.

'Haven't seen her! Then go at once, and get her authority to appear.'

'I have been to the prison, but she won't see me. I suppose she is ill.'

A look of positive pleasure crossed the face of the elder man.

'Ill—no, but innocent!' he exclaimed. 'I can understand her refusing to see you. You have played with her life for the prize of infamy, and you deserve that she should discard you. This is the best thing I have heard yet. Why, I could almost forgive you now for telling me. I will go this instant and offer my services: they will be those of a plain, honest man.'

And, flinging off his wig and gown, he rushed out of the place in a very unwonted state of excitement.

Tressamer was left, bewildered and enraged,

to curse his own folly in betraying his defeat to a rival.

When Eleanor was summoned by the gaoler to see Mr. Prescott, she at first thought there must be some mistake.

'Are you sure you don't mean Mr. Tressamer?' she asked.

'No; he said Prescott.'

A faint smile rose in her face. She eagerly assented to the interview, and in a couple of minutes the two were closeted together.

At first there was a brief, awkward silence. Then Prescott broke it by speaking in calm, precise words:

'It is nearly five years since we met, Miss Owen, but I hope you have not quite forgotten me.'

'No, indeed,' she answered; 'but you should have forgotten me. I know I ought to thank you for this visit, and for dealing so leniently with the case yesterday, but I cannot find the right words. It is all so strange—so terrible and so strange.'

Prescott was afraid to look at her, lest the tears should come into his eyes.

'Don't thank me, please. I wish I could forgive myself for taking that wretched brief at all. I can only say I did so for fear it might fall into the hands of some abler and bitterer prosecutor. The solicitors were your enemies.'

'Yes; I refused their services. I have wondered since if I was wise. It was Mr. Tressamer who advised me.'

'And why? Why did you trust yourself so entirely to that man? But I forgot. I believe you are or were engaged.'

Eleanor raised her eyes, and looked long and searchingly at her questioner. Suddenly she said:

'Before I tell you, why did you come here—for any special object, I mean?'

'Yes. I came, hearing you had refused—and in my opinion rightly refused—to see Mr. Tressamer. I came, taking the privilege of an old friend of your father's and your own, to ask if I might appear for you in the court to which your case is being taken.'

'Ah, then there is a Providence. I am not quite deserted!'

She spoke in half irony, and then all at once

broke down, and began sobbing as if her heart would break.

'Miss Owen!—don't, Eleanor!' cried her friend in alarm and distress. 'Do try and be calm. All will end happily yet, believe me. I swear to you I will never rest till your innocence is established by the discovery of the real criminal!'

For some time she wept on without replying. At last the sobs grew feebler, and she lifted her head.

'Oh, if you knew,' she said, 'what I have gone through these last two months—no, I ought to say these last two years, since my father died, and that you are the first to speak to me in tones that I can trust, you would not wonder that I weep. Sometimes I have felt it too much to bear, and I have actually thought before now of writing to you to tell you all my troubles.'

'To me! Why, do you—are you——'

She checked him gently.

'To you, as to my oldest friend, whose memory I could recall with trust and confidence. I am speaking now of a time that has passed. Now I shall never consent to claim anyone as my friend—

if I live—until this horrible stain has been wiped off my name.'

'I will wipe it off. Only trust me fully meanwhile, and if you won't claim my friendship, at least so far rely on it as to unburden yourself to me freely. Tell me all, because I feel that you may hold in some way the clue to this mystery. I cannot think that all the circumstances piled up against you were purely accidental, and I must know everything before I can see my way clearly.'

She shook her head doubtfully.

'I am afraid that my story will not throw much light on the murder. Indeed, I fear I am abusing your kindness in troubling you with my affairs. It is a father-confessor I want, not a lawyer.' And she smiled faintly.

But Prescott was in earnest, and at length he persuaded her to speak. Making allowance for some repetitions and some slips of memory, her story was something like this:

'When my father died I was only seventeen. In spite of his being rector, we had lived a very retired life and seen few visitors. The only people

I knew at all intimately were Miss Lewis and the Tressamers.

'Miss Lewis had been in the habit of inviting me to her house ever since I can remember. She used to give me valuable presents, too. In fact, she treated me more like a niece or some near relation than a mere acquaintance. I can never forget her kindness—never, never!'

She had to stop a moment or two to overcome her emotion.

'I dare say you remember as much about the Tressamers as I could tell you. You know that I was constantly at their house. George Tressamer and I were always friends, and he showed me great kindness when I was a mere child. I remember I used to look forward to his coming home for the holidays. Neither of us had any brothers or sisters, and so we were more ready to seek each other's company, I suppose.

'But I never quite understood him. I could see, even at an early age, that there was something in his feeling towards me quite different from ordinary friendship. And yet it was only friendship that I felt for him—yes, even to the very last, I assure you. I never felt for him any warmer feeling than gratitude and affection.

'When my dear father died, I was at first in despair. Only two people would I listen to—my aunt Lewis, as she liked me to call her, and George. My own relations were all far away. I had never seen them, and they were too poor to do anything for me. So when Miss Lewis offered me a home, I had no choice but to accept. And I was very, very grateful for it.

'But in the meantime George had shown me a great deal of kindness. He came down from London on purpose directly he heard of my father's death. He made all the arrangements for the funeral, and wound up all my father's affairs. I believe he must have paid some money out of his own pocket, as I know my poor father always spent every penny of his income, and was often hard pressed for money. But there were no demands ever made on me. All the things I expressed a wish for were saved, and after the rest were sold, and all debts settled, George brought me a sum of two hundred pounds, which he said was mine.'

Prescott frowned thoughtfully, and drummed with the toe of his boot on the floor.

'I suppose he didn't give you any accounts?' he said.

'No; I never asked for any. I felt sure that my father couldn't really have left me so much as that, and I told Miss Lewis I thought so. But she seemed to think it was all right, and I was really too distressed at his death to think much about money matters, one way or the other.

'Well, that wasn't all. Not only did he see to these business affairs for me, but he did everything he could to console me besides. He brought me books to read, he persuaded me to come out walks, and, in fact, he succeeded in making me get over my first grief sooner than I had thought it possible. The result was that I came to rely on him very much. I looked for him constantly, and felt a disappointment if a day passed without bringing him to see me.

'This was in the vacation time. At last he had to go up to London, and left me, feeling very lonely. He offered to write to me, and I was glad to accept. We corresponded the whole term, nearly every week, and at Christmas he came down again.

'By this time some months had gone by since my father's loss, and I was beginning to recover my ordinary spirits. George saw this; he gave me more of his company than ever, and finally, before the Christmas holidays were over, he told me that he loved me.

'You will think I ought to have been prepared for this. Perhaps another girl would have been, but I can only say that it took me completely by surprise. You see, I had never known any other young man at all intimately, and George I had looked upon more as a brother than anything else. When he spoke of love, my first feeling was one of annoyance and fear. I shrank from answering, and when he pressed me I asked him to let me have time to think it over. He wisely dropped the subject, and before we got home he was chatting to me as familiarly as ever.

'The result was that I began to think that the love which he offered me was nothing very deep, but only a warm friendship like what I felt for him. Then I reflected on my own position, as an orphan, dependent on one who was no relation and might cast me adrift at any moment. I realised what a loss it would be to be deprived of George's friendship. I had never really felt anything that I could call love for anyone else, and, in short, I reconciled myself by degrees to the idea. At Easter of that year I accepted him.

'In all this I had made one great mistake. I thought George's feeling towards me was a mild one. The moment we were engaged I found the very opposite.

'When I first uttered the words which gave him the right to do so, he clasped me to him with a transport which frightened me. It was actually fierce in its intensity. He lost all that studied control which he had maintained for so long, and fairly gave himself up to the intoxication of his passion. Had I dreamed what his state of feeling really was, I don't believe that I should ever have promised myself to him. But it was too late to draw back. He had obtained a power over me, from which I shrank, but of which I had no right to complain. I became in a sense his slave, and he did with me what he chose.

'From that moment, unhappily, my own feelings towards him underwent a rapid change. I ceased to look forward to his coming. I got in time to actually dread it. Instead of taking pleasure in his society, I feared him. I disliked the little tokens of proprietorship which are common in the case of an engaged couple. I did not even tell Miss Lewis that we were engaged, though I believe she looked upon it as an understood thing. In fact, I suppose it would not have done for me to see so much of George otherwise. Neither did I dare to tell her of the aversion which had begun to replace my former feelings towards him. To tell the truth, I was ashamed of it. In common gratitude, after all George had done for me, I ought not to have allowed myself to feel so. I did try to check it. I told myself of all his good qualities. I recalled how long I had known him, and how friendly we had always been. But it was no use.

'Sometimes he seemed to realise that I was alienated by his passionate displays. Then he would return for awhile to his old manner, and be cheerful and cynical with me. Then my confidence in him returned, and I enjoyed his company. But this would not last long. When I was least expecting it, he would break into a strain of what I can only call love-frenzy, and disturb me more than ever.

'It was impossible for me to hide what was going on in my mind from him always. He began to find out that I avoided him. Instead of openly coming and calling for me to go out with him, he took to lying in wait as it were, and joining me when I was out by myself. Of course nothing was said between us. I did not complain of his stratagems, and he did not complain of my excuses. But I think we understood each other.

'Then he managed to get Miss Lewis on his side. He used to come into the room where we both were and give me an invitation for a walk or sail or other excursion in his company. And if I tried to get out of it, he appealed to Miss Lewis to give me leave, and, of course, she then urged me to go. The way in which he went to work inspired me with a queer sort of admiration for him. I thought that he showed powers of intrigue that would have made him a great man if he had been able to apply them on some vast stage.'

'Yes, yes,' said Prescott, as she paused a few moments for breath; 'he has great ability, strange powers in many things, but——'

He shrugged his shoulders, and turned a pitying eye on Eleanor. He had known Tressamer well enough to be able to understand her experience.

She went on again.

'Strange to say, you were the cause of our first open quarrel, about six months ago.'

'I? How?'

'You know you had not been to Rivermouth for some four years or more. But I remembered you perfectly, and used always to ask George about you when he came down from London. At last, on this occasion, he happened to say he had a recent photograph of you. I got him to show it to me, and then I wanted to keep it. He objected; I persisted, and finally his jealousy was aroused.

'"You always liked Prescott better than me," he said.

'"I haven't even seen him for five years," I said. "I remember him as an old friend, and I don't see why you should mind my taking an interest in him."

'"Taking an interest!" he scoffed back. "I wish you would take an interest in me. You have never asked me for my photograph, that I recollect."

'But I needn't tell you all that we said. It ended in his accusing me of not loving him, and in my saying that he was at liberty to find someone else, if he was dissatisfied with me.

'But he—he would not take the release. He altered his tone all at once and fell at my feet, protesting that he loved me above all others, and that nothing should ever separate us.

'So things went on, he alternately courting me and threatening me, I turning from coldness to dislike, and from dislike to detestation. But I hadn't the courage to break my bondage, intolerable as I sometimes felt it. Perhaps I should never have shaken myself free but for his own action in bringing things to a crisis. Our letters had been friendly for some time, and, at last, in the month of May, he threw out a suggestion in one that it was time to think of our marriage.

'I took no notice of this. He repeated it more distinctly. Then I wrote, objecting that I was far too young to think of such a thing for some time to come. He took the alarm, came down by the next train, and sought me out. We went together to a lonely part of the shore, and there we came to a full explanation.

'Don't ask me what passed between us. He may be able to tell you. I never can. Enough, that after four hours' agonized entreaty and storm on his part, and agonized endurance on mine, we parted. I told him I could never hold intercourse with him again on any footing, and left him apparently resigned. That was just two days before my friend was murdered.

'He left the place next day, and I did not see him again till after I had been lodged in prison.

'There he came to me, asking no return to the old relations, but simply the privilege of befriending and defending me in my fearful trouble. I was crushed by his generosity, and freely gave myself to his guidance.

'But even in that first interview he threw out a suggestion which shocked and repelled me. He seemed to take it for granted that the jury would convict me, and to rely upon getting me off on a law point. I told him that life would not be worth anything to me under such conditions, and in reply he hinted that his devotion would still be mine, if I cared for it.

'Since then you have seen how it has happened exactly as he foretold. Now, it seems a dreadful thing to say, but the suspicion has forced itself into my mind, and I cannot get rid of it, that he wished all along that I might be blighted in my reputation, and just be saved at the last from actual condemnation, so that I might be driven to take refuge with him.'

She spoke these last sentences in a whisper, as if afraid to hear such suggestions even from her own lips.

Prescott gave a groan.

'Would to Heaven I could contradict you!' he said, 'but I believe it myself.'

And he related to her what had passed between his friend of old and himself. Then he went on to ask:

'By the way, can you can tell me anything more

about that night than what came out in court? It was you who went out the first time, I take it?'

'Yes. I had been quite unwell for some time, owing to my trouble with George Tressamer. After our final meeting I had a terrible headache, and could not sleep at all. I went out each night about the same hour, but I haven't the faintest idea where I wandered to or how long I was gone. I got a little sleep after I came in, towards the morning.'

'And what do you think yourself of this man, Lewis?'

'I can hardly say. He has shown himself my enemy, and, of course, I cannot like him.'

'But as to suspecting him?'

'Oh dear no! I suspect no one.'

'Not one of the servants? Rebecca, for instance?'

'No. I haven't any inkling whatever as to who committed the crime.'

'Well, I suppose I must leave you. I will do whatever is in my power for your deliverance, not merely from danger, but from disgrace, and if I fail I will never venture in your sight again.'

CHAPTER XII.

THE C.C.R.

THE Court for Crown Cases Reserved is a modern institution, whose workings are not always quite understood by the public.

In every case which is tried before a jury there are two questions to be decided. The first is whether the evidence produced by the plaintiff alone is sufficient in point of law to justify a verdict. The second is whether the balance of evidence at the end of the trial is in favour of the plaintiff or the defendant.

The first of these questions is for the judge, the second for the jury. From the verdict of the jury there is, strictly speaking, no appeal. From the decision of the judge an appeal may be carried right up to the House of Lords.

But in criminal cases, where the Queen is treated as plaintiff, there was anciently no such method of reviewing the judge's decision. Now a special court has been established, embracing all the common law judges of the High Court, who sit in a body to decide these questions. It was to this tribunal that Tressamer had intended to resort.

But though the prisoner's legal advisers, both her former and her present one, looked to this court for their client's deliverance from the extreme penalty of the law, the general public turned to a very different remedy, that of agitation, to be exerted upon a very different authority, an impressionable politician in the Home Office.

Up to the hour of her conviction public opinion had run strongly against Eleanor. Whether this was deliberately aimed at by Tressamer or not, it was the consequence of the policy adopted by him. But no sooner had the law pronounced her doom than the tide turned with startling rapidity, and a gigantic agitation was at once set on foot for a reprieve.

Clergymen of mild manners and susceptible hearts went round canvassing their parishioners for signatures to petitions. Legal gentlemen, whose practice did not yet correspond to their own opinion of their deserts, rushed into print with gratuitous opinions on the evidence and the various points in the case. Newspaper reporters, sensitively alive to the first symptoms of a 'boom,' wrote up the tragic situation with graphic pens. They described the youth and beauty of the prisoner, her gentle bringing up, her desolate condition. Even her relations with the counsel for the defence, of which some inkling had transpired, were freely glanced at, and the reader was invited to sympathize with the despair of the lover as well as of the beloved.

Then the illustrated journals took it up. They had already given pictures of the scene of the crime, of the deceased, and of other characters, including the prisoner. But they now threw away the blocks representing Eleanor, and which had originally done service in America, where they represented a female temperance lecturer of moderate attractiveness, and came out with full-page illustrations, taken in one case from the portrait of the most charming actress on the

Parisian stage, and all calculated to feed the growing flame of sympathy with the victim of what was now boldly referred to as a 'miscarriage of justice.'

The sporting fraternity, too, rallied round Eleanor almost to a man. A tremendous number of wagers had been made as to her fate, and those whose success was involved in her escape neglected no means of bringing about the desired end. And as public sentiment has not yet sunk quite so low as to tolerate petitions and meetings against clemency, the natural effect of all this was to make it appear that the suffrages of the whole community were on one side.

Even the jurymen began to repent their verdict. Several of them allowed themselves to be interviewed by pressmen, and went so far as to state that they had given their verdict with much misgiving, and hoped that a commutation of sentence would follow.

Petitions flowed in upon the Home Secretary. Meetings were held, not only in Porthstone and the neighbouring towns, but all over the country. Finally the excitement culminated in a monster meeting in London itself, in one of the largest public halls of the Metropolis, at which the chair was taken by a nobleman, and the speakers included a canon of the Church of England, a Roman cardinal, a leading light of the Wesleyan denomination, a major-general (on half-pay), and an ex-colonial judge.

The office of Home Secretary happened to be held at this time by an experienced member of the legal profession, and it is well known that trained lawyers are far more cautious in condemning, and usually milder in punishing, than laymen. The Home Secretary wavered. He sent for the judge who had presided at the trial, and Sir Daniel Buller, who had had time to recover from his little pique against the prisoner's counsel, infused his own doubt into the Home Secretary's mind.

At last the Minister issued a decision. It was a thorough specimen of the not-guilty-but-don't-do-it-again order of judgment. It stated that the Home Secretary saw no reason to doubt the substantial guilt of Eleanor Owen, but that as, in his opinion, the evidence was of an imperfect character, and failed to throw a clear light upon all the circumstances of the case, including the motive for the crime, he had advised her Majesty to commute the sentence to one of imprisonment for life.

The very day that this unsatisfactory announcement appeared, thirteen judges sat side by side at the Royal Law Courts to consider the point reserved.

Charles Prescott represented the prisoner. If the judges felt any surprise at this change of sides they were careful not to express it. Young Mr. Pollard appeared on behalf of the Crown, but he was led by the great Appleby, Q.C., and, as a matter of fact, was not allowed to open his lips once during the proceedings.

Prescott's argument was long and elaborate. A crowded bar were present to hear the celebrated case, and the feeling was universal among them that he had never shone so conspicuously on any former occasion. He took up the history of the law of murder from its earliest stages, and along with it he traced the gradual evolution of circumstantial evidence. He showed with what suspicion and reluctance the latter had been gradual'y admitted into our courts, and how succeeding judges had been careful to fence it in and restrain its application. Then he turned to the particular rule of law which Tressamer had relied on in the Assize Court, and repeated and emphasized the arguments made use of by him. He wound up with an impressive appeal to the judges to lean in the prisoner's favour, reminding them of the old maxim that a statute must be construed in favour of life, and asking them to apply the same principle in expounding the common law.

Then Appleby, Q.C., addressed the court. In reply to Prescott's last observations, he said that imperfection of evidence was a good ground for commutation of sentence, but none for releasing the prisoner altogether. This was, of course, a reminder to the judges of the Home Secretary's decision, announced that morning. Then he proceeded to argue the case on general lines.

He began by stigmatizing Hale's precept as a mere piece of advice to juries, rather than a maxim of law. He went on to say:

'The most serious difficulty in following this

rule is to know how far to apply it. How much of the deceased's body is it necessary to produce in order to justify a conviction? If the head had been discovered, surely my learned friend would not venture to argue that that was not sufficient. It seems clear that it must be a question of fact in each case, and a question of fact is eminently one for the jury, and where they are satisfied that a death has taken place, it would be the height of folly for their verdict to be set aside because there was not exactly what would enable a coroner to hold an inquest.

'In the present case, however, as a matter of fact, an inquest has been held. The proceedings have gone on all along on the assumption which every reasonable man must have formed, namely, that the body of the deceased had been committed to the waves. To set aside the conviction under such circumstances is simply to encourage crime, and to hold out a guarantee of safety to every murderer who will take a little trouble to conceal the remains of his victim.'

When Appleby had finished, Prescott made a brief reply. He confined himself to saying that this was a case of interpreting the law, and not of framing it anew on the ground of expediency. But, he added, even if the court had to decide without reference to authority, he should still be prepared to urge that the danger of convicting one innocent person must always outweigh that of granting immunity to any number of felons, and he reminded their lordships how very rarely such a circumstance as the present occurred in actual experience.

When the judges came to give their opinions it was at once evident that the court was divided. In accordance with old etiquette, the youngest judge delivered himself first, and he, with some hesitation, declared in favour of the prisoner. But the next three all took the opposite side, and did so with great firmness. After them came another who supported Prescott's view, and then one who sided against him. Sir Daniel Buller repeated his decision at the trial, and Sir John Wiseman dwelt with elaboration on the reasons which swayed his cautious mind to the opposite view.

But the member of the court who was listened to with most attention by his brethren was Sir

Stephen James, who had made a European reputation by his studies in criminal law. His works on the subject were in every library, and his mere dictum carried almost as much weight as a decided case. When it began to be evident that he was going in the prisoner's favour, Prescott took courage again.

His lordship's decision was brief, and to the point.

'When I am asked to apply a rule of law to a state of facts,' he said, 'and it appears doubtful whether or no the facts are included in the strict wording of the rule, I think it rational to look behind the words to the meaning, and to ask whether the reason for the rule applies with equal force to the facts now before me. Now, the reason I am able to discover for Sir Matthew Hale's rule is the danger of condemning anyone on a capital charge when you cannot be quite sure that a capital crime has been committed. It is no use to say to me that the jury believe this, that, or the other. The jury may believe it will be a fine day to-morrow, but that does not justify me in condemning a man to death on the assumption that it will be a fine day. The question is whether the jury are justified in coming to their verdict by cogent and decisive evidence. In this case I can see nothing of the sort. An eccentric old lady, with a mania for hoarding jewels, has disappeared in the night, carrying her jewels with her. A hand, identified as hers, because of the rings on it, was found on the beach next day. On those grounds, practically, we are asked to say that she is dead. I can only say that I decline to come to any such conclusion, and furthermore, I am quite satisfied that if Sir Matthew Hale were sitting on this bench to-day he would be in favour of quashing this conviction.'

Two other judges at once subscribed this judgment, and finally, when all but the Chief Justice had spoken, it appeared that the court so far was evenly divided, and that Lord Christobel held the fate of the prisoner in his hands.

Possibly his lordship was not ill-pleased at this. He was a past master of dramatic effect, and in his hands the ancient dignity of Lord Chief Justice of England lost nothing of its imposing character. It may be added that it lost nothing of that higher dignity conferred upon it by the Gascoignes of another age. Lord Christobel had shown on more than one occasion that all ranks, even the highest, were equal in the eye of the law as administered by him. He was the scourge of truckling magistrates, and a thorn in the side of those petty tyrants whom our peculiar system allows to flourish in rural districts in the degraded robes of justice.

He did not long keep the court in suspense. In a gracefully-worded judgment he endorsed the arguments of the prisoner's counsel, and pronounced the conviction of Eleanor Owen to be void in law. The prisoner was to be discharged forthwith.

Hardly did Prescott wait for the closing words of the judgment before rushing out to the telegraph office at the entrance to the Law Courts, and despatching a message to Eleanor, who was still in Abertaff gaol.

He followed this up by thrusting a few things into a bag, cashing a cheque, and hurrying to Paddington, where he caught an express for the county town.

Within four hours he was in Eleanor's presence.

She had waited for him in the prison, and now put on some outdoor things. He led her to the door, where the governor took a courteous leave of them, and they passed through the gates.

When she found herself for the first time in the open air, Eleanor's limbs shook beneath her. She looked wildly round, as if fearing to behold some disagreeable object, and then begged Prescott to take her to a seat.

They had emerged into a wide, dirty street, formed by the prison wall on one side and a row of shabby little houses and shops on the other. A few boys were playing marbles on the path, and Eleanor never saw the game afterwards without remembering that evening.

The sun was about to set as they took their way by the quietest route to a little public garden in the neighbourhood, where was a grass plot and some seats. There they stopped, and sat down for a short time to decide on Eleanor's future steps.

Eleanor's first words struck heavily in the ears of her companion.

'I almost wish myself back again. Where am I to go now?' And she shivered slightly.

'Oh, Eleanor, don't say that! To-night you must go to some hotel in the town, but to-morrow we will go up to town together, and I will find you lodgings for a time.'

She turned and looked at him sorrowfully, not reproachfully, and shook her head.

'No, no. You forget what I said to you before. I have accepted your friendship, and I need not tell you how grateful I am for it, and for your efforts in obtaining my release. But I am still where I was, as far as the world is concerned. They will go on believing me guilty, and while they do I cannot let you associate with me.'

'Oh, why not? Surely you know by this time what you are to me? Need I tell you, Eleanor——'

She put up her hand.

'Hush, Charles!'

The word sent a thrill through him. He looked round. Some children were engrossed in a game a hundred yards and more away. The sunlight was fading from gold to crimson across the roofs and chimneys beyond. The whole scene was still and Sabbath-like. A great peace seemed to speak to him, and bid him take courage and hope for better things. He turned again to Eleanor.

'Thank you,' he said, in acknowledgment of her tacit confession. 'But oh! if I am satisfied, what need you care for others? Listen: I have some money—more than enough to keep us for some years. We will go to Australia, where they have not heard of us; or, if they have, we will change our names. I can join the bar there, and do as well as here. Are you not my only happiness? What are other things compared to that?'

Again she looked at him sorrowfully. Again she shook her head. Then she turned and gazed into the green and crimson of the sunset while she spoke.

'You would not speak like that if you knew me. Do you suppose I have not thought of all these things during my weary prison hours? I have done nothing else since I saw you, since I saw you and knew you loved me, Charles. But I must be strong where you are weak. I must decide in this matter without heeding your wishes.

I must decide as your mother would, if you asked her. Would she wish you to marry a convicted murderess? I have to speak plainly, because I want you to understand me at once, Charles, and spare me the pain of further talk like this. I shall go to London by myself, and I shall let you have my address on the strict condition that you are never to come and see me till my character stands clear again. You may write to me sometimes, not often, but if you break the condition and come to me, I shall move somewhere else and hide myself from you altogether. Now let us go and find a hotel for me, different from yours.'

She made a movement to rise. Charles looked round once more. The children had finished their game and disappeared. The brilliancy of the sunset was dropping into dusk and gray. They were alone in the twilight, beneath the faded trees.

'Eleanor, one pledge that you will not forsake me!'

She turned. Their eyes met; then their lips. The silent, close embrace lasted but a minute, though to both of them it seemed longer than the whole of their previous life. Then they arose and went forth out of their poor paradise, like Adam and Eve, with the world lying empty and desolate in front of them.

CHAPTER XIII.

UNDER THE GREAT SEAL.

SHORTLY after Prescott had returned to town, he was surprised to get a letter from Tressamer to this effect:

'I want you to give me Eleanor's address. I must see her once more, as I have something of importance to say to her.'

Without an instant's hesitation he sat down and wrote an answer, in which he said ·

'You have no further claim on my friendship, nor on Miss Owen's. Fortunately, she is now under my protection, and in a place where you are not likely to find her. Do not expect for one moment that I shall do anything to bring her again within the reach of your dangerous character. Only the memory of our old kindness restrains me from writing in a very much stronger way. I am sorry that I must ask you never to hold communication with me again.'

Meanwhile Prescott had been doing his utmost to obtain some further light upon the mystery. But neither his inquiries nor those of the skilled detective whom he sent down at his own expense to investigate had resulted so far in finding the smallest clue to what had happened on the night of the first of June.

He had not seen Eleanor since they parted at Abertaff. He now received a letter from her, in which she fulfilled her promise of letting him know her address. But her letter was so despondent, and showed her to feel her situation so deeply, that Prescott was greatly shocked and grieved.

Two days after he was roused by seeing in the papers this announcement:

'THE PORTHSTONE MURDER: DISCOVERY OF THE LOST JEWELS.—Last night, while dragging for fish along the shore of Newton Bay, some fishermen brought to land in their net a chest which had evidently been in the water some time. On being opened, it was found to be full of valuable gems. The police were at once communicated with, it being supposed that they were those missing since the night of the murder. They sent for Mr. Lewis, but as he was unable to speak to their identity, Mr. Williams, of Abertaff, who had supplied deceased with jewellery, was wired for, and he came down by the next train and identified the contents of the chest as the missing jewels. It will be remembered that a part of the body was discovered at or about the same place.

'The importance of the discovery is in negativing the theory that the crime was committed for the sake of robbery. But it cannot be said that the mystery which has enshrouded this murder from first to last is in any degree dispelled by this new incident.'

While Prescott was still pondering over this

discovery, and its bearing on the position of Eleanor and the facts in the case, he received a second letter from Tressamer.

His first impulse was to return it unopened, but he thought this might be doing an injustice, as the letter might contain some explanation, though hardly any excuse for his strange conduct. He therefore opened it.

The letter was a long one, taking up many sheets of paper. After the opening words, it went on:

'I know not what opinion you have formed of me and of my conduct towards Eleanor Owen. Neither do I write in any hope of excusing myself. I am past that now, and I shall soon be past the reach of your anger and of hers.

'Let me begin at the beginning. You remember our childhood, and you know, none better, the bonds between Eleanor and myself. But you do not know that, as children, we were united by those pledges which children sometimes make in imitation of the serious engagements of later life. Of course, as we grew older that passed more or less out of sight, but the memory of it remained—at least, with me.

'I think it was you who first came between us, even at that early age. I used to think she liked you better than me. But why dwell on these things? Let me come on to a later time, the time of her father's death, when I had passed into manhood, and she was passing into young womanhood.

'That was my first opportunity of showing her my devotion, and I did so. I paid off her father's debts, and by the time I had settled everything, and handed over a little sum to her, I had spent some hundreds of pounds of my own.

'Eleanor was grateful. Whether she had any warmer feeling for me at that time, I cannot say. But I thought then that she had, and that she returned my love—not in the degree that I gave it; no, that could not be. Still, the pleasure she took in my company, the trust with which she seemed to lean on me, certainly filled me with the hope of some day winning her.

'I went to work cautiously. I dreaded her being afraid of my passion if I let her see its whole force. I never did. I chained it up when I was with her, and played a mild and cheerful part. I had my reward. At last, the Christmas after her father's death, I ventured to speak. She heard me with no delight, but yet, it seemed, with no great repugnance. Time soon reconciled her to the idea, and before long, I had the rapture of hearing her consent to be mine.

'Then it was that I betrayed myself. I let my mad passion peep forth for an instant, and in that instant I was undone. I saw I had terrified and shocked her. I would have given worlds to recall that volcanic outburst, but it was too late. Her feelings, mild hitherto, were soured by the lightning of my intense love. From that hour she turned from me with deeper and deeper aversion, and from that hour my passion grew and grew upon me with the force of mania, till it usurped the functions of reason, morality, prudence, and every motive that guides and controls the life of man, and left me with but one dominating, desperate idea, that I must possess Eleanor Owen, or perish.

'I need not dwell on what happened during the

next year. How I saw her turning from me, with a sickening heart; how I hungered.for the tokens of even that mild friendship she had shown me of old, and how even that was denied; how I brooded upon my wrongs till I scarce knew whether I loved or hated her, whether it was passion or revenge that inspired my mad resolve to kill her rather than forfeit my right to her.

'You, yes, you, came between us again. God help me, I sometimes think she must have loved you all along, unconsciously. She asked me for your portrait; I refused. She persisted. Then my wrath broke out in an ungovernable transport of jealousy, and I showed—I must have shown—something of the black stuff that was working in my heart. I saw her lose. colour. I saw her tremble, and I rushed away to calm myself if I could.

'From that moment I could see that all friendly feeling was at an end between us. She hated me and I hated her. But I would not give her up. The very animosity between us seemed only to feed my fierce desire to have her and make her my slave. Am I writing wildly? Do you start back and shudder at all this? Go on; you have not yet come to a glimmering of the worst!

'I began to grow impatient for a final end to this state of things, and I pressed her to name a day for the marriage. She replied, putting me off. I went down by the next train to have it out with her. And then at last we spoke freely.

'I accused her of having ceased to love me. She said she had never really felt love for me, but only affection, and that I had extinguished that by my own behaviour.

'I asked her what behaviour. She was silent. Then the flood-gates of my wrath broke loose, and I put all her weakness and wickedness before her. Ah, how I spoke! You may think you have heard me eloquent. But you never have. I was that afternoon as one inspired. I stood there on the bare sands, alone with her, with the wind rushing past us, and the sea roaring in front, and the wild seabirds wheeling and screaming far away. Oh, it was a grand hour for me! The frenzy mounted to my brain. I felt like a destroying angel. I took her miserable girl's heart in my hands and rent it in twain, and cast its miserable pretences to the earth. I showed her myself, my manhood, my ardour, my passion, my devotion. I terrified her, awed her, fascinated her. For a time I think I had almost won upon her to yield.

'But my power forsook me. No sooner did I see the first symptom of returning tenderness in her, or what I mistook for it, than my hatred and rage departed; I was melted in a moment; I flung myself in front of her on my face, and implored her with sobs and tears to give me one little spark of love. Fool that I was! Fool! Fool!

'She took advantage of my weakness. Doubtless she despised me for it. She made me one of those mincing, lying answers that women know how to make to us in our madness, and she took courage at last to rise and leave me lying there—lying there with my face upon the wet sand, and the wet rain beating down upon my head, and the moaning tempest rising over me in the heavens, like the awful eruption of maniacal hatred that was working its way into my being within.

'I got up at night and came away. I suppose I still looked and acted as if I were sane. At all events, the people I passed said nothing to me. I packed up and left for Abertaff that night.

'With me I took an object which I had picked up on the sands where Eleanor had sat. It was the key of the house where she lived. When I caught sight of it it seemed like an inspiration. In an instant I resolved to make use of it to execute my vengeance. Since I could not marry Eleanor, I would kill her.

'But in the train a more subtle scheme presented itself. If I killed her, she would be lost to me for ever, and I still longed for her as madly as at any time. The new idea which I had got was this. I would kill, not Eleanor, but her friend and benefactress, and I would do it in such a way as to cast the stain of guilt on Eleanor herself. You see the plot. Her life was to be in no real danger. The body was to disappear, and hence she was to escape a trial. But the horror and condemnation of the whole world were to be turned upon her, and then, in her hour of blackest misery, I was to come forward and say: "I love you still. I believe in your innocence. Come with me to a foreign land as my wife, and I will make you happy."

'I need not tell you much more. I came back by road for greater secrecy, and did not arrive in Porthstone till eleven at night. I was not tired. Some superhuman power had taken possession of me, and in all I did I felt as if I were but a passive instrument in its hands.

'I approached the house at twelve, expecting all its inmates to be asleep. Just as I was about to enter it the door opened, and to my astonishment Eleanor herself emerged. I gazed at her retreating figure with a sort of stupid fascination for some time, and then recovered myself, and went in. I had taken off my boots outside, and hence, I suppose my footsteps sounded light as I went upstairs.

'Well, do you want more? Do you care to hear how I killed her; how I stabbed her in her sleep, lowered her through the window, and came down with the jewel chest in my arms? I had to mutilate the corpse; the weight would have been too great for me at once. As it was, I made three journeys before I had disposed of all, and thrown everything, including the latchkey, into the sea.

'Then I walked back to Abertaff—twenty miles it was, and I got there before ten the next morning. I had breakfast, and was still walking the streets when the news came that the murder was discovered.

'It overwhelmed me. I assure you, Charles Prescott, on the oath of a dying man, that I knew not what I did, till that moment. I was possessed as surely as any of the Galilean sufferers of old. Madness, your modern science calls it. It is all the same. I passed out of it into my ordinary state with a terrible shock, and then I set about playing the part I had looked forward to, of delivering Eleanor, and carrying her off.

'But it was not to be. I had forgotten that she was not mad, too; I had made no allowance for her, and now I found that my protection, my confidence, was of no value to her, when she had lost the good opinion of the world.

'Of the world, do I say? Verily, I believe it was you; I believe you unconsciously thwarted me then, as before.

'I gave way to my frenzy again in secret.

Again the demon came back and resumed his sway. He has held me ever since. He holds me now.

'Yet I can act my part. I deceive all. I just rang for my clerk, and told him I should want him to carry this to your chambers. Fool! He had no suspicion that he was never going to hear me speak again.

'Good-bye. 'Twere folly to ask you to forgive. I do not wish it. Yet, Eleanor—Eleanor——'

The letter ended abruptly at this point. The reader put on his hat and rushed round to Tressamer's chambers. It was too late. He found him sitting in a chair, stark and dead, with a dagger driven through his heart.

* * * * *

When a year had elapsed, a quiet wedding took place, in an out-of-the-way city church, between Charles Prescott and Eleanor Owen. The only dowry brought by the bride was her restored beauty, and a parchment under the Great Seal of

England, pardoning her from all accusations that had been or might be raised against her on account of the tragedy which had so nearly involved her in a felon's doom.

THE END.

BILLING AND SONS, PRINTERS, GUILDFORD.

The Dawn of Light between her last Moments and Eternity.

"As clouds of adversity gathered around, *Marie Antoinette* displayed a Patience and Courage in *Unparalleled Sufferings* such as few Saints and *Martyrs have equalled*. . . . The *Pure Ore* of her nature was but hidden under the cross of worldliness, and the scorching fire of suffering revealed one of the tenderest hearts, and one of the *Bravest Natures* that history records,

(Which will haunt all who have studied that tremendous drama,
THE FRENCH REVOLUTION.)"

. . . . "When one reflects that a century which considered itself enlightened, of the most refined civilization, *ends* with public acts of such *barbarity*, one begins to doubt of *Human Nature itself*, ond *fear* that the *brute which is always* in *Human Nature*, *has the ascendancy!*"—GOWER.

"Power itself hath not *one-half* the Might of Gentleness."

"She who Rocks the Cradle *Rules the World*."

"Extinguish all emotions of heart and what differences will remain? I do *not* say between man *and brute*, but between *Man* and mere *inanimate Clod!*"
—CICERO.

The Unspeakable Grandeur of the Human Heart.

The Drying up of a single tear has more Honest Fame than Shedding SEAS OF GORE!!!

All Hope of Succour but from Thee is Past!

What is Ten Thousand Times more Horrible than Revolution or War?

☞ OUTRAGED NATURE! ☜

"O World! O men! what are we, and our best designs, that we must work by crime to punish crime, and slay, as if death had but this one gate?"—BYRON.

"What is Ten Thousand Times more Terrible than *Revolution* or War? Outraged Nature! She kills and kills, and is never tired of killing, till she has taught man the terrible lesson he is so slow to learn—that Nature is only conquered by obeying her . . . . Man has his courtesies in Revolution and War; he spares the *woman and child*. But Nature is fierce when she is offended; she spares neither *woman nor child*. She has no pity, for some awful but most good reason. She is *not* allowed to have any pity. Silently she strikes the sleeping child with as little remorse as she would strike the strong man with musket or the pickaxe in his hand. Oh! would to God that some man had the pictorial eloquence to put before the mothers of England the *mass of preventible suffering*, the mass of preventible agony of mind which exists in England year after year."—KINGSLEY.

MORAL.—Life is a Battle, not a Victory. Disobey ye who will, but ye who disobey must suffer.

[SEE OVER.

LIGHT versus DARKNESS.

"It is very characteristic of the late Prince Consort—*a man himself of the purest mind, who powerfully impressed and influenced others by sheer force of his own benevolent nature*—when drawing up the conditions of the annual prize to be given by Her Majesty at Wellington College, to determine that it should be awarded Not to the Cleverest Boy, nor the most Bookish Boy, nor to the most Precise, Diligent, and Prudent Boy, but to the Noblest Boy, to the Boy who should show the most promise of becoming a Large-Hearted, High-Motived Man."—*Smiles.*

"*How noble in reason! how infinite in faculty! in action how like an Angel! in apprehension how like a God.*"

"**SHAKESPEARE**, the Greatest Genius who has ever yet lived," taught the **Divineness of Forgiveness**, of **Perpetual Mercy**, of **Constant Patience**, of **Endless Peace**, of **Perpetual Gentleness**. If you can show me one who knew things better than this man, show him!! I know him not!! If he had appeared as a Divine, they would have **Burned Him**; as a Politician, they would have **Beheaded Him**.

"He Taught that Kindness is Nobler than Revenge!!"
The REV. GEORGE DAWSON, M.A.

"Earthly power doth then show likest God's   And that same prayer doth teach us all to render
When mercy seasons justice,   The Deeds of Mercy."—SHAKESPEARE.

"And such is Human Life; so gliding on,
It glimmers like a meteor, and is gone!"

What higher aim can man attain than conquest over human pain?

JEOPARDY OF LIFE, THE GREAT DANGER OF DELAY.
You can change the trickling stream, but not the Raging Torrent.

WHAT EVERYBODY SHOULD READ.—How important it is to every individual to have at hand some simple, effective, and palatable remedy, such as ENO'S "FRUIT SALT," to check disease at the onset!!! For this is the time. With very little trouble you can change the course of the trickling mountain stream, but not the rolling river. It will defy all your tiny efforts. I feel I cannot sufficiently impress this important information upon all householders, ship captains, or Europeans generally, who are visiting or residing in any hot or foreign climate. Whenever a change is contemplated likely to disturb the condition of health, let ENO'S "FRUIT SALT" be your companion, for under any circumstances its use is beneficial, and never can do harm. When you feel out of sorts, restless, sleepless, yet unable to say why, frequently without any warning you are suddenly seized with lassitude, disinclination for bodily or mental exertion, loss of appetite, sickness, pain in the forehead, dull aching of back and limbs, coldness of the surface, and often shivering, &c., &c., then your whole body is out of order, the spirit of danger has been kindled, but you do not know where it may end; it is a real necessity to have a simple remedy at hand. The pilot can so steer and direct as to bring the ship into safety, but he cannot quell the raging storm. The common idea when not feeling well is: "I will wait and see, perhaps I shall be better to-morrow," whereas had a supply of ENO'S "FRUIT SALT" been at hand, and use made of it at the onset, all calamitous results might have been avoided. What dashes to the earth so many hopes, breaks so many sweet alliances, blasts so many auspicious enterprises, as untimely Death?

"I used my 'FRUIT SALT' in my last severe attack of fever, and I have every reason to say I believe it saved my life."—J. C. ENO.

ENO'S "FRUIT SALT" prevents any over-acid state of the blood. It should be kept in every bedroom, in readiness for any emergency. Be careful to avoid rash acidulated salines, and use ENO'S "FRUIT SALT" to prevent the bile becoming too thick and (impure) producing a gummy, viscous, clammy stickiness or adhesiveness in the mucous membrane of the intestinal canal, frequently the pivot of diarrhœa and disease. ENO'S "FRUIT SALT" prevents and removes diarrhœa in the early stages.

CAUTION.—*Examine each Bottle and see the CAPSULE is marked ENO'S "FRUIT SALT." Without it you have been imposed on by a worthless imitation. Prepared only at*

ENO'S "FRUIT SALT" WORKS, LONDON, S.E., by J. C. ENO'S Patent.

A List of Books Published by
CHATTO & WINDUS
214, Piccadilly, London, W.

ABOUT (EDMOND).—THE FELLAH: An Egyptian Novel. Translated by Sir RANDAL ROBERTS. Post 8vo, illustrated boards, 2s.

ADAMS (W. DAVENPORT), WORKS BY.
A DICTIONARY OF THE DRAMA: The Plays, Playwrights, Players, and Playhouses of the United Kingdom and America. Cr. 8vo, half-bound, 12s. 6d. [*Preparing.*
QUIPS AND QUIDDITIES. Selected by W. D. ADAMS. Post 8vo, cloth limp, 2s. 6d.

AGONY COLUMN (THE) OF "THE TIMES," from 1800 to 1870. Edited, with an Introduction, by ALICE CLAY. Post 8vo, cloth limp, 2s. 6d.

AIDE (HAMILTON), WORKS BY. Post 8vo, illustrated boards, 2s. each.
CARR OF CARRLYON. | CONFIDENCES.

ALBERT (MARY).—BROOKE FINCHLEY'S DAUGHTER. Post 8vo, picture boards, 2s.; cloth limp, 2s. 6d.

ALDEN (W. L.).—A LOST SOUL. Fcap. 8vo, cloth boards, 1s. 6d.

ALEXANDER (MRS.), NOVELS BY. Post 8vo, illustrated boards, 2s. each.
MAID, WIFE, OR WIDOW? | VALERIE'S FATE.

ALLEN (F. M.).—GREEN AS GRASS. With a Frontispiece by J. SMYTH. Crown 8vo, cloth extra, 3s. 6d.

ALLEN (GRANT), WORKS BY.
THE EVOLUTIONIST AT LARGE. Crown 8vo, cloth extra, 6s.
POST-PRANDIAL PHILOSOPHY. Crown 8vo, art linen, 3s. 6d.

Crown 8vo, cloth extra, 3s. 6d. each; post 8vo, illustrated boards, 2s. each.
PHILISTIA.	THE DEVIL'S DIE.	THE DUCHESS OF
BABYLON.	THIS MORTAL COIL.	POWYSLAND.
STRANGE STORIES.	THE TENTS OF SHEM.	BLOOD ROYAL.
BECKONING HAND.	THE GREAT TABOO.	IVAN GREET'S MASTER-
FOR MAIMIE'S SAKE.	DUMARESQ'S DAUGH-	PIECE.
IN ALL SHADES.	TER.	THE SCALLYWAG.

DR. PALLISER'S PATIENT. Fcap. 8vo, cloth extra, 1s. 6d.
AT MARKET VALUE. Two Vols., crown 8vo, cloth, 10s. net.
UNDER SEALED ORDERS. Three Vols., crown 8vo, cloth, 15s. net.

ARNOLD (EDWIN LESTER), STORIES BY.
THE WONDERFUL ADVENTURES OF PHRA THE PHŒNICIAN. With 12 Illusts. by H. M. PAGET. Crown 8vo, cloth extra, 3s. 6d.; post 8vo, illust. boards, 2s.
THE CONSTABLE OF ST. NICHOLAS. With Front. by S. WOOD. Cr. 8vo, cl., 3s. 6d.

ARTEMUS WARD'S WORKS. With Portrait and Facsimile. Crown 8vo, cloth extra, 7s. 6d.—Also a POPULAR EDITION, post 8vo, picture boards, 2s.
THE GENIAL SHOWMAN: Life and Adventures of ARTEMUS WARD. By EDWARD P. HINGSTON. With a Frontispiece. Crown 8vo, cloth extra, 3s. 6d.

ASHTON (JOHN), WORKS BY. Crown 8vo, cloth extra, 7s. 6d. each.
HISTORY OF THE CHAP-BOOKS OF THE 18th CENTURY. With 334 Illusts.
SOCIAL LIFE IN THE REIGN OF QUEEN ANNE. With 85 Illustrations.
HUMOUR, WIT, AND SATIRE OF SEVENTEENTH CENTURY. With 82 Illusts.
ENGLISH CARICATURE AND SATIRE ON NAPOLEON THE FIRST. 115 Illusts.
MODERN STREET BALLADS. With 57 Illustrations.

BACTERIA, YEAST FUNGI, AND ALLIED SPECIES, A SYNOPSIS OF. By W. B. GROVE, B.A. With 87 Illustrations. Crown 8vo, cloth extra, 3s. 6d.

BARDSLEY (REV. C. W.), WORKS BY.
ENGLISH SURNAMES: Their Sources and Significations. Cr. 8vo, cloth, 7s. 6d.
CURIOSITIES OF PURITAN NOMENCLATURE. Crown 8vo, cloth extra, 6s.

BARING GOULD (S., Author of "John Herring," &c.), **NOVELS BY.**
Crown 8vo, cloth extra, 3s. 6d. each; post 8vo, illustrated boards, 2s. each.
RED SPIDER. | EVE.

BARR (ROBERT: LUKE SHARP), STORIES BY. Cr. 8vo, cl., 3s. 6d. ex.
IN A STEAMER CHAIR. With Frontispiece and Vignette by DEMAIN HAMMOND.
FROM WHOSE BOURNE, &c. With 47 Illustrations.

BARRETT (FRANK), NOVELS BY.
Post 8vo, illustrated boards, 2s. each; cloth, 2s. 6d. each.
FETTERED FOR LIFE. | A PRODIGAL'S PROGRESS.
THE SIN OF OLGA ZASSOULICH. | JOHN FORD; and HIS HELPMATE.
BETWEEN LIFE AND DEATH. | A RECOILING VENGEANCE.
FOLLY MORRISON. | HONEST DAVIE. | LIEUT. BARNABAS. | FOUND GUILTY.
LITTLE LADY LINTON. | FOR LOVE AND HONOUR.
THE WOMAN OF THE IRON BRACELETS. Crown 8vo, cloth, 3s. 6d.

BEACONSFIELD, LORD. By T. P. O'CONNOR, M.P. Cr. 8vo, cloth, 5s.

BEAUCHAMP (S).—GRANTLEY GRANGE. Post 8vo, illust. boards, 2s.

BEAUTIFUL PICTURES BY BRITISH ARTISTS: A Gathering from the Picture Galleries, engraved on Steel. Imperial 4to, cloth extra, gilt edges, 21s.

BECHSTEIN (LUDWIG).—AS PRETTY AS SEVEN, and other German Stories. With Additional Tales by the Brothers GRIMM, and 98 Illustrations by RICHTER. Square 8vo, cloth extra, 6s. 6d.; gilt edges, 7s. 6d.

BESANT (WALTER), NOVELS BY.
Cr. 8vo, cl. ex., 3s. 6d. each; post 8vo, illust. bds., 2s. each; cl. limp, 2s. 6d. each.
ALL SORTS AND CONDITIONS OF MEN. With Illustrations by FRED. BARNARD.
THE CAPTAINS' ROOM, &c. With Frontispiece by E. J. WHEELER.
ALL IN A GARDEN FAIR. With 6 Illustrations by HARRY FURNISS.
DOROTHY FORSTER. With Frontispiece by CHARLES GREEN.
UNCLE JACK, and other Stories. | CHILDREN OF GIBEON.
THE WORLD WENT VERY WELL THEN. With 12 Illustrations by A. FORESTIER.
HERR PAULUS: His Rise, his Greatness, and his Fall.
FOR FAITH AND FREEDOM. With Illustrations by A. FORESTIER and F. WADDY.
TO CALL HER MINE, &c. With 9 Illustrations by A. FORESTIER.
THE BELL OF ST. PAUL'S.
THE HOLY ROSE, &c. With Frontispiece by F. BARNARD.
ARMOREL OF LYONESSE: A Romance of To-day. With 12 Illusts. by F. BARNARD.
ST. KATHERINE'S BY THE TOWER. With 12 page Illustrations by C. GREEN.
VERBENA CAMELLIA STEPHANOTIS, &c. | THE IVORY GATE: A Novel.
THE REBEL QUEEN.
BEYOND THE DREAMS OF AVARICE. Crown 8vo, cloth extra, 6s.
IN DEACON'S ORDERS, &c. With Frontispiere. Crown 8vo, cloth, 6s. [May.
FIFTY YEARS AGO. With 144 Plates and Woodcuts. Crown 8vo, cloth extra, 5s.
THE EULOGY OF RICHARD JEFFERIES. With Portrait. Cr. 8vo, cl. extra, 6s.
LONDON. With 125 Illustrations. New Edition. Demy 8vo, cloth extra, 7s. 6d.
SIR RICHARD WHITTINGTON. Frontispiece. Crown 8vo, art linen, 3s. 6d.
GASPARD DE COLIGNY. With a Portrait. Crown 8vo, art linen, 3s. 6d.
AS WE ARE: AS WE MAY BE: Social Essays. Crown 8vo, linen, 6s. [Shortly.
THE ART OF FICTION. Demy 8vo, 1s.

BESANT (WALTER) AND JAMES RICE, NOVELS BY.
Cr. 8vo, cl. ex., 3s. 6d. each; post 8vo, illust. bds., 2s. each; cl. limp, 2s. 6d. each.
READY-MONEY MORTIBOY. | BY CELIA'S ARBOUR.
MY LITTLE GIRL. | THE CHAPLAIN OF THE FLEET.
WITH HARP AND CROWN. | THE SEAMY SIDE.
THIS SON OF VULCAN. | THE CASE OF MR. LUCRAFT, &c.
THE GOLDEN BUTTERFLY. | 'TWAS IN TRAFALGAR'S BAY, &c.
THE MONKS OF THELEMA. | THE TEN YEARS' TENANT, &c.

*** There is also a LIBRARY EDITION of the above Twelve Volumes, handsomely set in new type on a large crown 8vo page, and bound in cloth extra, 6s. each; and a POPULAR EDITION of THE GOLDEN BUTTERFLY, medium 8vo, 6d.; cloth, 1s.

CHATTO & WINDUS, PUBLISHERS, PICCADILLY. 3

BEERBOHM (JULIUS).—WANDERINGS IN PATAGONIA; or, Life among the Ostrich Hunters. With Illustrations. Crown 8vo, cloth extra, 3s. 6d.

BELLEW (FRANK).—THE ART OF AMUSING: A Collection of Graceful Arts, Games, Tricks, Puzzles, and Charades. 300 Illusts. Cr. 8vo, cl. ex., 4s. 6d.

BENNETT (W. C., LL.D.), WORKS BY. Post 8vo, cloth limp, 2s. each.
A BALLAD HISTORY OF ENGLAND. | SONGS FOR SAILORS.

BEWICK (THOMAS) AND HIS PUPILS. By AUSTIN DOBSON. With 95 Illustrations. Square 8vo, cloth extra, 6s.

BIERCE (AMBROSE).—IN THE MIDST OF LIFE: Tales of Soldiers and Civilians. Crown 8vo, cloth extra, 6s.; post 8vo, illustrated boards, 2s.

BILL NYE'S HISTORY OF THE UNITED STATES. With 146 Illustrations by F. OPPER. Crown 8vo, cloth extra, 3s. 6d.

BLACKBURN'S (HENRY) ART HANDBOOKS.
ACADEMY NOTES, 1875, 1877–86, 1889, 1890, 1892-1895, each 1s. [May.
ACADEMY NOTES, 1875–79. Complete in One Vol., with 600 Illusts. Cloth, 6s.
ACADEMY NOTES, 1880–84. Complete in One Vol., with 700 Illusts. Cloth, 6s.
GROSVENOR NOTES, 1877. 6d.
GROSVENOR NOTES, separate years, from 1878-1890, each 1s.
GROSVENOR NOTES, Vol. I., 1877–82. With 300 Illusts. Demy 8vo, cloth, 6s.
GROSVENOR NOTES, Vol. II., 1883–87. With 300 Illusts. Demy 8vo, cloth, 6s.
GROSVENOR NOTES, Vol. III., 1888-90. With 230 Illusts. Demy 8vo, cloth, 3s. 6d.
THE NEW GALLERY, 1888–1895. With numerous Illustrations, each 1s. [May.
THE NEW GALLERY, Vol. I., 1858-1892. With 250 Illustrations. Demy 8vo, cloth, 6s.
ENGLISH PICTURES at the NATIONAL GALLERY. With 114 Illustrations. 1s.
OLD MASTERS AT THE NATIONAL GALLERY. With 128 Illustrations. 1s. 6d.
ILLUSTRATED CATALOGUE TO THE NATIONAL GALLERY. 242 Illusts., cl., 3s.
THE PARIS SALON, 1834. With Facsimile Sketches. 3s.

BLIND (MATHILDE), Poems by. Crown 8vo, cloth extra, 5s. each.
THE ASCENT OF MAN.
DRAMAS IN MINIATURE. With a Frontispiece by FORD MADOX BROWN.
SONGS AND SONNETS. Fcap. 8vo, vellum and gold.

BOURNE (H. R. FOX), WORKS BY.
ENGLISH MERCHANTS: Memoirs in Illustration of the Progress of British Commerce. With numerous Illustrations. Crown 8vo, cloth extra, 7s. 6d.
ENGLISH NEWSPAPERS: The History of Journalism. Two Vols., demy 8vo, cl., 25s.
THE OTHER SIDE OF THE EMIN PASHA RELIEF EXPEDITION. Cr. 8vo, 6s.

BOWERS (GEORGE).—LEAVES FROM A HUNTING JOURNAL. Oblong folio, half-bound, 21s.

BOYLE (FREDERICK), WORKS BY. Post 8vo, illustrated boards, 2s. each.
CHRONICLES OF NO-MAN'S LAND. | CAMP NOTES. | SAVAGE LIFE.

BRAND (JOHN).—OBSERVATIONS ON POPULAR ANTIQUITIES; chiefly illustrating the Origin of our Vulgar Customs, Ceremonies, and Superstitions. With the Additions of Sir HENRY ELLIS, and Illusts. Cr. 8vo, cloth extra, 7s. 6d.

BREWER (REV. DR.), WORKS BY.
THE READER'S HANDBOOK OF ALLUSIONS, REFERENCES, PLOTS, AND STORIES. Seventeenth Thousand. Crown 8vo, cloth extra, 7s. 6d.
AUTHORS AND THEIR WORKS, WITH THE DATES: Being the Appendices to "The Reader's Handbook," separately printed. Crown 8vo, cloth limp, 2s.
A DICTIONARY OF MIRACLES. Crown 8vo, cloth extra, 7s. 6d.

BREWSTER (SIR DAVID), WORKS BY. Post 8vo, cl. ex., 4s. 6d. each.
MORE WORLDS THAN ONE: Creed of Philosopher and Hope of Christian. Plates

BRET HARTE, WORKS BY.
BRET HARTE'S COLLECTED WORKS. Arranged and Revised by the Author.
LIBRARY EDITION. In Eight Volumes, crown 8vo, cloth extra, 6s. each.
Vol.   I. COMPLETE POETICAL AND DRAMATIC WORKS. With Steel Portrait.
Vol.   II. LUCK OF ROARING CAMP—BOHEMIAN PAPERS—AMERICAN LEGENDS.
Vol. III. TALES OF THE ARGONAUTS—EASTERN SKETCHES.
Vol. IV. GABRIEL CONROY. | Vol. V. STORIES—CONDENSED NOVELS, &c.
Vol. VI. TALES OF THE PACIFIC SLOPE.
Vol. VII. TALES OF THE PACIFIC SLOPE—II. With Portrait by JOHN PETTIE, R.A.
Vol.VIII. TALES OF THE PINE AND THE CYPRESS.
THE SELECT WORKS OF BRET HARTE, in Prose and Poetry. With Introductory Essay by J. M. BELLEW, Portrait of Author, and 50 Illusts. Cr. 8vo, cl. ex., 7s. 6d.
BRET HARTE'S POETICAL WORKS. Hand-made paper & buckram. Cr. 8vo, 4s. 6d.
THE QUEEN OF THE PIRATE ISLE. With 28 original Drawings by KATE GREENAWAY, reproduced in Colours by EDMUND EVANS. Small 4to, cloth, 5s.

Crown 8vo, cloth extra, 3s. 6d. each; post 8vo, picture boards, 2s. each.
A WAIF OF THE PLAINS. With 60 Illustrations by STANLEY L. WOOD.
A WARD OF THE GOLDEN GATE. With 59 Illustrations by STANLEY L. WOOD.

Crown 8vo, cloth extra, 3s. 6d. each.
A SAPPHO OF GREEN SPRINGS, &c. With Two Illustrations by HUME NISBET.
COLONEL STARBOTTLE'S CLIENT, AND SOME OTHER PEOPLE. Frontisp.
SUSY: A Novel. With Frontispiece and Vignette by J. A. CHRISTIE.
SALLY DOWS, &c. With 47 Illustrations by W. D. ALMOND, &c.
A PROTÉGÉE OF JACK HAMLIN'S. With 26 Illustrations by W. SMALL, &c.
THE BELL-RINGER OF ANGEL'S, &c. 39 Illusts. by DUDLEY HARDY, &c.
CLARENCE: A Story of the War. With Illustrations. [Shortly.

Post 8vo, illustrated boards, 2s. each.
GABRIEL CONROY. | **THE LUCK OF ROARING CAMP, &c.**
AN HEIRESS OF RED DOG, &c. | **CALIFORNIAN STORIES.**

Post 8vo, illustrated boards, 2s. each; cloth limp, 2s. 6d. each.
FLIP. | **MARUJA.** | **A PHYLLIS OF THE SIERRAS.**

Fcap. 8vo, picture cover, 1s. each.
SNOW-BOUND AT EAGLE'S. | **JEFF BRIGGS'S LOVE STORY.**

BRYDGES (HAROLD).—UNCLE SAM AT HOME. Post 8vo, illustrated boards, 2s.; cloth limp, 2s. 6d.

BUCHANAN (ROBERT), WORKS BY. Crown 8vo, cloth extra, 6s. each.
SELECTED POEMS OF ROBERT BUCHANAN. With Frontispiece by T. DALZIEL.
THE EARTHQUAKE; or, Six Days and a Sabbath.
THE CITY OF DREAM: An Epic Poem. With Two Illustrations by P. MACNAB.
THE WANDERING JEW: A Christmas Carol. Second Edition.
THE OUTCAST: A Rhyme for the Time. With 15 Illustrations by RUDOLF BLIND, PETER MACNAB, and HUME NISBET. Small demy 8vo, cloth extra, 8s.
ROBERT BUCHANAN'S COMPLETE POETICAL WORKS. With Steel-plate Portrait. Crown 8vo, cloth extra, 7s. 6d.

Crown 8vo, cloth extra, 3s. 6d. each; post 8vo, illustrated boards, 2s. each.
THE SHADOW OF THE SWORD. | **LOVE ME FOR EVER.** Frontispiece.
A CHILD OF NATURE. Frontispiece. | **ANNAN WATER. | FOXGLOVE MANOR.**
GOD AND THE MAN. With 11 Illustrations by FRED. BARNARD. | **THE NEW ABELARD.**
THE MARTYRDOM OF MADELINE. With Frontispiece by A. W. COOPER. | **MATT:** A Story of a Caravan. Frontisp.
 | **THE MASTER OF THE MINE.** Front.
 | **THE HEIR OF LINNE.**

Crown 8vo, cloth extra, 3s. 6d. each.
WOMAN AND THE MAN. | **RED AND WHITE HEATHER.**
RACHEL DENE. Crown 8vo, cloth extra, 3s. 6d. [Sept.
LADY KILPATRICK. Crown 8vo, cloth extra, 6s. [Shortly.
THE CHARLATAN. By ROBERT BUCHANAN and HENRY MURRAY. Two Vols., crown 8vo, 10s. net.

CAINE (T. HALL), NOVELS BY. Crown 8vo, cloth extra, 3s. 6d. each; post 8vo, illustrated boards, 2s. each; cloth limp, 2s. 6d. each.
SHADOW OF A CRIME. | **A SON OF HAGAR.** | **THE DEEMSTER.**

CAMERON (COMMANDER V. LOVETT).—THE CRUISE OF THE "BLACK PRINCE" PRIVATEER. Post 8vo, picture boards, 2s.

CAMERON (MRS. H. LOVETT), NOVELS BY. Post 8vo, Illust. bds., 2s. each.
JULIET'S GUARDIAN. | **DECEIVERS EVER.**

CARLYLE (JANE WELSH), LIFE OF. By Mrs. ALEXANDER IRELAND. With Portrait and Facsimile Letter. Small demy 8vo, cloth extra, 7s. 6d.

CHATTO & WINDUS, PUBLISHERS, PICCADILLY. 5

CARLYLE (THOMAS) on the CHOICE of BOOKS. Post 8vo, 1s. 6d.
CORRESPONDENCE OF THOMAS CARLYLE AND R. W. EMERSON, 1834 to 1872.
Edited by C. E. NORTON. With Portraits. Two Vols., crown 8vo, cloth, 24s.

CHAPMAN'S (GEORGE) WORKS.—Vol. I., Plays.—Vol. II., Poems and Minor Translations, with Essay by A. C. SWINBURNE.—Vol. III., Translations of the Iliad and Odyssey. Three Vols., crown 8vo, cloth, 6s. each.

CHAPPLE (J. MITCHELL).—THE MINOR CHORD; A Story of a Prima Donna. Crown 8vo, art linen, 3s. 6d.

CHATTO (W. A.) AND J. JACKSON. — A TREATISE ON WOOD ENGRAVING. With 450 fine Illustrations. Large 4to, half-leather, 28s.

CHAUCER FOR CHILDREN: A Golden Key. By Mrs. H. R. HAWEIS.
With 8 Coloured Plates and 30 Woodcuts. Small 4to, cloth extra, 3s. 6d.
CHAUCER FOR SCHOOLS. By Mrs. H. R. HAWEIS. Demy 8vo, cloth limp, 2s. 6d.

CHESS BOOKS.
THE LAWS AND PRACTICE OF CHESS. With an Analysis of the Openings.
By HOWARD STAUNTON. Edited by R. B. WORMALD. Crown 8vo, cloth, 5s.
THE MINOR TACTICS OF CHESS: A Treatise on the Deployment of the Forces.
By F. K. YOUNG and E. C. HOWELL. Long fcap. 8vo, cloth, 2s. 6d.

CLARE (A.).—FOR THE LOVE OF A LASS. Post 8vo, 2s. ; cl., 2s. 6d.

CLIVE (MRS. ARCHER), NOVELS BY. Post 8vo, illust. boards 2s. each.
PAUL FERROLL. | WHY PAUL FERROLL KILLED HIS WIFE.

CLODD (EDWARD, F.R.A.S.).—MYTHS AND DREAMS. Cr.8vo,3s.6d.

COBBAN (J. MACLAREN), NOVELS BY.
THE CURE OF SOULS. Post 8vo, illustrated boards, 2s.
THE RED SULTAN. Crown 8vo, cl. extra, 3s. 6d. ; post 8vo, illustrated bds., 2s.
THE BURDEN OF ISABEL. Crown 8vo, cloth extra, 3s. 6d.

COLEMAN (JOHN).—PLAYERS AND PLAYWRIGHTS I HAVE KNOWN. Two Vols., demy 8vo, cloth, 24s.

COLERIDGE (M. E.).—SEVEN SLEEPERS OF EPHESUS. 1s. 6d.

COLLINS (C. ALLSTON).—THE BAR SINISTER. Post 8vo, 2s.

COLLINS (JOHN CHURTON, M.A.), BOOKS BY.
ILLUSTRATIONS OF TENNYSON. Crown 8vo, cloth extra, 6s.
JONATHAN SWIFT: A Biographical and Critical Study. Crown 8vo, cloth extra, 8s.

COLLINS (MORTIMER AND FRANCES), NOVELS BY.
Crown 8vo, cloth extra, 3s. 6d. each; post 8vo, illustrated boards, 2s. each.
FROM MIDNIGHT TO MIDNIGHT. | BLACKSMITH AND SCHOLAR.
TRANSMIGRATION. | YOU PLAY ME FALSE. | A VILLAGE COMEDY.
Post 8vo, illustrated boards, 2s. each.
SWEET ANNE PAGE. | FIGHT WITH FORTUNE. | SWEET & TWENTY. | FRANCES.

COLLINS (WILKIE), NOVELS BY.
Cr. 8vo, cl. ex., 3s. 6d. each ; post 8vo, illust. bds., 2s. each; cl. limp, 2s. 6d. each.
ANTONINA. With a Frontispiece by Sir JOHN GILBERT, R.A.
BASIL. Illustrated by Sir JOHN GILBERT, R.A., and J. MAHONEY.
HIDE AND SEEK. Illustrated by Sir JOHN GILBERT, R.A., and J. MAHONEY.
AFTER DARK. Illustrations by A. B. HOUGHTON. | THE TWO DESTINIES.
THE DEAD SECRET. With a Frontispiece by Sir JOHN GILBERT, R.A.
QUEEN OF HEARTS. With a Frontispiece by Sir JOHN GILBERT, R.A.
THE WOMAN IN WHITE. With Illusts. by Sir J. GILBERT, R.A., and F. A. FRASER.
NO NAME. With Illustrations by Sir J. E. MILLAIS, R.A., and A. W. COOPER.
MY MISCELLANIES. With a Steel-plate Portrait of WILKIE COLLINS.
ARMADALE. With Illustrations by G. H. THOMAS.
THE MOONSTONE. With Illustrations by G. DU MAURIER and F. A. FRASER.
MAN AND WIFE. With Illustrations by WILLIAM SMALL.

COLMAN'S (GEORGE) HUMOROUS WORKS: "Broad Grins," "My Nightgown and Slippers," &c. With Life and Frontis. Cr. 8vo, cl. extra, 7s. 6d.

COLQUHOUN (M. J.).—EVERY INCH A SOLDIER: A Novel. Post 8vo, illustrated boards, 2s.

CONVALESCENT COOKERY: A Family Handbook. By CATHERINE RYAN. Crown 8vo, 1s.; cloth limp, 1s. 6d.

CONWAY (MONCURE D.), WORKS BY.
DEMONOLOGY AND DEVIL-LORE. 65 Illustrations. Two Vols. 8vo, cloth, 28s.
GEORGE WASHINGTON'S RULES OF CIVILITY. Fcap. 8vo, Jap. vellum, 2s. 6d.

COOK (DUTTON), NOVELS BY.
PAUL FOSTER'S DAUGHTER. Cr. 8vo, cl. ex., 3s. 6d.; post 8vo, illust. boards, 2s.
LEO. Post 8vo, illustrated boards, 2s.

COOPER (EDWARD H.)—GEOFFORY HAMILTON. Cr. 8vo, 3s. 6d.

CORNWALL.—POPULAR ROMANCES OF THE WEST OF ENGLAND; or, The Drolls, Traditions, and Superstitions of Old Cornwall. Collected by ROBERT HUNT, F.R.S. Two Steel-plates by GEO. CRUIKSHANK. Cr. 8vo, cl., 7s. 6d.

COTES (V. CECIL).—TWO GIRLS ON A BARGE. With 44 Illustrations by F. H. TOWNSEND. Post 8vo, cloth, 2s. 6d.

CRADDOCK (C. EGBERT), STORIES BY.
PROPHET OF THE GREAT SMOKY MOUNTAINS. Post 8vo, illustrated boards, 2s.
HIS VANISHED STAR. Crown 8vo, cloth extra, 3s. 6d.

CRELLIN (H. N.), BOOKS BY.
ROMANCES of the OLD SERAGLIO. 28 Illusts. by S. L. WOOD. Cr. 8vo, cl., 3s. 6d.
THE NAZARENES: A Drama. Crown 8vo, 1s.

CRIM (MATT.).—ADVENTURES OF A FAIR REBEL. Crown 8vo, cloth extra, with a Frontispiece, 3s. 6d.; post 8vo, illustrated boards, 2s.

CROKER (MRS. B. M.), NOVELS BY. Crown 8vo, cloth extra, 3s. 6d. each; post 8vo, illustrated boards, 2s. each; cloth limp, 2s. 6d. each.
PRETTY MISS NEVILLE. | DIANA BARRINGTON.
A BIRD OF PASSAGE. | PROPER PRIDE.
A FAMILY LIKENESS. | "TO LET."
MR. JERVIS. Three Vols., crown 8vo, cloth, 15s. net.
VILLAGE TALES AND JUNGLE TRAGEDIES. Crown 8vo, cloth, 3s. 6d.

CRUIKSHANK'S COMIC ALMANACK. Complete in Two SERIES: The FIRST from 1835 to 1843; the SECOND from 1844 to 1853. A Gathering of the BEST HUMOUR of THACKERAY, HOOD, MAYHEW, ALBERT SMITH, A'BECKETT, ROBERT BROUGH, &c. With numerous Steel Engravings and Woodcuts by CRUIKSHANK, HINE, LANDELLS, &c. Two Vols., crown 8vo, cloth gilt, 7s. 6d. each.
THE LIFE OF GEORGE CRUIKSHANK. By BLANCHARD JERROLD. With 84 Illustrations and a Bibliography. Crown 8vo, cloth extra, 6s.

CUMMING (C. F. GORDON), WORKS BY. Demy 8vo, cl. ex., 8s. 6d. each.
IN THE HEBRIDES. With Antotype Facsimile and 23 Illustrations.
IN THE HIMALAYAS AND ON THE INDIAN PLAINS. With 42 Illustrations.
TWO HAPPY YEARS IN CEYLON. With 28 Illustrations.
VIA CORNWALL TO EGYPT. With Photogravure Frontis. Demy 8vo, cl., 7s. 6d.

CUSSANS (JOHN E.).—A HANDBOOK OF HERALDRY; with Instructions for Tracing Pedigrees and Deciphering Ancient MSS., &c.; 408 Woodcuts and 2 Coloured Plates. Fourth edition, revised, crown 8vo, cloth extra, 6s.

CYPLES (W.)—HEARTS of GOLD. Cr. 8vo, cl., 3s. 6d.; post 8vo, bds., 2s.

DANIEL (GEORGE).—MERRIE ENGLAND IN THE OLDEN TIME. With Illustrations by ROBERT CRUIKSHANK. Crown 8vo, cloth extra, 3s. 6d.

DAUDET (ALPHONSE).—THE EVANGELIST; or, Port Salvation. Crown 8vo, cloth extra, 3s. 6d.; post 8vo, illustrated boards, 2s.

DAVIDSON (HUGH COLEMAN).—MR. SADLER'S DAUGHTERS. With a Frontispiece by STANLEY WOOD. Crown 8vo, cloth extra, 3s. 6d.

DAVIES (DR. N. E. YORKE-), WORKS BY. Cr. 8vo, 1s. ea.; cl., 1s. 6d. ea.
ONE THOUSAND MEDICAL MAXIMS AND SURGICAL HINTS.
NURSERY HINTS: A Mother's Guide in Health and Disease.
FOODS FOR THE FAT: A Treatise on Corpulency, and a Dietary for its Cure.
AIDS TO LONG LIFE. Crown 8vo, 2s.; cloth limp, 2s. 6d.

CHATTO & WINDUS, PUBLISHERS, PICCADILLY.   7

DAVIES' (SIR JOHN) COMPLETE POETICAL WORKS. Collected
and Edited, with Memorial-Introduction and Notes, by the Rev. A. B. GROSART, D.D.
Two Vols., crown 8vo, cloth boards, 12s.

DAWSON (ERASMUS, M.B.).—THE FOUNTAIN OF YOUTH. Crown
8vo, cloth extra, 3s. 6d.; post 8vo, illustrated boards, 2s.

DE GUERIN (MAURICE), THE JOURNAL OF. Edited by G. S.
TREBUTIEN. With a Memoir by SAINTE-BEUVE. Translated from the 20th French
Edition by JESSIE P. FROTHINGHAM. Fcap. 8vo, half-bound, 2s. 6d.

DE MAISTRE (XAVIER).—A JOURNEY ROUND MY ROOM. Translated by HENRY ATTWELL. Post 8vo, cloth limp, 2s. 6d.

DE MILLE (JAMES).—A CASTLE IN SPAIN. With a Frontispiece.
Crown 8vo, cloth extra, 3s. 6d.; post 8vo, illustrated boards, 2s.

DERBY (THE).—THE BLUE RIBBON OF THE TURF. With Brief
Accounts of THE OAKS. By LOUIS HENRY CURZON. Cr. 8vo, cloth limp, 2s. 6d.

DERWENT (LEITH), NOVELS BY. Cr.8vo,cl., 3s.6d. ea.; post 8vo,bds.,2s.ea.
OUR LADY OF TEARS. | CIRCE'S LOVERS.

DEWAR (T. R.).—A RAMBLE ROUND THE GLOBE. With 220
Illustrations. Crown 8vo, cloth extra, 7s. 6d.

DICKENS (CHARLES), NOVELS BY. Post 8vo, illustrated boards, 2s. each.
SKETCHES BY BOZ. | NICHOLAS NICKLEBY. | OLIVER TWIST.

THE SPEECHES OF CHARLES DICKENS, 1841-1870. With a New Bibliography
Edited by RICHARD HERNE SHEPHERD. Crown 8vo, cloth extra. 6s.
ABOUT ENGLAND WITH DICKENS. By ALFRED RIMMER. With 57 Illustrations
by C. A. VANDERHOOF, ALFRED RIMMER, and others. Sq. 8vo, cloth extra, 7s. 6d.

DICTIONARIES.
A DICTIONARY OF MIRACLES: Imitative, Realistic, and Dogmatic. By the Rev.
E. C. BREWER, LL.D. Crown 8vo, cloth extra, 7s. 6d.
THE READER'S HANDBOOK OF ALLUSIONS, REFERENCES, PLOTS, AND
STORIES. By the Rev. E. C. BREWER, LL.D. With an ENGLISH BIBLIOGRAPHY.
Seventeenth Thousand. Crown 8vo, cloth extra 7s. 6d.
AUTHORS AND THEIR WORKS, WITH THE DATES. Cr. 8vo, cloth limp, 2s.
FAMILIAR SHORT SAYINGS OF GREAT MEN. With Historical and Explanatory Notes. By SAMUEL A. BENT, A.M. Crown 8vo, cloth extra, 7s. 6d.
SLANG DICTIONARY: Etymological, Historical, and Anecdotal. Cr. 8vo, cl., 6s. 6d.
WOMEN OF THE DAY: A Biographical Dictionary. By F. HAYS. Cr.8vo, cl., 5s.
WORDS, FACTS, AND PHRASES: A Dictionary of Curious, Quaint, and Out-of-the-Way Matters. By ELIEZER EDWARDS. Crown 8vo, cloth extra, 7s. 6d.

DIDEROT.—THE PARADOX OF ACTING. Translated, with Notes,
by WALTER HERRIES POLLOCK. With a Preface by HENRY IRVING. Crown 8vo,
parchment, 4s. 6d.

DOBSON (AUSTIN), WORKS BY.
THOMAS BEWICK & HIS PUPILS. With 95 Illustrations. Square 8vo, cloth. 6s.
FOUR FRENCHWOMEN. With 4 Portraits. Crown 8vo, buckram, gilt top, 6s.
EIGHTEENTH CENTURY VIGNETTES. Two SERIES. Cr. 8vo, buckram, 6s. each.

DOBSON (W. T.)—POETICAL INGENUITIES AND ECCENTRICITIES. Post 8vo, cloth limp, 2s. 6d.

DONOVAN (DICK), DETECTIVE STORIES BY.
Post 8vo, illustrated boards, 2s. each; cloth limp, 2s. 6d. each.
THE MAN-HUNTER. | WANTED! | A DETECTIVE'S TRIUMPHS.
CAUGHT AT LAST!   IN THE GRIP OF THE LAW.
TRACKED AND TAKEN.   FROM INFORMATION RECEIVED.
WHO POISONED HETTY DUNCAN?   LINK BY LINK. | DARK DEEDS.
SUSPICION AROUSED.   THE LONG ARM OF THE LAW. [Shortly.

Crown 8vo, cloth, 3s. 6d. each; post 8vo, boards, 2s. each; cloth, 2s. 6d. each.
THE MAN FROM MANCHESTER. With 23 Illustrations.
TRACKED TO DOOM. With 6 full-page Illustrations by GORDON BROWNE.

DOYLE (A. CONAN).—THE FIRM OF GIRDLESTONE: A Romance
of the Unromantic. Crown 8vo, cloth extra, 3s. 6d.

8 CHATTO & WINDUS, PUBLISHERS, PIC

DRAMATISTS, THE OLD. With Vignette Portraits. Cr. 8
BEN JONSON'S WORKS. With Notes Critical and Exp
graphical Memoir by WM. GIFFORD. Edited by Col. CUN:
CHAPMAN'S WORKS. Complete in Three Vols. Vol. I
complete; Vol. II., Poems and Minor Translations, with
by A. C. SWINBURNE; Vol. III., Translations of the Iliad a
MARLOWE'S WORKS. Edited, with Notes, by Col. CUNNING
MASSINGER'S PLAYS. From GIFFORD'S Text. Edit by Col.C

DUNCAN (SARA JEANNETTE): Mrs. EVERARD COT
Crown 8vo, cloth extra, **7s. 6d.** each.
A SOCIAL DEPARTURE: How Orthodocia and I Went roun
selves. With 111 Illustrations by F. H. TOWNSEND.
AN AMERICAN GIRL IN LONDON. With 80 Illustrations
THE SIMPLE ADVENTURES OF A MEMSAHIB. Illustrated
Crown 8vo, cloth extra, **3s. 6d.** each.
A DAUGHTER OF TO-DAY. | VERNON'S AUNT. 47 l

DYER (T. F. THISELTON, M.A.).—THE FOLK-LO
Crown 8vo, cloth extra, **6s.**

EARLY ENGLISH POETS. Edited, with Introduct
tions, by Rev. A. B. GROSART, D.D. Crown 8vo, cloth boards
FLETCHER'S (GILES) COMPLETE POEMS. One Vol.
DAVIES' (SIR JOHN) COMPLETE POETICAL WORKS.
HERRICK'S (ROBERT) COMPLETE COLLECTED POEMS.
SIDNEY'S (SIR PHILIP) COMPLETE POETICAL WORKS

EDGCUMBE (E. R. PEARCE).—ZEPHYRUS: A Ho
on the River Plate. With 41 Illustrations. Crown 8vo, cloth

EDISON, THE LIFE & INVENTIONS OF THOMAS A
A. DICKSON. With 200 Illustrations by R. F. OUTCALT, &c. Den

EDWARDES (MRS. ANNIE), NOVELS BY.
A POINT OF HONOUR. Post 8vo, illustrated boards, **2s.**
ARCHIE LOVELL. Crown 8vo, cloth extra, **3s. 6d.**; post 8

EDWARDS (ELIEZER).—WORDS, FACTS, AND
Dictionary of Quaint Matters. Crown 8vo, cloth, **7s. 6d.**

EDWARDS (M. BETHAM-), NOVELS BY.
KITTY. Post 8vo, **2s.**; cloth, **2s. 6d.** | FELICIA. Pos

EGERTON (REV. J. C.).—SUSSEX FOLK AND S
With Introduction by Rev. Dr. H. WACE, and 4 Illustrations.

EGGLESTON (EDWARD).—ROXY: A Novel. Post 8

ENGLISHMAN'S HOUSE, THE: A Practical Guide
Selecting or Building a House; with Estimates of Cost, Qu
RICHARDSON. With Coloured Frontispiece and 600 Illusts. Cro

EWALD (ALEX. CHARLES, F.S.A.), WORKS BY
THE LIFE AND TIMES OF PRINCE CHARLES STUAR
(THE YOUNG PRETENDER). With a Portrait. Crown 8vo,
STORIES FROM THE STATE PAPERS. With an Autotype.

EYES, OUR: How to Preserve Them from Infancy
JOHN BROWNING, F.R.A.S. With 70 Illusts. Twenty-fourth T

FAMILIAR SHORT SAYINGS OF GREAT MEN. B
BENT, A.M. Fifth Edition, Revised and Enlarged. Crown 8v

FARADAY (MICHAEL), WORKS BY. Post 8vo, cloth
THE CHEMICAL HISTORY OF A CANDLE: Lectures deliv
Audience. Edited by WILLIAM CROOKES, F.C.S. With n
ON THE VARIOUS FORCES OF NATURE, AND THE
EACH OTHER. Edited by WILLIAM CROOKES, F.C.S. V

FARRER (J. ANSON), WORKS BY.
MILITARY MANNERS AND CUSTOMS. Crown 8vo, cloth e
WAR: Three Essays, reprinted from "Military Manners." Cr

FENN (G. MANVILLE), NOVELS BY.
Crown 8vo, cloth extra, **3s. 6d.** each; post 8vo, illustrate
THE NEW MISTRESS. | WITNESS TO TH
Crown 8vo, cloth extra, **3s. 6d.** each.
THE TIGER LILY: Tale of Two Passions. | THE WHIT

FIN-BEC.—THE CUPBOARD PAPERS: Observations on the Art of Living and Dining. Post 8vo, cloth limp, 2s. 6d.

FIREWORKS, THE COMPLETE ART OF MAKING; or, The Pyrotechnist's Treasury. By THOMAS KENTISH. With 267 Illustrations. Cr. 8vo, cl., 5s.

FIRST BOOK, MY. By WALTER BESANT, JAMES PAYN, W. CLARK RUSSELL, GRANT ALLEN, HALL CAINE, GEORGE R. SIMS, RUDYARD KIPLING, A. CONAN DOYLE, M. E. BRADDON, F. W. ROBINSON, H. RIDER HAGGARD, R. M. BALLANTYNE, I. ZANGWILL, MORLEY ROBERTS, D. CHRISTIE MURRAY, MARIE CORELLI, J. K. JEROME, JOHN STRANGE WINTER, BRET HARTE, "Q.," ROBERT BUCHANAN, and R. L. STEVENSON. With a Prefatory Story by JEROME K. JEROME, and 185 Illustrations. Small demy 8vo, cloth extra, 7s. 6d.

FITZGERALD (PERCY), WORKS BY.
THE WORLD BEHIND THE SCENES. Crown 8vo, cloth extra, 3s. 6d.
LITTLE ESSAYS: Passages from Letters of CHARLES LAMB. Post 8vo, cl., 2s. 6d.
A DAY'S TOUR: Journey through France and Belgium. With Sketches. Cr. 4to, 1s.
FATAL ZERO. Crown 8vo, cloth extra, 3s. 6d.; post 8vo, illustrated boards, 2s.

Post 8vo, illustrated boards, 2s. each.
BELLA DONNA. | LADY OF BRANTOME. | THE SECOND MRS. TILLOTSON.
POLLY. | NEVER FORGOTTEN. | SEVENTY-FIVE BROOKE STREET.
LIFE OF JAMES BOSWELL (of Auchinleck). With an Account of his Sayings, Doings, and Writings; and Four Portraits. Two Vols., demy 8vo, cloth, 24s.
THE SAVOY OPERA. With 60 Illustrations and Portraits. Cr. 8vo, cloth, 3s. 6d.

FLAMMARION (CAMILLE), WORKS BY.
POPULAR ASTRONOMY: A General Description of the Heavens. Translated by J. ELLARD GORE, F.R.A.S. With 3 Plates and 288 Illusts. Medium 8vo, cloth, 10s.
URANIA: A Romance. With 87 Illustrations. Crown 8vo, cloth extra, 5s.

FLETCHER'S (GILES, B.D.) COMPLETE POEMS: Christ's Victorie in Heaven, Christ's Victorie on Earth, Christ's Triumph over Death, and Minor Poems. With Notes by Rev. A. B. GROSART, D.D. Crown 8vo, cloth boards, 6s.

FONBLANQUE (ALBANY).—FILTHY LUCRE. Post 8vo, illust. bds., 2s.

FRANCILLON (R. E.), NOVELS BY.
Crown 8vo, cloth extra, 3s. 6d. each; post 8vo, illustrated boards, 2s. each.
ONE BY ONE. | A REAL QUEEN. | KING OR KNAVE?
ROPES OF SAND. Illustrated. | A DOG AND HIS SHADOW.

Post 8vo, illustrated boards, 2s. each.
QUEEN COPHETUA. | OLYMPIA. | ROMANCES OF THE LAW.

JACK DOYLE'S DAUGHTER. Crown 8vo, cloth, 3s. 6d.
ESTHER'S GLOVE. Fcap. 8vo, picture cover, 1s.

FREDERIC (HAROLD), NOVELS BY. Post 8vo, illust. bds., 2s. each.
SETH'S BROTHER'S WIFE. | THE LAWTON GIRL.

FRENCH LITERATURE, A HISTORY OF. By HENRY VAN LAUN. Three Vols., demy 8vo, cloth boards, 7s. 6d. each.

FRISWELL (HAIN).—ONE OF TWO: A Novel. Post 8vo, illust. bds., 2s.

FROST (THOMAS), WORKS BY. Crown 8vo, cloth extra, 3s. 6d. each.
CIRCUS LIFE AND CIRCUS CELEBRITIES. | LIVES OF THE CONJURERS.
THE OLD SHOWMEN AND THE OLD LONDON FAIRS.

FRY'S (HERBERT) ROYAL GUIDE TO THE LONDON CHARITIES.
Edited by JOHN LANE. Published Annually. Crown 8vo, cloth, 1s. 6d.

GARDENING BOOKS. Post 8vo, 1s. each; cloth limp, 1s. 6d. each.
A YEAR'S WORK IN GARDEN AND GREENHOUSE. By GEORGE GLENNY.
HOUSEHOLD HORTICULTURE. By TOM and JANE JERROLD. Illustrated.
THE GARDEN THAT PAID THE RENT. By TOM JERROLD.
MY GARDEN WILD. By FRANCIS G. HEATH. Crown 8vo, cloth extra, 6s.

GARRETT (EDWARD).—THE CAPEL GIRLS: A Novel. Crown 8vo, cloth extra, 3s. 6d.; post 8vo, illustrated boards, 2s.

GAULOT (PAUL).—THE RED SHIRTS: A Story of the Revolution. Translated by J. A. J. DE VILLIERS. Crown 8vo, cloth, 3s. 6d.

GENTLEMAN'S ANNUAL, THE. Published Annually in November. 1s.

GENTLEMAN'S MAGAZINE, THE. 1s. Monthly. With Stories, Articles upon Literature, Science, and Art, and **"TABLE TALK"** by SYLVANUS URBAN.
⁎ *Bound Volumes for recent years kept in stock,* 8s. 6d. *each. Cases for binding,* 2s.

GERMAN POPULAR STORIES. Collected by the Brothers GRIMM and Translated by EDGAR TAYLOR. With Introduction by JOHN RUSKIN, and 22 Steel Plates after GEORGE CRUIKSHANK. Square 8vo, cloth, 6s. 6d.; gilt edges, 7s. 6d.

GIBBON (CHARLES), NOVELS BY.
Crown 8vo, cloth extra, 3s. 6d. each; post 8vo, illustrated boards, 2s. each.
ROBIN GRAY. | THE GOLDEN SHAFT.
LOVING A DREAM. | OF HIGH DEGREE.
Post 8vo, illustrated boards, 2s. *each.*
THE FLOWER OF THE FOREST. | IN LOVE AND WAR.
THE DEAD HEART. | A HEART'S PROBLEM.
FOR LACK OF GOLD. | BY MEAD AND STREAM.
WHAT WILL THE WORLD SAY? | THE BRAES OF YARROW.
FOR THE KING. | A HARD KNOT. | FANCY FREE.
QUEEN OF THE MEADOW. | IN HONOUR BOUND.
IN PASTURES GREEN. | HEART'S DELIGHT. | BLOOD-MONEY.

GIBNEY (SOMERVILLE).—SENTENCED! Cr. 8vo, 1s.; cl., 1s. 6d.

GILBERT (WILLIAM), NOVELS BY. *Post 8vo, illustrated boards,* 2s. *each.*
DR. AUSTIN'S GUESTS. | JAMES DUKE, COSTERMONGER.
THE WIZARD OF THE MOUNTAIN. |

GILBERT (W. S.), ORIGINAL PLAYS BY. Three Series, 2s. 6d. each.
The FIRST SERIES contains: The Wicked World—Pygmalion and Galatea—Charity—The Princess—The Palace of Truth—Trial by Jury.
The SECOND SERIES: Broken Hearts—Engaged—Sweethearts—Gretchen—Dan'l Druce—Tom Cobb—H.M.S. "Pinafore"—The Sorcerer—Pirates of Penzance.
The THIRD SERIES: Comedy and Tragedy—Foggerty's Fairy—Rosencrantz and Guildenstern—Patience—Princess Ida—The Mikado—Ruddigore—The Yeomen of the Guard—The Gondoliers—The Mountebanks—Utopia.

EIGHT ORIGINAL COMIC OPERAS written by W. S. GILBERT. Containing: The Sorcerer—H.M.S. "Pinafore"—Pirates of Penzance—Iolanthe—Patience—Princess Ida—The Mikado—Trial by Jury. Demy 8vo, cloth limp, 2s. 6d.
THE "GILBERT AND SULLIVAN" BIRTHDAY BOOK: Quotations for Every Day in the Year, Selected from Plays by W. S. GILBERT set to Music by Sir A. SULLIVAN. Compiled by ALEX. WATSON. Royal 16mo, Jap. leather, 2s. 6d.

GLANVILLE (ERNEST), NOVELS BY.
Crown 8vo, cloth extra, 3s. 6d. each; post 8vo, illustrated boards, 2s. each.
THE LOST HEIRESS: A Tale of Love, Battle, and Adventure. With 2 Illusts.
THE FOSSICKER: A Romance of Mashonaland. With 2 Illusts. by HUME NISBET.
A FAIR COLONIST.

GLENNY (GEORGE).—A YEAR'S WORK in GARDEN and GREEN-HOUSE: Practical Advice to Amateur Gardeners as to the Management of the Flower, Fruit and Frame Garden. Post 8vo, 1s.; cloth limp, 1s. 6d.

GODWIN (WILLIAM).—LIVES OF THE NECROMANCERS. Post 8vo, cloth limp, 2s.

GOLDEN TREASURY OF THOUGHT, THE: An Encyclopædia of QUOTATIONS. Edited by THEODORE TAYLOR. Crown 8vo, cloth gilt, 7s. 6d.

GONTAUT, MEMOIRS OF THE DUCHESSE DE (Gouvernante to the Children of France), 1773-1836. With Photogravure Frontispieces. Two Vols., small demy 8vo, cloth extra, 21s.

GOODMAN (E. J.).—THE FATE OF HERBERT WAYNE. Crown 8vo, cloth extra, 3s. 6d.

GRAHAM (LEONARD).—THE PROFESSOR'S WIFE: A Story. Fcap. 8vo, picture cover, 1s.

GREEKS AND ROMANS, THE LIFE OF THE, described from Antique Monuments. By ERNST GUHL and W. KONER. Edited by Dr. F. HUEFFER. With 545 Illustrations. Large crown 8vo, cloth extra, 7s. 6d.

GREVILLE (HENRY), NOVELS BY:
NIKANOR. Translated by ELIZA E. CHASE. Post 8vo, illustrated boards, 2s.
A NOBLE WOMAN. Crown 8vo, cloth extra, 5s.; post 8vo, illustrated boards, 2s.

CHATTO & WINDUS, PUBLISHERS, PICCADILLY.   11

GREENWOOD (JAMES), WORKS BY. Cr. 8vo, cloth extra, 3s. 6d. each.
THE WILDS OF LONDON. | LOW-LIFE DEEPS.

GRIFFITH (CECIL).—CORINTHIA MARAZION: A Novel. Crown
8vo, cloth extra, 3s. 6d.; post 8vo, illustrated boards, 2s.

GRUNDY (SYDNEY).—THE DAYS OF HIS VANITY: A Passage in
the Life of a Young Man. Crown 8vo, cloth extra, 3s. 6d.; post 8vo, boards, 2s.

HABBERTON (JOHN, Author of "Helen's Babies"), NOVELS BY.
Post 8vo, illustrated boards 2s. each; cloth limp, 2s. 6d. each.
BRUETON'S BAYOU. | COUNTRY LUCK.

HAIR, THE: Its Treatment in Health, Weakness, and Disease. Translated from the German of Dr. J. PINCUS. Crown 8vo, 1s.; cloth, 1s. 6d.

HAKE (DR. THOMAS GORDON), POEMS BY. Cr. 8vo, cl. ex., 6s. each.
NEW SYMBOLS. | LEGENDS OF THE MORROW. | THE SERPENT PLAY.
MAIDEN ECSTASY. Small 4to, cloth extra, 8s.

HALL (MRS. S. C.).—SKETCHES OF IRISH CHARACTER. With
numerous Illustrations on Steel and Wood by MACLISE, GILBERT, HARVEY, and
GEORGE CRUIKSHANK. Small demy 8vo, cloth extra, 7s. 6d.

HALLIDAY (ANDREW).—EVERY-DAY PAPERS. Post 8vo, 2s.

HANDWRITING, THE PHILOSOPHY OF. With over 100 Facsimiles
and Explanatory Text. By DON FELIX DE SALAMANCA. Post 8vo, cloth limp, 2s. 6d.

HANKY-PANKY: Easy Tricks, White Magic, Sleight of Hand, &c.
Edited by W. H. CREMER. With 200 Illustrations. Crown 8vo, cloth extra, 4s. 6d.

HARDY (LADY DUFFUS).—PAUL WYNTER'S SACRIFICE. 2s.

HARDY (THOMAS).—UNDER THE GREENWOOD TREE. Crown
8vo, cloth extra, with Portrait and 15 Illustrations, 3s. 6d.; post 8vo, illustrated
boards, 2s.; cloth limp, 2s. 6d.

HARPER (CHARLES G.), WORKS BY. Demy 8vo, cloth extra, 16s. each.
THE BRIGHTON ROAD. With Photogravure Frontispiece and 90 Illustrations.
FROM PADDINGTON TO PENZANCE: The Record of a Summer Tramp. 105 Illusts.

HARWOOD (J. BERWICK).—THE TENTH EARL. Post 8vo,
illustrated boards, 2s.

HAWEIS (MRS. H. R.), WORKS BY. Square 8vo, cloth extra, 6s. each.
THE ART OF BEAUTY. With Coloured Frontispiece and 91 Illustrations.
THE ART OF DECORATION. With Coloured Frontispiece and 74 Illustrations.
THE ART OF DRESS. With 32 Illustrations. Post 8vo, 1s.; cloth, 1s. 6d.
CHAUCER FOR SCHOOLS. Demy 8vo, cloth limp, 2s. 6d.
CHAUCER FOR CHILDREN. 38 Illusts. (8 Coloured). Sm. 4to, cl. extra, 3s. 6d.

HAWEIS (Rev. H. R., M.A.).—AMERICAN HUMORISTS: WASHINGTON
IRVING, OLIVER WENDELL HOLMES, JAMES RUSSELL LOWELL, ARTEMUS WARD,
MARK TWAIN, and BRET HARTE. Third Edition. Crown 8vo, cloth extra, 6s.

HAWLEY SMART.—WITHOUT LOVE OR LICENCE: A Novel.
Crown 8vo, cloth extra, 3s. 6d.; post 8vo, illustrated boards, 2s.

HAWTHORNE (JULIAN), NOVELS BY.
Crown 8vo, cloth extra, 3s. 6d. each; post 8vo, illustrated boards, 2s. each.
GARTH. | ELLICE QUENTIN. | BEATRIX RANDOLPH. | DUST.
SEBASTIAN STROME. | DAVID POINDEXTER.
FORTUNE'S FOOL. | THE SPECTRE OF THE CAMERA.
Post 8vo, illustrated boards, 2s. each.
MISS CADOGNA. | LOVE—OR A NAME.
MRS. GAINSBOROUGH'S DIAMONDS. Fcap. 8vo. illustrated cover, 1s.

HAWTHORNE (NATHANIEL).—OUR OLD HOME. Annotated with
Passages from the Author's Note-books, and Illustrated with 31 Photogravures
Two Vols., crown 8vo, buckram, gilt top, 15s.

HEATH (FRANCIS GEORGE).—MY GARDEN WILD, AND WHAT
I GREW THERE. Crown 8vo, cloth extra, gilt edges, 6s.

HELPS (SIR ARTHUR), WORKS BY. Post 8vo, cloth limp, 2s. 6d. each
ANIMALS AND THEIR MASTERS. | SOCIAL PRESSURE.
IVAN DE BIRON: A Novel. Cr. 8vo, cl. extra, 3s. 6d.; post 8vo, illust. bds., 2s.

HENDERSON (ISAAC).—AGATHA PAGE: A Novel. Crown 8vo, cloth extra, 3s. 6d.

HENTY (G. A.), NOVELS BY. Crown 8vo, cloth extra, 3s. 6d. each.
RUJUB THE JUGGLER. 8 Illusts. by STANLEY L. WOOD. PRESENTATION ED., 5s.
DOROTHY'S DOUBLE.

HERMAN (HENRY).—A LEADING LADY. Post 8vo, illustrated boards, 2s.; cloth extra, 2s. 6d.

HERRICK'S (ROBERT) HESPERIDES, NOBLE NUMBERS, AND COMPLETE COLLECTED POEMS. With Memorial-Introduction and Notes by the Rev. A. B. GROSART, D.D.; Steel Portrait, &c. Three Vols., crown 8vo, cl. bds., 18s.

HERTZKA (Dr. THEODOR).—FREELAND: A Social Anticipation. Translated by ARTHUR RANSOM. Crown 8vo, cloth extra, 6s.

HESSE-WARTEGG (CHEVALIER ERNST VON).—TUNIS: The Land and the People. With 22 Illustrations. Crown 8vo, cloth extra, 3s. 6d.

HILL (HEADON).—ZAMBRA THE DETECTIVE. Post 8vo, illustrated boards, 2s.; cloth, 2s. 6d.

HILL (JOHN), WORKS BY.
TREASON-FELONY. Post 8vo, 2s. | THE COMMON ANCESTOR. Cr. 8vo, 3s. 6d.

HINDLEY (CHARLES), WORKS BY.
TAVERN ANECDOTES AND SAYINGS: Including Reminiscences connected with Coffee Houses, Clubs, &c. With Illustrations. Crown 8vo, cloth, 3s. 6d.
THE LIFE AND ADVENTURES OF A CHEAP JACK. Cr. 8vo, cloth ex., 3s. 6d.

HOEY (MRS. CASHEL).—THE LOVER'S CREED. Post 8vo, 2s.

HOLLINGSHEAD (JOHN).—NIAGARA SPRAY. Crown 8vo, 1s.

HOLMES (GORDON, M.D.).—THE SCIENCE OF VOICE PRODUCTION AND VOICE PRESERVATION. Crown 8vo, 1s.

HOLMES (OLIVER WENDELL), WORKS BY.
THE AUTOCRAT OF THE BREAKFAST-TABLE. Illustrated by J. GORDON THOMSON. Post 8vo, cloth limp, 2s. 6d.—Another Edition, post 8vo, cloth, 2s.
THE AUTOCRAT OF THE BREAKFAST-TABLE and THE PROFESSOR AT THE BREAKFAST-TABLE. In One Vol. Post 8vo, half-bound, 2s.

HOOD'S (THOMAS) CHOICE WORKS, in Prose and Verse. With Life of the Author, Portrait, and 200 Illustrations. Crown 8vo, cloth extra, 7s. 6d.
HOOD'S WHIMS AND ODDITIES. With 85 Illusts. Post 8vo, half-bound, 2s.

HOOD (TOM).—FROM NOWHERE TO THE NORTH POLE: A Noah's Arkæological Narrative. With 25 Illustrations by W. BRUNTON and E. C. BARNES. Square 8vo, cloth extra, gilt edges, 6s.

HOOK'S (THEODORE) CHOICE HUMOROUS WORKS; including his Ludicrous Adventures, Bons Mots, Puns, and Hoaxes. With Life of the Author, Portraits, Facsimiles, and Illustrations. Crown 8vo, cloth extra, 7s. 6d.

HOOPER (MRS. GEO.).—THE HOUSE OF RABY. Post 8vo, bds., 2s.

HOPKINS (TIGHE). — "'TWIXT LOVE AND DUTY:" A Novel. Post 8vo, illustrated boards, 2s.

HORNE (R. HENGIST).—ORION: An Epic Poem. With Photographic Portrait by SUMMERS. Tenth Edition. Crown 8vo, cloth extra, 7s.

HUNGERFORD (MRS., Author of "Molly Bawn,"), **NOVELS BY.**
Post 8vo, illustrated boards, 2s. each; cloth limp, 2s. 6d. each.
A MAIDEN ALL FORLORN. | IN DURANCE VILE. | A MENTAL STRUGGLE.
MARVEL. | A MODERN CIRCE.
LADY VERNER'S FLIGHT. Cr. 8vo, cloth, 3s. 6d.; post 8vo, illust. boards, 2s.
THE RED-HOUSE MYSTERY. Crown 8vo, cloth extra, 3s. 6d.
THE THREE GRACES. Two Vols., 10s. nett. [Shortly.

HUNT (MRS. ALFRED), NOVELS BY.
Crown 8vo, cloth extra, 3s. 6d. each; post 8vo, illustrated boards, 2s. each.
THE LEADEN CASKET. | SELF-CONDEMNED. | THAT OTHER PERSON.
THORNICROFT'S MODEL. Post 8vo, illustrated boards, 2s.
MRS. JULIET. Crown 8vo, cloth extra, 3s. 6d.

HUNT'S (LEIGH) ESSAYS: A TALE FOR A CHIMNEY CORNER, &c. Edited by EDMUND OLLIER. Post 8vo, printed on laid paper and half-bd., 2s.

CHATTO & WINDUS, PUBLISHERS, PICCADILLY. 13

HUTCHISON (W. M.).—HINTS ON COLT-BREAKING. With 25 Illustrations. Crown 8vo, cloth extra, 3s. 6d.

HYDROPHOBIA: An Account of M. PASTEUR'S System; Technique of his Method, and Statistics. By RENAUD SUZOR, M.B. Crown 8vo, cloth extra, 6s.

HYNE (C. J. CUTCLIFFE).—HONOUR OF THIEVES. Crown 8vo, cloth extra, 3s. 6d. [*Shortly*.

IDLER (THE): A Monthly Magazine. Profusely Illustr. 6d. Monthly. The first SIX VOLS. now ready, cl. extra, 5s. each; Cases for Binding, 1s. 6d. each.

INDOOR PAUPERS. By ONE OF THEM. Crown 8vo, 1s.; cloth, 1s. 6d.

INGELOW (JEAN).—FATED TO BE FREE. Post 8vo, illustrated bds., 2s.

INNKEEPER'S HANDBOOK (THE) AND LICENSED VICTUALLER'S MANUAL. By J. TREVOR-DAVIES. Crown 8vo, 1s.; cloth, 1s. 6d.

IRISH WIT AND HUMOUR, SONGS OF. Collected and Edited by A. PERCEVAL GRAVES. Post 8vo, cloth limp, 2s. 6d.

JAMES (C. T. C.).—A ROMANCE OF THE QUEEN'S HOUNDS. Post 8vo, picture cover, 1s.; cloth limp, 1s. 6d.

JAMESON (WILLIAM).—MY DEAD SELF. Post 8vo, illustrated boards, 2s.; cloth, 2s. 6d.

JAPP (ALEX. H., LL.D.).—DRAMATIC PICTURES, SONNETS, &c. Crown 8vo, cloth extra, 5s.

JAY (HARRIETT), NOVELS BY. Post 8vo, illustrated boards, 2s. each.
THE DARK COLLEEN. | THE QUEEN OF CONNAUGHT.

JEFFERIES (RICHARD), WORKS BY. Post 8vo, cloth limp, 2s. 6d. each.
NATURE NEAR LONDON. | THE LIFE OF THE FIELDS. | THE OPEN AIR.
⁎ Also the HAND-MADE PAPER EDITION, crown 8vo, buckram, gilt top, 6s. each.

THE EULOGY OF RICHARD JEFFERIES. By WALTER BESANT. With a Photograph Portrait. Crown 8vo, cloth extra, 6s.

JENNINGS (HENRY J.), WORKS BY.
CURIOSITIES OF CRITICISM. Post 8vo, cloth limp, 2s. 6d.
LORD TENNYSON: A Biographical Sketch. Post 8vo, 1s.; cloth, 1s. 6d.

JEROME (JEROME K.), BOOKS BY.
STAGELAND. With 64 Illusts. by J. BERNARD PARTRIDGE. Fcap. 4to, pict. cov., 1s.
JOHN INGERFIELD, &c. With 9 Illusts. by A. S. BOYD and JOHN GULICH. Fcap. 8vo, picture cover, 1s. 6d.

JERROLD (DOUGLAS).—THE BARBER'S CHAIR; and THE HEDGEHOG LETTERS. Post 8vo, printed on laid paper and half-bound, 2s.

JERROLD (TOM), WORKS BY. Post 8vo, 1s. each; cloth limp, 1s. 6d. each.
THE GARDEN THAT PAID THE RENT.
HOUSEHOLD HORTICULTURE: A Gossip about Flowers. Illustrated.

JESSE (EDWARD).—SCENES AND OCCUPATIONS OF A COUNTRY LIFE. Post 8vo, cloth limp, 2s.

JONES (WILLIAM, F.S.A.), WORKS BY. Cr. 8vo, cl. extra, 7s. 6d. each.
FINGER-RING LORE: Historical, Legendary, and Anecdotal. With nearly 300 Illustrations. Second Edition, Revised and Enlarged.
CREDULITIES, PAST AND PRESENT. Including the Sea and Seamen, Miners, Talismans, Word and Letter Divination, Exorcising and Blessing of Animals,

KERSHAW (MARK).—COLONIAL FACTS & FICTIONS: Humorous Sketches. Post 8vo, illustrated boards, 2s.; cloth, 2s. 6d.

KEYSER (ARTHUR).—CUT BY THE MESS: A Novel. Crown 8vo, picture cover, 1s.; cloth limp, 1s. 6d.

KING (R. ASHE), NOVELS BY. Cr. 8vo, cl., 3s. 6d. ea.; post 8vo, bds., 2s. ea.
A DRAWN GAME. | "THE WEARING OF THE GREEN."
Post 8vo, illustrated boards, 2s. each.
PASSION'S SLAVE. | BELL BARRY.

KNIGHT (WILLIAM, M.R.C.S., and EDWARD, L.R.C.P.).—THE PATIENT'S VADE MECUM: How to Get Most Benefit from Medical Advice. Crown 8vo, 1s.; cloth limp, 1s. 6d.

KNIGHTS (THE) OF THE LION: A Romance of the Thirteenth Century. Edited, with an Introduction, by the MARQUESS of LORNE, K.T. Cr. 8vo. cl. ex. 6s.

LAMB'S (CHARLES) COMPLETE WORKS, in Prose and Verse, including "Poetry for Children" and "Prince Dorus." Edited, with Notes and Introduction, by R. H. SHEPHERD. With Two Portraits and Facsimile of a page of the "Essay on Roast Pig." Crown 8vo, half-bound, 7s. 6d.
THE ESSAYS OF ELIA. Post 8vo, printed on laid paper and half-bound, 2s.
LITTLE ESSAYS: Sketches and Characters by CHARLES LAMB, selected from his Letters by PERCY FITZGERALD. Post 8vo, cloth limp, 2s. 6d.
THE DRAMATIC ESSAYS OF CHARLES LAMB. With Introduction and Notes by BRANDER MATTHEWS, and Steel-plate Portrait. Fcap. 8vo, hf.-bd., 2s. 6d.

LANDOR (WALTER SAVAGE).—CITATION AND EXAMINATION OF WILLIAM SHAKSPEARE, &c., before Sir THOMAS LUCY, touching Deer-stealing, 19th September, 1582. To which is added, A CONFERENCE OF MASTER EDMUND SPENSER with the Earl of Essex, touching the State of Ireland, 1595. Fcap. 8vo, half-Roxburghe, 2s. 6d.

LANE (EDWARD WILLIAM). — THE THOUSAND AND ONE NIGHTS, commonly called in England THE ARABIAN NIGHTS' ENTERTAINMENTS. Translated from the Arabic, with Notes. Illustrated by many hundred Engravings from Designs by HARVEY. Edited by EDWARD STANLEY POOLE. With a Preface by STANLEY LANE-POOLE, Three Vols., demy 8vo, cloth extra, 7s. 6d. each.

LARWOOD (JACOB), WORKS BY.
THE STORY OF THE LONDON PARKS. With Illusts. Cr. 8vo, cl. extra, 3s. 6d.
ANECDOTES OF THE CLERGY. Post 8vo, laid paper, half-bound, 2s.
Post 8vo, cloth limp, 2s. 6d. each.
FORENSIC ANECDOTES. | THEATRICAL ANECDOTES.

LEHMANN (R. C.), WORKS BY. Post 8vo, pict. cover, 1s. ea.; cloth, 1s. 6d. ea.
HARRY FLUDYER AT CAMBRIDGE.
CONVERSATIONAL HINTS FOR YOUNG SHOOTERS: A Guide to Polite Talk.

LEIGH (HENRY S.), WORKS BY.
CAROLS OF COCKAYNE. Printed on hand-made paper, bound in buckram, 5s.
JEUX D'ESPRIT. Edited by HENRY S. LEIGH. Post 8vo, cloth limp, 2s. 6d.

LEPELLETIER (EDMOND).—MADAME SANS-GENE. Translated from the French by J. A. J. DE VILLIERS. Crown 8vo, cloth extra, 3s. 6d.

LEYS (JOHN).—THE LINDSAYS: A Romance. Post 8vo, illust. bds., 2s.

LINDSAY (HARRY).—RHODA ROBERTS: A Welsh Mining Story. Crown 8vo, cloth, 3s. 6d. [Shortly.

LINTON (E. LYNN), WORKS BY. Post 8vo, cloth limp, 2s. 6d. each.
WITCH STORIES. | OURSELVES: ESSAYS ON WOMEN.
Crown 8vo, cloth extra, 3s. 6d. each; post 8vo, illustrated boards, 2s. each.
PATRICIA KEMBALL. | IONE. | UNDER WHICH LORD?
ATONEMENT OF LEAM DUNDAS. | "MY LOVE!" | SOWING THE WIND.
THE WORLD WELL LOST. | PASTON CAREW, Millionaire & Miser.
Post 8vo, illustrated boards, 2s. each.
THE REBEL OF THE FAMILY. | WITH A SILKEN THREAD.
THE ONE TOO MANY. Crown 8vo, cloth extra, 3s. 6d.
FREESHOOTING: Extracts from Works of Mrs. LINTON. Post 8vo, cloth, 2s. 6d.

LUCY (HENRY W.).—GIDEON FLEYCE: A Novel. Crown 8vo, cloth extra, 3s. 6d.; post 8vo, illustrated boards, 2s.

VERY), NOVELS BY.
 Crown 8vo, cloth extra, 1s.
 With 6 Illusts. by W. J. HENNESSY. Crown 8vo, cloth extra, 6s.

STIN, M.P.), WORKS BY.
OUR OWN TIMES, from the Accession of Queen Victoria to the
ion of 1880. Four Vols. demy 8vo, cloth extra, 12s. each.—Also
DITION, in Four Vols., crown 8vo, cloth extra, 6s. each.—And a
ION, with an Appendix of Events to the end of 1886, in Two Vols.,
vo, cloth extra, 7s. 6d. each.
RY OF OUR OWN TIMES. One Vol., crown 8vo, cloth extra, 6s.
P POPULAR EDITION, post 8vo, cloth limp, 2s. 6d.
THE FOUR GEORGES. Four Vols. demy 8vo, cloth extra,
[Vols. I. & II. ready.

6d. each; post 8vo, illust. bds., 2s. each; cl. limp, 2s. 6d. each.
LE NEIGHBOURS. | DONNA QUIXOTE.
AUGHTER. | THE COMET OF A SEASON.
| MAID OF ATHENS.
RD. | CAMIOLA: A Girl with a Fortune.
DAIN. | THE DICTATOR.
OPE. | RED DIAMONDS.
NOURABLE." By JUSTIN MCCARTHY, M.P., and Mrs. CAMPBELL
n 8vo, cloth extra, 6s.

STIN HUNTLY), WORKS BY.
EVOLUTION. Four Vols., 8vo, 12s. each. [Vols. I. & II. ready.
THE HISTORY OF IRELAND. Crown 8vo, 1s.; cloth, 1s. 6d.
THE UNION: Irish History, 1798-1886. Crown 8vo, cloth, 6s.
ON: Poems. Small 8vo, gold cloth, 3s. 6d.
: Poems. Small 4to, Japanese vellum, 8s.
NOVEL. Crown 8vo, picture cover, 1s.; cloth limp, 1s. 6d.
ic Episode. Crown 8vo, picture cover, 1s.
. Crown 8vo, picture cover, 1s.; cloth limp, 1s. 6d.
omance. Crown 8vo, picture cover, 1s.; cloth limp, 1s. 6d.
AND ONE DAYS. 2 Photogravures. Two Vols., cr. 8vo, 12s.
END. Three Vols., crown 8vo, 15s. net.

H), NOVELS BY.
SEALED PACKET. Post 8vo, illustrated boards, 2s.
CK. Crown 8vo, cloth extra, 6s.

EORGE, LL.D.), WORKS BY.
CY AND IMAGINATION. Ten Vols., 16mo, cl., gilt edges, in cloth
)r the Vols. may be had separately, in grolier cl., at 2s. 6d. each.
D WITHOUT.—THE HIDDEN LIFE.
PLE.—THE GOSPEL WOMEN.—BOOK OF SONNETS.—ORGAN SONGS.
NGS.—SONGS OF THE DAYS AND NIGHTS.—A BOOK OF DREAMS.—
POEMS.—POEMS FOR CHILDREN.
—BALLADS.—SCOTCH SONGS.
STES: A Faerie Romance. | Vol. VII. THE PORTENT.
PRINCESS.—THE GIANT'S HEART.—SHADOWS.
POSES.—THE GOLDEN KEY.—THE CARASOYN.—LITTLE DAYLIGHT.
L PAINTER.—THE WOW O' RIVVEN.—THE CASTLE.—THE BROKEN
.—THE GRAY WOLF.—UNCLE CORNELIUS.
KS OF GEORGE MACDONALD. Collected and arranged by the
ls., crown 8vo, buckram, 12s.
ORD. Edited by GEORGE MACDONALD. Post 8vo, cloth, 5s.
SNOW! A Novel. Crown 8vo, cloth extra, 3s. 6d.
Faerie Romance. With 25 Illustrations by J. BELL. Crown 8vo,
. 6d.
nce. Crown 8vo, cloth extra, 6s. [Shortly.

GNES).—QUAKER COUSINS. Post 8vo, boards, 2s.

OBERT).—PASTIMES AND PLAYERS: Notes on
Post 8vo, cloth limp, 2s. 6d.

LES, LL.D.).—INTERLUDES AND UNDERTONES;
ght. Crown 8vo, cloth extra, 6s.

MACLISE PORTRAIT GALLERY (THE) OF ILLUSTRIOUS LITERARY CHARACTERS: 85 PORTRAITS; with Memoirs — Biographical, Critical, Bibliographical, and Anecdotal—illustrative of the Literature of the former half of the Present Century, by WILLIAM BATES, B.A. Crown 8vo, cloth extra, 7s. 6d.

MACQUOID (MRS.), WORKS BY. Square 8vo, cloth extra, 6s. each.
IN THE ARDENNES. With 50 Illustrations by THOMAS R. MACQUOID.
PICTURES AND LEGENDS FROM NORMANDY AND BRITTANY. 34 Illustrations.
THROUGH NORMANDY. With 92 Illustrations by T. R. MACQUOID, and a Map.
THROUGH BRITTANY. With 35 Illustrations by T. R. MACQUOID, and a Map.
ABOUT YORKSHIRE. With 67 Illustrations by T. R. MACQUOID.

Post 8vo, illustrated boards, 2s. each.
THE EVIL EYE, and other Stories. | LOST ROSE.

MAGICIAN'S OWN BOOK, THE: Performances with Eggs, Hats, &c. Edited by W. H. CREMER. With 200 Illustrations. Crown 8vo, cloth extra, 4s. 6d.

MAGIC LANTERN, THE, and its Management: including full Practical Directions. By T. C. HEPWORTH. 10 Illustrations. Cr. 8vo, 1s.; cloth, 1s. 6d.

MAGNA CHARTA: An Exact Facsimile of the Original in the British Museum, 3 feet by 2 feet, with Arms and Seals emblazoned in Gold and Colours, 5s.

MALLOCK (W. H.), WORKS BY.
THE NEW REPUBLIC. Post 8vo, picture cover, 2s.; cloth limp, 2s. 6d.
THE NEW PAUL & VIRGINIA: Positivism on an Island. Post 8vo, cloth, 2s. 6d.
POEMS. Small 4to, parchment, 8s.
IS LIFE WORTH LIVING? Crown 8vo, cloth extra, 6s.
A ROMANCE OF THE NINETEENTH CENTURY. Crown 8vo, cloth, 6s.; post 8vo, illustrated boards, 2s.

MALLORY (SIR THOMAS).—MORT D'ARTHUR: The Stories of King Arthur and of the Knights of the Round Table. (A Selection.) Edited by B. MONTGOMERIE RANKING. Post 8vo, cloth limp, 2s.

MARK TWAIN, WORKS BY. Crown 8vo, cloth extra, 7s. 6d. each.
THE CHOICE WORKS OF MARK TWAIN. Revised and Corrected throughout by the Author. With Life, Portrait, and numerous Illustrations.
ROUGHING IT, and INNOCENTS AT HOME. With 200 Illusts. by F. A. FRASER.
MARK TWAIN'S LIBRARY OF HUMOUR. With 197 Illustrations.

Crown 8vo, cloth extra (illustrated), 7s. 6d. each; post 8vo, illust. boards, 2s. each.
THE INNOCENTS ABROAD; or, New Pilgrim's Progress. With 234 Illustrations. (The Two-Shilling Edition is entitled MARK TWAIN'S PLEASURE TRIP.)
THE GILDED AGE. By MARK TWAIN and C. D. WARNER. With 212 Illustrations.
THE ADVENTURES OF TOM SAWYER. With 111 Illustrations.
A TRAMP ABROAD. With 314 Illustrations.
THE PRINCE AND THE PAUPER. With 190 Illustrations.
LIFE ON THE MISSISSIPPI. With 300 Illustrations.
ADVENTURES OF HUCKLEBERRY FINN. With 174 Illusts. by E. W. KEMBLE.
A YANKEE AT THE COURT OF KING ARTHUR. With 220 Illusts. by BEARD.

Post 8vo, illustrated boards, 2s. each.
THE STOLEN WHITE ELEPHANT. | MARK TWAIN'S SKETCHES.

Crown 8vo, cloth extra, 3s. 6d. each.
THE AMERICAN CLAIMANT. With 81 Illustrations by HAL HURST, &c.
TOM SAWYER ABROAD. With 26 Illustrations by DAN BEARD.
PUDD'NHEAD WILSON. With Portrait and Six Illustrations by LOUIS LOEB.

THE £1,000,000 BANK-NOTE. Cr. 8vo, cloth, 3s. 6d.; post 8vo, picture bds., 2s.

MARKS (H. S., R.A.), PEN AND PENCIL SKETCHES BY. With 4 Photogravures and 126 Illustrations. Two Vols., demy 8vo, cloth, 32s.

MARLOWE'S WORKS. Including his Translations. Edited, with Notes and Introductions, by Col. CUNNINGHAM. Crown 8vo, cloth extra, 6s.

MARRYAT (FLORENCE), NOVELS BY. Post 8vo, illust. boards, 2s. each.
A HARVEST OF WILD OATS. | FIGHTING THE AIR.
OPEN! SESAME! | WRITTEN IN FIRE.

MASSINGER'S PLAYS. From the Text of WILLIAM GIFFORD. Edited by Col. CUNNINGHAM. Crown 8vo, cloth extra. 6s.

MASTERMAN (J.).—HALF-A-DOZEN DAUGHTERS: A Novel. Post 8vo, illustrated boards, 2s.

MATTHEWS (BRANDER).—A SECRET OF THE SEA, &c. Post 8vo, illustrated boards, 2s.; cloth limp, 2s. 6d.

MAYHEW (HENRY).—LONDON CHARACTERS & THE HUMOROUS SIDE OF LONDON LIFE. With Illustrations. Crown 8vo, cloth, 3s. 6d.

MEADE (L. T.), NOVELS BY.
A SOLDIER OF FORTUNE. Crown 8vo, cloth, 3s. 6d.
IN AN IRON GRIP. Two Vols., crown 8vo, cloth, 10s. net.
THE VOICE OF THE CHARMER. Three Vols., 15s. net. [Shortly.

MERRICK (LEONARD).—THE MAN WHO WAS GOOD. Post 8vo, illustrated boards, 2s.

MEXICAN MUSTANG (ON A), through Texas to the Rio Grande. By A. E. SWEET and J. ARMOY KNOX. With 265 Illusts. Cr. 8vo, cloth extra, 7s. 6d.

MIDDLEMASS (JEAN), NOVELS BY. Post 8vo, illust. boards, 2s. each.
TOUCH AND GO. | MR. DORILLION.

MILLER (MRS. F. FENWICK).—PHYSIOLOGY FOR THE YOUNG; or, The House of Life. With Illustrations. Post 8vo, cloth limp, 2s. 6d.

MILTON (J. L.), WORKS BY. Post 8vo, 1s. each; cloth, 1s. 6d. each.
THE HYGIENE OF THE SKIN. With Directions for Diet, Soaps, Baths, &c.
THE BATH IN DISEASES OF THE SKIN.
THE LAWS OF LIFE, AND THEIR RELATION TO DISEASES OF THE SKIN.
THE SUCCESSFUL TREATMENT OF LEPROSY. Demy 8vo, 1s.

MINTO (WM.)—WAS SHE GOOD OR BAD? Cr. 8vo, 1s.; cloth, 1s. 6d.

MITFORD (BERTRAM), NOVELS BY. Crown 8vo, cloth extra, 3s. 6d. each.
THE GUN-RUNNER: A Romance of Zululand. With Frontispiece by S. L. WOOD.
THE LUCK OF GERARD RIDGELEY. With a Frontispiece by STANLEY L. WOOD.
THE KING'S ASSEGAI. With Six full-page Illustrations by STANLEY L. WOOD.
RENSHAW FANNING'S QUEST. With a Frontispiece by STANLEY. L. WOOD.

MOLESWORTH (MRS.), NOVELS BY.
HATHERCOURT RECTORY. Post 8vo, illustrated boards, 2s.
THAT GIRL IN BLACK. Crown 8vo, cloth, 1s. 6d.

MOORE (THOMAS), WORKS BY.
THE EPICUREAN; and ALCIPHRON. Post 8vo, half-bound, 2s.
PROSE AND VERSE. With Suppressed Passages from the MEMOIRS OF LORD BYRON. Edited by R. H. SHEPHERD. With Portrait. Cr. 8vo, cl. ex., 7s. 6d.

MUDDOCK (J. E.), STORIES BY.
STORIES WEIRD AND WONDERFUL. Post 8vo, illust. boards, 2s.; cloth, 2s. 6d.
THE DEAD MAN'S SECRET; or, The Valley of Gold. With Frontispiece by F. BARNARD. Crown 8vo, cloth extra, 5s.; post 8vo, illustrated boards, 2s.
FROM THE BOSOM OF THE DEEP. Post 8vo, illustrated boards, 2s.
MAID MARIAN AND ROBIN HOOD: A Romance of Old Sherwood Forest. With 12 Illustrations by STANLEY L. WOOD. Crown 8vo, cloth extra, 3s. 6d.

MURRAY (D. CHRISTIE), NOVELS BY.
Crown 8vo, cloth extra, 3s. 6d. each; post 8vo, illustrated boards, 2s. each.
A LIFE'S ATONEMENT. | THE WAY OF THE WORLD. | A BIT OF HUMAN NATURE.
JOSEPH'S COAT. | A MODEL FATHER. | FIRST PERSON SINGULAR.
COALS OF FIRE. | OLD BLAZER'S HERO. | BOB MARTIN'S Little GIRL.
VAL STRANGE. | CYNIC FORTUNE. | TIME'S REVENGES.
HEARTS. | BY THE GATE OF THE SEA. | A WASTED CRIME.
Crown 8vo, cloth extra, 3s. 6d. each.
IN DIREST PERIL.
MOUNT DESPAIR, &c. With Frontispiece by G. GRENVILLE MANTON.
THE MAKING OF A NOVELIST: An Experiment in Autobiography. With a Collotype Portrait and Vignette. Crown 8vo, art linen, 6s.

MURRAY (D. CHRISTIE) & HENRY HERMAN, WORKS BY.
Crown 8vo, cloth extra, 3s. 6d. each; post 8vo, illustrated boards, 2s. each.
ONE TRAVELLER RETURNS. | PAUL JONES'S ALIAS. | THE BISHOPS' BIBLE.

MURRAY (HENRY), NOVELS BY. Post 8vo, illust. bds., 2s. ea.; cl., 2s. 6d. ea.
A GAME OF BLUFF. | A SONG OF SIXPENCE.

18   CHATTO & WINDUS, PUBLISHERS, PICCADILLY.

NEWBOLT (HENRY).—TAKEN FROM THE ENEMY. Fcap. 8vo, cloth boards, 1s. 6d.

NISBET (HUME), BOOKS BY.
"BAIL UP!" Crown 8vo, cloth extra, 3s. 6d.; post 8vo, illustrated boards, 2s.
DR. BERNARD ST. VINCENT. Post 8vo, illustrated boards, 2s.
LESSONS IN ART. With 21 Illustrations. Crown 8vo, cloth extra, 2s. 6d.
WHERE ART BEGINS. With 27 Illustrations. Square 8vo, cloth extra, 7s. 6d.

NORRIS (W. E.).—ST. ANN'S: A Novel. Crown 8vo, cloth, 3s. 6d.

O'HANLON (ALICE), NOVELS BY. Post 8vo, illustrated boards, 2s. each.
THE UNFORESEEN. | CHANCE? OR FATE?

OHNET (GEORGES), NOVELS BY. Post 8vo, illustrated boards, 2s. each.
DOCTOR RAMEAU. | A LAST LOVE.
A WEIRD GIFT. Crown 8vo, cloth, 3s. 6d.; post 8vo, picture boards, 2s.

OLIPHANT (MRS.), NOVELS BY. Post 8vo, illustrated boards, 2s. each.
THE PRIMROSE PATH. | WHITELADIES.
THE GREATEST HEIRESS IN ENGLAND.

O'REILLY (HARRINGTON).—LIFE AMONG THE AMERICAN INDIANS: Fifty Years on the Trail. 100 Illusts. by P. FRENZENY. Crown 8vo, 3s. 6d.

O'REILLY (MRS.).—PHŒBE'S FORTUNES. Post 8vo, illust. bds., 2s.

OUIDA, NOVELS BY. Cr. 8vo, cl., 3s. 6d. each; post 8vo, illust. bds., 2s. each.
HELD IN BONDAGE.   FOLLE-FARINE.   MOTHS. | PIPISTRELLO.
TRICOTRIN.   A DOG OF FLANDERS.   A VILLAGE COMMUNE.
STRATHMORE.   PASCAREL. | SIGNA.   IN MAREMMA. | WANDA.
CHANDOS.   TWO WOODEN SHOES.   BIMBI. | SYRLIN.
CECIL CASTLEMAINE.   IN A WINTER CITY.   FRESCOES. | OTHMAR.
UNDER TWO FLAGS.   ARIADNE.   PRINCESS NAPRAXINE.
PUCK. | IDALIA.   FRIENDSHIP.   GUILDEROY. | RUFFINO.

Square 8vo, cloth extra, 5s. each.
BIMBI. With Nine Illustrations by EDMUND H. GARRETT.
A DOG OF FLANDERS, &c. With Six Illustrations by EDMUND H. GARRETT.
SANTA BARBARA. &c. Square 8vo, cloth, 6s.; crown 8vo, cloth, 3s. 6d.; post 8vo, illustrated boards, 2s.
TWO OFFENDERS. Square 8vo, cloth extra, 6s.; crown 8vo, cloth extra, 3s. 6d.
WISDOM, WIT, AND PATHOS, selected from the Works of OUIDA by F. SYDNEY MORRIS. Post 8vo, cloth extra, 5s. CHEAP EDITION, illustrated boards, 2s.

PAGE (H. A.), WORKS BY.
THOREAU: His Life and Aims. With Portrait. Post 8vo, cloth limp, 2s. 6d.
ANIMAL ANECDOTES. Arranged on a New Principle. Crown 8vo, cloth extra, 5s.

PAYN (JAMES), NOVELS BY.
Crown 8vo, cloth extra, 3s. 6d. each; post 8vo, illustrated boards, 2s. each.
LOST SIR MASSINGBERD.   FROM EXILE. | HOLIDAY TASKS.
WALTER'S WORD.   [ED.   THE CANON'S WARD.
LESS BLACK THAN WE'RE PAINT-   THE TALK OF THE TOWN.
BY PROXY. | FOR CASH ONLY.   GLOW-WORM TALES.
HIGH SPIRITS.   THE MYSTERY OF MIRBRIDGE.
UNDER ONE ROOF.   THE WORD AND THE WILL.
A CONFIDENTIAL AGENT.   THE BURNT MILLION.
A GRAPE FROM A THORN.   SUNNY STORIES. | A TRYING PATIENT.

Post 8vo, illustrated boards, 2s. each.
HUMOROUS STORIES.   FOUND DEAD.
THE FOSTER BROTHERS.   GWENDOLINE'S HARVEST.
THE FAMILY SCAPEGRACE.   A MARINE RESIDENCE.
MARRIED BENEATH HIM.   MIRK ABBEY.
BENTINCK'S TUTOR.   SOME PRIVATE VIEWS.
A PERFECT TREASURE.   NOT WOOED, BUT WON.
A COUNTY FAMILY.   TWO HUNDRED POUNDS REWARD.
LIKE FATHER, LIKE SON.   THE BEST OF HUSBANDS.
A WOMAN'S VENGEANCE.   HALVES.
CARLYON'S YEAR. | CECIL'S TRYST. FALLEN FORTUNES.
MURPHY'S MASTER.   WHAT HE COST HER.
AT HER MERCY.   KIT: A MEMORY.
THE CLYFFARDS OF CLYFFE.   A PRINCE OF THE BLOOD.

IN PERIL AND PRIVATION: Stories of MARINE ADVENTURE. With 17 Illustrations. Crown 8vo, cloth extra, 3s. 6d.
NOTES FROM THE "NEWS." Crown 8vo, portrait cover, 1s.; cloth, 1s. 6d.

CHATTO & WINDUS, PUBLISHERS, PICCADILLY. 19

PANDURANG HARI; or, Memoirs of a Hindoo. With Preface by Sir BARTLE FRERE. Crown 8vo, cloth, 3s. 6d.; post 8vo, illustrated boards, 2s.

PASCAL'S PROVINCIAL LETTERS. A New Translation, with Historical Introduction and Notes by T. M'CRIE, D.D. Post 8vo, cloth limp, 2s.

PAUL (MARGARET A.).—GENTLE AND SIMPLE. With Frontispiece by HELEN PATERSON. Crown 8vo, cloth, 3s. 6d.; post 8vo, illust. boards, 2s.

PENNELL (H. CHOLMONDELEY), WORKS BY. Post 8vo, cl., 2s. 6d. each.
PUCK ON PEGASUS. With Illustrations.
PEGASUS RE-SADDLED. With Ten full-page Illustrations by G. DU MAURIER.
THE MUSES OF MAYFAIR. Vers de Société, Selected by H. C. PENNELL.

PHELPS (E. STUART), WORKS BY. Post 8vo 1s. each; cloth 1s. 6d. each.
BEYOND THE GATES. | OLD MAID'S PARADISE. | BURGLARS IN PARADISE.
JACK THE FISHERMAN. Illustrated by C. W. REED. Cr. 8vo, 1s.; cloth, 1s. 6d.

PIRKIS (C. L.), NOVELS BY.
TROOPING WITH CROWS. Fcap. 8vo, picture cover, 1s.
LADY LOVELACE. Post 8vo, illustrated boards, 2s.

PLANCHE (J. R.), WORKS BY.
THE PURSUIVANT OF ARMS. With Six Plates, and 209 Illusts. Cr. 8vo, cl. 7s. 6d.
SONGS AND POEMS, 1819-1879. Introduction by Mrs. MACKARNESS. Cr. 8vo, cl., 6s.

PLUTARCH'S LIVES OF ILLUSTRIOUS MEN. With Notes and Life of Plutarch by J. and WM. LANGHORNE. Portraits. Two Vols., demy 8vo, 10s. 6d.

POE'S (EDGAR ALLAN) CHOICE WORKS, in Prose and Poetry. Introduction by CHAS. BAUDELAIRE, Portrait, and Facsimiles. Cr. 8vo, cloth, 7s. 6d.
THE MYSTERY OF MARIE ROGET, &c. Post 8vo, illustrated boards, 2s.

POPE'S POETICAL WORKS. Post 8vo, cloth limp, 2s.

PRAED (MRS. CAMPBELL), NOVELS BY. Post 8vo, illust. bds., 2s. ea.
THE ROMANCE OF A STATION. | THE SOUL OF COUNTESS ADRIAN.
OUTLAW AND LAWMAKER. Crown 8vo, cloth, 3s. 6d.; post 8vo, boards, 2s.
CHRISTINA CHARD. Crown 8vo, cloth extra, 3s. 6d.

PRICE (E. C.), NOVELS BY.
Crown 8vo, cloth extra, 3s. 6d. each; post 8vo, illustrated boards, 2s. each.
VALENTINA. | THE FOREIGNERS. | MRS. LANCASTER'S RIVAL.
GERALD. Post 8vo, illustrated boards, 2s.

PRINCESS OLGA.—RADNA: A Novel. Crown 8vo, cloth extra, 6s.

PROCTOR (RICHARD A., B.A.), WORKS BY.
FLOWERS OF THE SKY. With 55 Illusts. Small crown 8vo, cloth extra, 3s. 6d.
EASY STAR LESSONS. With Star Maps for Every Night in the Year. Cr. 8vo, 6s.
FAMILIAR SCIENCE STUDIES. Crown 8vo, cloth extra, 6s.
SATURN AND ITS SYSTEM. With 13 Steel Plates. Demy 8vo, cloth ex., 10s. 6d.
MYSTERIES OF TIME AND SPACE. With Illustrations. Cr. 8vo, cloth extra, 6s.
THE UNIVERSE OF SUNS. With numerous Illustrations. Cr. 8vo, cloth ex., 6s.
WAGES AND WANTS OF SCIENCE WORKERS. Crown 8vo, 1s. 6d.

PRYCE (RICHARD).—MISS MAXWELL'S AFFECTIONS. Frontispiece by HAL LUDLOW. Crown 8vo, cloth, 3s. 6d.; post 8vo, illust. boards, 2s.

RAMBOSSON (J.). — POPULAR ASTRONOMY. With Coloured Plate and numerous Illustrations. Crown 8vo, cloth extra, 7s. 6d.

RANDOLPH (LIEUT.-COL. GEORGE, U.S.A.).—AUNT ABIGAIL DYKES: A Novel. Crown 8vo, cloth extra, 7s. 6d.

RIDDELL (MRS. J. H.), NOVELS BY.
WEIRD STORIES. Crown 8vo, cloth extra, 3s. 6d.; post 8vo, illustrated bds., 2s.
Post 8vo, illustrated boards, 2s. each.
THE UNINHABITED HOUSE. | FAIRY WATER.
THE PRINCE OF WALES'S GARDEN | HER MOTHER'S DARLING.
PARTY. | THE NUN'S CURSE.
MYSTERY IN PALACE GARDENS. | IDLE TALES.

RIVES (AMELIE).—BARBARA DERING: A Sequel to "The Quick or the Dead?" Crown 8vo, cloth extra, 3s. 6d.; post 8vo, illustrated boards, 2s.

READE (CHARLES), NOVELS BY.
Crown 8vo, cloth extra, illustrated, 3s. 6d. each; post 8vo, illust. bds., 2s. each.
PEG WOFFINGTON. Illustrated by S. L. FILDES, R.A.—Also a POCKET EDITION, set in New Type, in Elzevir style, fcap. 8vo, half-leather, 2s. 6d.—And a Cheap POPULAR EDITION of PEG WOFFINGTON and CHRISTIE JOHNSTONE, the two Stories in One Volume, medium 8vo. 6d.; cloth, 1s.
CHRISTIE JOHNSTONE. Illustrated by WILLIAM SMALL.—Also a POCKET EDITION, set in New Type, in Elzevir style, fcap. 8vo, half-leather, 2s. 6d.
IT IS NEVER TOO LATE TO MEND. Illustrated by G. J. PINWELL.—Also the Cheap POPULAR EDITION, medium 8vo, portrait cover, 6d.; cloth, 1s.
COURSE OF TRUE LOVE NEVER DID RUN SMOOTH. Illust. HELEN PATERSON.
THE AUTOBIOGRAPHY OF A THIEF, &c. Illustrated by MATT STRETCH.
LOVE ME LITTLE, LOVE ME LONG. Illustrated by M. ELLEN EDWARDS.
THE DOUBLE MARRIAGE. Illusts. by Sir JOHN GILBERT, R.A., and C. KEENE.
THE CLOISTER AND THE HEARTH. Illustrated by CHARLES KEENE.—Also the ELZEVIR EDITION, with an Introduction by WALTER BESANT, 4 vols., post 8vo each with Frontispiece, cloth extra, gilt top, 14s. the set; and the Cheap POPULAR EDITION, medium 8vo, 6d.; cloth, 1s.
HARD CASH. Illustrated by F. W. LAWSON.
GRIFFITH GAUNT. Illustrated by S. L. FILDES, R.A., and WILLIAM SMALL.
FOUL PLAY. Illustrated by GEORGE DU MAURIER.
PUT YOURSELF IN HIS PLACE. Illustrated by ROBERT BARNES.
A TERRIBLE TEMPTATION. Illustrated by EDWARD HUGHES and A. W. COOPER.
A SIMPLETON. Illustrated by KATE CRAUFURD.
THE WANDERING HEIR. Illust. by H. PATERSON, S. L. FILDES, C. GREEN, &c.
A WOMAN-HATER. Illustrated by THOMAS COULDERY.
SINGLEHEART AND DOUBLEFACE. Illustrated by P. MACNAB.
GOOD STORIES OF MEN AND OTHER ANIMALS. Illust. by E. A. ABBEY, &c.
THE JILT, and other Stories. Illustrated by JOSEPH NASH.
A PERILOUS SECRET. Illustrated by FRED. BARNARD.
READIANA. With a Steel-plate Portrait of CHARLES READE.
BIBLE CHARACTERS: Studies of David, Paul, &c. Fcap. 8vo, leatherette, 1s.
SELECTIONS FROM THE WORKS OF CHARLES READE. Crown 8vo, with Portrait, buckram, 6s.; post 8vo, cloth limp, 2s. 6d.

RIMMER (ALFRED), WORKS BY. Square 8vo, cloth gilt, 7s. 6d. each.
OUR OLD COUNTRY TOWNS. With 55 Illustrations.
RAMBLES ROUND ETON AND HARROW. With 50 Illustrations.
ABOUT ENGLAND WITH DICKENS. With 58 Illusts. by C. A. VANDERHOOF, &c.

ROBINSON CRUSOE. By DANIEL DEFOE. (MAJOR'S EDITION.) With 37 Illustrations by GEORGE CRUIKSHANK. Post 8vo, half-bound, 2s.

ROBINSON (F. W.), NOVELS BY.
WOMEN ARE STRANGE. Post 8vo, illustrated boards, 2s.
THE HANDS OF JUSTICE. Cr. 8vo, cloth ex., 3s. 6d.; post 8vo, illust. bds., 2s.

ROBINSON (PHIL), WORKS BY. Crown 8vo, cloth extra, 6s. each.
THE POETS' BIRDS. | THE POETS' BEASTS.
THE POETS AND NATURE: REPTILES, FISHES, AND INSECTS.

ROCHEFOUCAULD'S MAXIMS AND MORAL REFLECTIONS. With Notes, and an Introductory Essay by SAINTE-BEUVE. Post 8vo, cloth limp, 2s.

ROLL OF BATTLE ABBEY, THE: A List of the Principal Warriors who came from Normandy with William the Conqueror. Handsomely printed, 5s.

ROSENGARTEN (A.).—HANDBOOK OF ARCHITECTURAL STYLES.
Translated by W. COLLETT-SANDARS. With 639 Illusts. Cr. 8vo, cloth extra, 7s. 6d.

ROWLEY (HON. HUGH), WORKS BY. Post 8vo, cloth, 2s. 6d. each.
PUNIANA: RIDDLES AND JOKES. With numerous Illustrations.
MORE PUNIANA. Profusely Illustrated.

RUSSELL (W. CLARK), BOOKS AND NOVELS BY:
Cr. 8vo, cloth extra, 6s. each; post 8vo, illust. boards, 2s. each; cloth limp, 2s. 6d. ea.
ROUND THE GALLEY-FIRE, | A BOOK FOR THE HAMMOCK.
IN THE MIDDLE WATCH. | MYSTERY OF THE "OCEAN STAR."
A VOYAGE TO THE CAPE. | THE ROMANCE OF JENNY HARLOWE.

Cr. 8vo, cl. extra, 3s. 6d. ea.; post 8vo, illust. boards, 2s. ea.; cloth limp, 2s. 6d. ea.
AN OCEAN TRAGEDY. | MY SHIPMATE LOUISE.
ALONE ON A WIDE WIDE SEA.

ON THE FO'K'SLE HEAD. Post 8vo, illust. boards, 2s.; cloth limp, 2s. 6d.
THE GOOD SHIP "MOHOCK." Two Vols., crown 8vo, cloth, 10s. net.
THE PHANTOM DEATH, &c. With Frontispiece. Crown 8vo, 3s. 6d.
THE CONVICT SHIP. Three Vols., crown 8vo, 15s. net. [Shortly.

CHATTO & WINDUS, PUBLISHERS, PICCADILLY.   21

RUNCIMAN (JAMES), STORIES BY. Post 8vo, bds., 2s. ea.; cl., 2s. 6d. ea.
SKIPPERS AND SHELLBACKS. | GRACE BALMAIGN'S SWEETHEART.
SCHOOLS AND SCHOLARS.

RUSSELL (DORA), NOVELS BY.
A COUNTRY SWEETHEART. Crown 8vo, cloth extra, 3s. 6d.   [Sept.
THE DRIFT OF FATE. Three Vols., crown 8vo, 15s. net.

SAINT AUBYN (ALAN), NOVELS BY.
Crown 8vo, cloth extra, 3s. 6d. each; post 8vo, illust. boards, 2s. each.
A FELLOW OF TRINITY. Note by OLIVER WENDELL HOLMES and Frontispiece.
THE JUNIOR DEAN. | MASTER OF ST. BENEDICT'S. | TO HIS OWN MASTER
Fcap. 8vo, cloth boards, 1s. 6d. each.
THE OLD MAID'S SWEETHEART. | MODEST LITTLE SARA.
Crown 8vo, cloth extra, 3s. 6d. each.
ORCHARD DAMEREL. | IN THE FACE OF THE WORLD. [Shortly.
THE TREMLETT DIAMONDS. Two Vols., 10s. net.   [Shortly.

SALA (G. A.).—GASLIGHT AND DAYLIGHT. Post 8vo, boards, 2s.

SANSON.—SEVEN GENERATIONS OF EXECUTIONERS: Memoirs of the Sanson Family (1688 to 1847). Crown 8vo, cloth extra, 3s. 6d.

SAUNDERS (JOHN), NOVELS BY.
Crown 8vo, cloth extra, 3s. 6d. each; post 8vo, illustrated boards, 2s. each.
GUY WATERMAN. | THE LION IN THE PATH. | THE TWO DREAMERS.
BOUND TO THE WHEEL. Crown 8vo, cloth extra, 3s. 6d.

SAUNDERS (KATHARINE), NOVELS BY.
Crown 8vo, cloth extra, 3s. 6d. each; post 8vo, illustrated boards, 2s. each.
MARGARET AND ELIZABETH. | HEART SALVAGE.
THE HIGH MILLS. | SEBASTIAN.
JOAN MERRYWEATHER. Post 8vo, illustrated boards, 2s.
GIDEON'S ROCK. Crown 8vo, cloth extra, 3s. 6d.

SCOTLAND YARD, Past and Present: Experiences of 37 Years. By Ex-Chief-Inspector CAVANAGH. Post 8vo, illustrated boards, 2s.; cloth, 2s. 6d.

SECRET OUT, THE: One Thousand Tricks with Cards; with Entertaining Experiments in Drawing-room or "White Magic." By W. H. CREMER. With 300 Illustrations. Crown 8vo, cloth extra, 4s. 6d.

SEGUIN (L. G.), WORKS BY.
THE COUNTRY OF THE PASSION PLAY (OBERAMMERGAU) and the Highlands of Bavaria. With Map and 37 Illustrations. Crown 8vo, cloth extra, 3s. 6d.
WALKS IN ALGIERS. With 2 Maps and 16 Illusts. Crown 8vo, cloth extra, 6s.

SENIOR (WM.).—BY STREAM AND SEA. Post 8vo, cloth, 2s. 6d.

SERGEANT (A.).—DR. ENDICOTT'S EXPERIMENT. 2 vols., 10s. net.

SHAKESPEARE FOR CHILDREN: LAMB'S TALES FROM SHAKESPEARE. With Illusts., coloured and plain, by J. MOYR SMITH. Cr. 4to, 3s. 6d.

SHARP (WILLIAM). — CHILDREN OF TO-MORROW: A Novel. Crown 8vo, cloth extra, 6s.

SHELLEY (PERCY BYSSHE), THE COMPLETE WORKS IN VERSE AND PROSE OF. Edited, Prefaced, and Annotated by R. HERNE SHEPHERD. Five Vols., crown 8vo, cloth boards, 3s. 6d. each.
• POETICAL WORKS, In Three Vols.:
Vol. I. Introduction by the Editor; Posthumous Fragments of Margaret Nicholson; Shelley's Correspondence with Stockdale; The Wandering Jew; Queen Mab, with the Notes; Alastor, and other Poems; Rosalind and Helen; Prometheus Unbound; Adonais, &c.

SHERIDAN'S (RICHARD BRINSLEY) COMPLETE WORKS. With Life and Anecdotes. Including his Dramatic Writings, his Works in Prose and Poetry, Translations, Speeches and Jokes. 10 Illusts. Cr. 8vo, hf.-bound, 7s. 6d.
THE RIVALS, THE SCHOOL FOR SCANDAL, and other Plays. Post 8vo, printed on laid paper and half-bound, 2s.
SHERIDAN'S COMEDIES: THE RIVALS and THE SCHOOL FOR SCANDAL. Edited, with an Introduction and Notes to each Play, and a Biographical Sketch, by BRANDER MATTHEWS. With Illustrations. Demy 8vo, half-parchment, 12s. 6d.

SIDNEY'S (SIR PHILIP) COMPLETE POETICAL WORKS, including all those in "Arcadia." With Portrait, Memorial-Introduction, Notes, &c. by the Rev. A. B. GROSART, D.D. Three Vols., crown 8vo, cloth boards, 18s.

SIGNBOARDS: Their History. With Anecdotes of Famous Taverns and Remarkable Characters. By JACOB LARWOOD and JOHN CAMDEN HOTTEN. With Coloured Frontispiece and 94 Illustrations. Crown 8vo, cloth extra, 7s. 6d.

SIMS (GEO. R.), WORKS BY. Post 8vo, illust. bds., 2s. ea; cl. limp, 2s. 6d. ea.
ROGUES AND VAGABONDS. | TALES OF TO-DAY.
THE RING O' BELLS. | DRAMAS OF LIFE. With 60 Illustrations.
MARY JANE'S MEMOIRS. | MEMOIRS OF A LANDLADY.
MARY JANE MARRIED. | MY TWO WIVES.
TINKLETOP'S CRIME. | SCENES FROM THE SHOW.
ZEPH: A Circus Story, &c.
    Crown 8vo, picture cover, 1s. each; cloth, 1s. 6d. each.
HOW THE POOR LIVE; and HORRIBLE LONDON.
THE DAGONET RECITER AND READER: being Readings and Recitations in Prose and Verse, selected from his own Works by GEORGE R. SIMS.
THE CASE OF GEORGE CANDLEMAS. | DAGONET DITTIES.
DAGONET ABROAD. Crown 8vo, cloth, 3s. 6d. [Shortly.

SISTER DORA: A Biography. By MARGARET LONSDALE. With Four Illustrations. Demy 8vo, picture cover, 4d.; cloth, 6d.

SKETCHLEY (ARTHUR). — A MATCH IN THE DARK. Post 8vo, illustrated boards, 2s.

SLANG DICTIONARY (THE): Etymological, Historical, and Anecdotal. Crown 8vo, cloth extra, 6s. 6d.

SMITH (J. MOYR), WORKS BY.
THE PRINCE OF ARGOLIS. With 130 Illusts. Post 8vo, cloth extra, 3s. 6d.
THE WOOING OF THE WATER WITCH. Illustrated. Post 8vo, cloth, 6s.

SOCIETY IN LONDON. Crown 8vo, 1s.; cloth, 1s. 6d.

SOCIETY IN PARIS: The Upper Ten Thousand. A Series of Letters from Count PAUL VASILI to a Young French Diplomat. Crown 8vo. cloth, 6s.

SOMERSET (LORD HENRY). — SONGS OF ADIEU. Small 4to, Japanese vellum, 6s.

SPALDING (T. A., LL.B.). — ELIZABETHAN DEMONOLOGY: An Essay on the Belief in the Existence of Devils. Crown 8vo, cloth extra, 5s.

SPEIGHT (T. W.), NOVELS BY.
            Post 8vo, illustrated boards, 2s. each.
THE MYSTERIES OF HERON DYKE. | THE GOLDEN HOOP.
BY DEVIOUS WAYS, &c. | BACK TO LIFE.
HOODWINKED; and THE SANDY- | THE LOUDWATER TRAGEDY.
CROFT MYSTERY. | BURGO'S ROMANCE.
            QUITTANCE IN FULL.
        Post 8vo, cloth limp, 1s. 6d. each.
A BARREN TITLE. | WIFE OR NO WIFE?
THE SANDYCROFT MYSTERY. Crown 8vo, picture cover, 1s.
A SECRET OF THE SEA. Crown 8vo, cloth extra, 3s. 6d.
THE GREY MONK. Three Vols., 15s. net.

SPENSER FOR CHILDREN. By M. H. TOWRY. With Illustrations by WALTER J. MORGAN. Crown 4to, cloth extra, 3s. 6d.

STARRY HEAVENS (THE): A POETICAL BIRTHDAY BOOK. Royal 16mo, cloth extra, 2s. 6d.

CHATTO & WINDUS, PUBLISHERS, PICCADILLY. 23

STERNDALE (R. ARMITAGE).—THE AFGHAN KNIFE: A Novel.
Crown 8vo, cloth extra, 3s. 6d.; post 8vo, illustrated boards, 2s.

STEVENSON (R. LOUIS), WORKS BY. Post 8vo, cl. limp, 2s. 6d. each
TRAVELS WITH A DONKEY. With a Frontispiece by WALTER CRANE.
AN INLAND VOYAGE. With a Frontispiece by WALTER CRANE.
Crown 8vo, buckram, gilt top, 6s. each.
FAMILIAR STUDIES OF MEN AND BOOKS.
THE SILVERADO SQUATTERS. With Frontispiece by J. D. STRONG.
THE MERRY MEN. | **UNDERWOODS:** Poems.
MEMORIES AND PORTRAITS.
VIRGINIBUS PUERISQUE, and other Papers. | **BALLADS.** | **PRINCE OTTO.**
ACROSS THE PLAINS, with other Memories and Essays.
NEW ARABIAN NIGHTS. Crown 8vo, buckram, gilt top, 6s.; post 8vo, illustrated boards, 2s.
THE SUICIDE CLUB; and **THE RAJAH'S DIAMOND.** (From NEW ARABIAN NIGHTS.) With 8 Illustrations by W. J. HENNESSY. Crown 8vo, cloth, 5s.
FATHER DAMIEN: An Open Letter to the Rev. Dr. Hyde. Crown 8vo, handmade and brown paper, 1s.
THE EDINBURGH EDITION OF THE WORKS OF ROBERT LOUIS STEVENSON. 20 Vols., demy 8vo. This Edition (which is limited to 1,000 copies) is sold only in Sets, the price of which may be learned from the Booksellers. The Vols. are appearing at the rate of one a month, beginning Nov. 1894.

STODDARD (C. WARREN).—SUMMER CRUISING IN THE SOUTH SEAS. Illustrated by WALLIS MACKAY. Crown 8vo, cloth extra, 3s. 6d.

STORIES FROM FOREIGN NOVELISTS. With Notices by HELEN and ALICE ZIMMERN. Crown 8vo, cloth extra, 3s. 6d.; post 8vo, illustrated boards, 2s.

STRANGE MANUSCRIPT (A) FOUND IN A COPPER CYLINDER.
Cr. 8vo, cloth extra, with 19 Illusts. by GILBERT GAUL, 5s.; post 8vo, illust. bds., 2s.

STRANGE SECRETS. Told by CONAN DOYLE, PERCY FITZGERALD, FLORENCE MARRYAT. &c. Post 8vo, illustrated boards, 2s.

STRUTT (JOSEPH).—THE SPORTS AND PASTIMES OF THE PEOPLE OF ENGLAND; including the Rural and Domestic Recreations, May Games, Mummeries, Shows, &c., from the Earliest Period to the Present Time. Edited by WILLIAM HONE. With 140 Illustrations. Crown 8vo, cloth extra, 7s. 6d.

SWIFT'S (DEAN) CHOICE WORKS, in Prose and Verse. With Memoir, Portrait, and Facsimiles of the Maps in "Gulliver's Travels." Cr. 8vo, cl., 7s. 6d.
GULLIVER'S TRAVELS, and **A TALE OF A TUB.** Post 8vo, half-bound, 2s.
JONATHAN SWIFT: A Study. By J. CHURTON COLLINS. Crown 8vo, cloth extra, 8s.

SWINBURNE (ALGERNON C.), WORKS BY.
SELECTIONS FROM POETICAL WORKS OF A. C. SWINBURNE. Fcap. 8vo, 6s.
ATALANTA IN CALYDON. Crown 8vo, 6s.
CHASTELARD: A Tragedy. Crown 8vo, 7s.
POEMS AND BALLADS. FIRST SERIES. Crown 8vo or fcap. 8vo, 9s.
POEMS AND BALLADS. SECOND SERIES. Crown 8vo or fcap. 8vo, 9s.
POEMS & BALLADS. THIRD SERIES. Cr. 8vo, 7s.
SONGS BEFORE SUNRISE. Crown 8vo, 10s. 6d.
BOTHWELL: A Tragedy. Crown 8vo, 12s. 6d.
SONGS OF TWO NATIONS. Crown 8vo, 6s.
GEORGE CHAPMAN. (See Vol. II. of G. CHAPMAN'S Works.) Crown 8vo, 6s.
ESSAYS AND STUDIES. Crown 8vo, 12s.
ERECHTHEUS; A Tragedy. Crown 8vo, 6s.
A NOTE ON CHARLOTTE BRONTE. Cr. 8vo, 6s.
SONGS OF THE SPRINGTIDES. Crown 8vo, 6s.
STUDIES IN SONG. Crown 8vo, 7s.
MARY STUART: A Tragedy. Crown 8vo, 8s.
TRISTRAM OF LYONESSE. Crown 8vo, 9s.
A CENTURY OF ROUNDELS. Crown 4to, 8s.
A MIDSUMMER HOLIDAY. Crown 8vo, 7s.
MARINO FALIERO: A Tragedy. Crown 8vo, 6s.
A STUDY OF VICTOR HUGO. Crown 8vo, 6s.
MISCELLANIES. Crown 8vo, 12s.
LOCRINE: A Tragedy. Crown 8vo, 6s.
A STUDY OF BEN JONSON. Crown 8vo, 7s.
THE SISTERS: A Tragedy. Crown 8vo, 6s.
ASTROPHEL, &c. Crown 8vo, 7s.
STUDIES IN PROSE AND POETRY. Crown 8vo, 9s.

SYNTAX'S (DR.) THREE TOURS: In Search of the Picturesque, in Search of Consolation, and in Search of a Wife. With ROWLANDSON'S Coloured Illustrations, and Life of the Author by J. C. HOTTEN. Crown 8vo, cloth extra, 7s. 6d.

TAINE'S HISTORY OF ENGLISH LITERATURE. Translated by HENRY VAN LAUN. Four Vols., small demy 8vo, cl. bds., 30s.—POPULAR EDITION, Two Vols., large crown 8vo, cloth extra, 15s.

TAYLOR (DR. J. E., F.L.S.), WORKS BY. Crown 8vo, cloth, 5s. each.
THE SAGACITY AND MORALITY OF PLANTS: A Sketch of the Life and Conduct of the Vegetable Kingdom. With a Coloured Frontispiece and 100 Illustrations.
OUR COMMON BRITISH FOSSILS, and Where to Find Them. 331 Illustrations.
THE PLAYTIME NATURALIST. With 366 Illustrations.

TAYLOR (BAYARD).—DIVERSIONS OF THE EC
lesques of Modern Writers. Post 8vo, cloth limp, 2s.

TAYLOR (TOM).—HISTORICAL DRAMAS. Conta
"Jeanne Darc," "'Twixt Axe and Crown," "The Fool's Re
Wife," " Anne Boleyn," " Plot and Passion." Crown 8vo, clo
. The Plays may also be had separately, at 1s

TENNYSON (LORD): A Biographical Sketch. B)
Post 8vo, portrait cover, 1s.; cloth, 1s. 6d.

THACKERAYANA : Notes and Anecdotes. Illustrate
Sketches by WILLIAM MAKEPEACE THACKERAY. Crown 8vo.

THAMES, A NEW PICTORIAL HISTORY OF
KRAUSSE. With 340 Illustrations Post 8vo, 1s.; cloth, 1s.

THIERS (ADOLPHE).—HISTORY of the CONSULA
FRANCE UNDER NAPOLEON. Translated by D. FORBES
STEBBING. With 36 Steel Plates. 12 vols., demy 8vo, cloth e

THOMAS (BERTHA), NOVELS BY. Cr. 8vo, cl., 3s. 6d
THE VIOLIN-PLAYER. | PROUD MAISIE
CRESSIDA. Post 8vo, illustrated boards, 2s.

THOMSON'S SEASONS, and CASTLE OF INDOLE
duction by ALLAN CUNNINGHAM, and 48 Illustrations. Post 8v

THORNBURY (WALTER), WORKS BY.
THE LIFE AND CORRESPONDENCE OF J. M. W. TUR
tions in Colours. Crown 8vo, cloth extra, 7s. 6d.
Post 8vo, illustrated boards, 2s. each.
OLD STORIES RE-TOLD. | TALES FOR THE

TIMBS (JOHN), WORKS BY. Crown 8vo, cloth extra,
THE HISTORY OF CLUBS AND CLUB LIFE IN LONDO
Famous Coffee-houses, Hostelries, and Taverns. With 42
ENGLISH ECCENTRICS AND ECCENTRICITIES: Stories
tures, Sporting Scenes, Eccentric Artists, Theatrical Folk

TROLLOPE (ANTHONY), NOVELS BY.
Crown 8vo, cloth extra, 3s. 6d. each; post 8vo, illustrated
THE WAY WE LIVE NOW. | MR. SCARBOROU(
FRAU FROHMANN. | THE LAND-LEAG
Post 8vo, illustrated boards, 2s. each.
KEPT IN THE DARK. | THE AMERICAN
THE GOLDEN LION OF GRANPERE. | JOHN CALDIGAT

TROLLOPE (FRANCES E.), NOVELS BY.
Crown 8vo, cloth extra, 3s. 6d. each; post 8vo, illustrated
LIKE SHIPS UPON THE SEA. | MABEL'S PROGRESS.

TROLLOPE (T. A.).—DIAMOND CUT DIAMOND. P

TROWBRIDGE (J. T.).—FARNELL'S FOLLY. Fo

TYTLER (C. C. FRASER-).—MISTRESS JUDITH:
8vo, cloth extra, 3s. 6d.; post 8vo, illustrated boards, 2s.

TYTLER (SARAH), NOVELS BY.
Crown 8vo, cloth extra, 3s. 6d. each; post 8vo, illustrated
THE BRIDE'S PASS. | BURIED DIAMON
LADY BELL. | THE BLACKHALI
Post 8vo, illustrated boards, 2s. each.
WHAT SHE CAME THROUGH. | BEAUTY AND TI
CITOYENNE JACQUELINE | DISAPPEARED. |
SAINT MUNGO'S CITY. | THE HUGUENOT
THE MACDONALD LASS. With Frontispiece. Cr. 8vo, clo

UPWARD (ALLEN), NOVELS BY.
THE QUEEN AGAINST OWEN. Crown 8vo, cloth, 3s. 6
THE PRINCE OF BALKISTAN. Crown 8vo, cloth extra,

VASHTI AND ESTHER. By the Writer of "Belle
World. Crown 8vo, cloth extra, 3s. 6d.

VILLARI (LINDA).—A DOUBLE BOND: A Story

VIZETELLY (ERNEST A.).—THE SCORPION: A Romance of Spain.
With a Frontispiece. Crown 8vo, cloth extra, 3s. 6d.

WALFORD (EDWARD, M.A.), WORKS BY.
WALFORD'S COUNTY FAMILIES OF THE UNITED KINGDOM (1895). Containing the Descent, Birth, Marriage, Education, &c., of 12,000 Heads of Families, their Heirs, Offices, Addresses, Clubs, &c. Royal 8vo, cloth gilt, 50s.
WALFORD'S SHILLING PEERAGE (1895). Containing a List of the House of Lords, Scotch and Irish Peers, &c. 32mo, cloth, 1s.
WALFORD'S SHILLING BARONETAGE (1895). Containing a List of the Baronets of the United Kingdom, Biographical Notices, Addresses, &c. 32mo, cloth, 1s.
WALFORD'S SHILLING KNIGHTAGE (1895). Containing a List of the Knights of the United Kingdom, Biographical Notices, Addresses, &c. 32mo, cloth, 1s.
WALFORD'S SHILLING HOUSE OF COMMONS (1895). Containing a List of all the Members of the New Parliament, their Addresses, Clubs, &c. 32mo, cloth, 1s.
WALFORD'S COMPLETE PEERAGE, BARONETAGE, KNIGHTAGE, AND HOUSE OF COMMONS (1895) Royal 32mo, cloth, gilt edges, 5s.
TALES OF OUR GREAT FAMILIES. Crown 8vo, cloth extra, 3s. 6d.

WALTON AND COTTON'S COMPLETE ANGLER; or, The Contemplative Man's Recreation, by IZAAK WALTON; and Instructions how to Angle for a Trout or Grayling in a clear Stream, by CHARLES COTTON. With Memoirs and Notes by Sir HARRIS NICOLAS, and 61 Illustrations. Crown 8vo, cloth antique, 7s. 6d.

WALT WHITMAN, POEMS BY. Edited, with Introduction, by WILLIAM M. ROSSETTI. With Portrait. Cr. 8vo, hand-made paper and buckram, 6s.

WARD (HERBERT).—MY LIFE WITH STANLEY'S REAR GUARD.
With a Map by F. S. WELLER. Post 8vo, 1s.; cloth, 1s. 6d.

WARNER (CHARLES DUDLEY).—A ROUNDABOUT JOURNEY.
Crown 8vo, cloth extra, 6s.

WARRANT TO EXECUTE CHARLES I. A Facsimile, with the 59 Signatures and Seals. Printed on paper 22 in. by 14 in. 2s.
WARRANT TO EXECUTE MARY QUEEN OF SCOTS. A Facsimile, including Queen Elizabeth's Signature and the Great Seal. 2s.

WASSERMANN (LILLIAS), NOVELS BY.
THE DAFFODILS. Crown 8vo, 1s.; cloth, 1s. 6d.
THE MARQUIS OF CARABAS. By AARON WATSON and LILLIAS WASSERMANN.
Post 8vo, illustrated boards, 2s.

WEATHER, HOW TO FORETELL THE, WITH THE POCKET SPECTROSCOPE. By F. W. CORY. With 10 Illustrations. Cr. 8vo, 1s.; cloth, 1s. 6d.

WEBBER (BYRON).—FUN, FROLIC, AND FANCY. With 43 Illustrations by PHIL MAY and CHARLES MAY. Fcap. 4to, picture cover, 1s.

WESTALL (WILLIAM). — TRUST-MONEY. Post 8vo, illustrated boards, 2s.; cloth limp, 2s. 6d.

WHIST, HOW TO PLAY SOLO. By ABRAHAM S. WILKS and CHARLES F. PARDON. Post 8vo, cloth limp, 2s.

WHITE (GILBERT).—THE NATURAL HISTORY OF SELBORNE.
Post 8vo, printed on laid paper and half-bound, 2s.

WILLIAMS (W. MATTIEU, F.R.A.S.), WORKS BY.
SCIENCE IN SHORT CHAPTERS. Crown 8vo, cloth extra, 7s. 6d.
A SIMPLE TREATISE ON HEAT. With Illustrations. Crown 8vo, cloth, 2s. 6d.
THE CHEMISTRY OF COOKERY. Crown 8vo, cloth extra, 6s.
THE CHEMISTRY OF IRON AND STEEL MAKING. Crown 8vo, cloth extra, 9s.
A VINDICATION OF PHRENOLOGY. With Portrait and 43 Illustrations. Demy 8vo, cloth extra, 12s. 6d.

WILLIAMSON (MRS. F. H.).—A CHILD WIDOW. Post 8vo, bds., 2s.

WILSON (DR. ANDREW, F.R.S.E.), WORKS BY.
CHAPTERS ON EVOLUTION. With 259 Illustrations. Cr. 8vo, cloth extra, 7s. 6d.
LEAVES FROM A NATURALIST'S NOTE-BOOK. Post 8vo, cloth limp, 2s. 6d.
LEISURE-TIME STUDIES. With Illustrations. Crown 8vo, cloth extra, 6s.
STUDIES IN LIFE AND SENSE. With numerous Illusts. Cr. 8vo, cl. ex., 6s.
COMMON ACCIDENTS: HOW TO TREAT THEM. Illusts. Cr. 8vo, 1s.; cl., 1s. 6d.
GLIMPSES OF NATURE. With 35 Illustrations. Crown 8vo, cloth extra, 3s. 6d.

WISSMANN (HERMANN VON).—MY SECOND JOURNEY THROUGH EQUATORIAL AFRICA. With 92 Illustrations. Demy 8vo, 16s.

WINTER (J. S.), STORIES BY. Post 8vo, illustr[ated]
cloth limp, 2s. 6d. each.
CAVALRY LIFE. | REGIMENTAL LE[GENDS.
A SOLDIER'S CHILDREN. With 34 Illustrations by E. G. 7[
HARDY. Crown 8vo, cloth extra, 3s. 6d.

WOOD (H. F.), DETECTIVE STORIES BY. Post 8v[o
PASSENGER FROM SCOTLAND YARD. | ENGLISHMAI[

WOOD (LADY).—SABINA : A Novel. Post 8vo,

**WOOLLEY (CELIA PARKER).—RACHEL ARM[S
and Theology. Post 8vo, illustrated boards, 2s. ; cloth, 2s.

WRIGHT (THOMAS), WORKS BY. Crown 8vo, cl[oth
CARICATURE HISTORY OF THE GEORGES. With 400
HISTORY OF CARICATURE AND OF THE GROTESQ[UE in LITERA-
TURE, SCULPTURE, AND PAINTING. Illustrated by

WYNMAN (MARGARET).—MY FLIRTATIONS.
tions by J. BERNARD PARTRIDGE. Crown 8vo, cloth extra, 3

YATES (EDMUND), NOVELS BY. Post 8vo, illustr[
LAND AT LAST. | THE FORLORN HOPE. |

ZANGWILL (I.)—GHETTO TRAGEDIES. With
by A. S. BOYD. Fcap. 8vo, picture cover, 1s. net.

ZOLA (EMILE), NOVELS BY. Crown 8vo, cloth e[xtra
THE DOWNFALL. Translated by E. A. VIZETELLY. Fou[
THE DREAM. Translated by ELIZA CHASE. With 8 Illus[
DOCTOR PASCAL. Translated by E. A. VIZETELLY, Wi[
MONEY. Translated by ERNEST A. VIZETELLY.
LOURDES. Translated by ERNEST A. VIZETELLY.
EMILE ZOLA: A Biography. By R. H. SHERARD. With
and Facsimile Letter. Demy 8vo, cloth extra, 12s.

SOME BOOKS CLASSIFIED IN
* *For fuller cataloguing, see alphabetical arrangem[ent.*

THE MAYFAIR LIBRARY. Post 8vo, cloth limp,
A Journey Round My Room. By X. DE MAISTRE.
Quips and Quiddities. By W. D. ADAMS.
The Agony Column of "The Times."
Melancholy Anatomised: An Abridgment of Burton's "Anatomy of Melancholy."
Poetical Ingenuities. By W. T. DOBSON.
The Cupboard Papers. By FIN-BEC.
W. S. Gilbert's Plays. THREE SERIES.
Songs of Irish Wit and Humour.
Animals and their Masters. By Sir A. HELPS.
Social Pressure. By Sir A. HELPS.
Curiosities of Criticism. By H. J. JENNINGS.
The Autocrat of the Breakfast-Table. By OLIVER WENDELL HOLMES.
Pencil and Palette. By R. KEMPT.
Little Essays: from LAMB'S Letters.
Forensic Anecdotes. By JACOB LARWOOD.

Theatrical Anecdote[s
Jeux d'Esprit. Edit[
Witch Stories. By E[
Ourselves. By E. L[
Pastimes and Player[s
New Paul and Virgin[ia
The New Republic.
Puck on Pegasus. B[y
Pegasus Re-saddled.
Muses of Mayfair.
Thoreau: His Life an[d
Puniana. By Hon. H[
More Puniana. By H[
The Philosophy of H[
By Stream and Sea.
Leaves from a Natu[
ANDREW WILSON.

THE GOLDEN LIBRARY. Post 8vo, cloth limp
Diversions of the Echo Club. BAYARD TAYLOR.
Ballad History of England. By W. C. BENNETT.
Songs for Sailors. By W. C. BENNETT.
Lives of the Necromancers. By W. GODWIN.
The Poetical Works of Alexander Pope.
Scenes of Country Life. By EDWARD JESSE.

The Autocrat of
OLIVER WENDELL
Tale for a Chimney
La Mort d'Arthur :
Provincial Letters o[f
Maxims and Reflecti[ons

THE WANDERER'S LIBRARY. Crown 8vo, cloth
Wanderings in Patagonia. By JULIUS BEERBOHM. Illustrated.
Camp Notes. By FREDERICK BOYLE.
Savage Life. By FREDERICK BOYLE.
Merrie England in the Olden Time. By G. DANIEL. Illustrated by CRUIKSHANK.
Circus Life. By THOMAS FROST.
Lives of the Conjurers. By THOMAS FROST.
The Old Showmen and the Old London Fairs. By THOMAS FROST.
Low-Life Deeps. By JAMES GREENWOOD.

Wilds of London. B[y
Tunis. By Chev. HE[
Life and Adventures
World Behind the Sc[
Tavern Anecdotes an[
The Genial Showman[
Story of London Par[
London Characters.
Seven Generations of
Summer Cruising i[
WARREN STODDA[RD.

CHATTO & WINDUS, PUBLISHERS, PICCADILLY.   27

)KS IN SERIES—*continued.*

HANDY NOVELS. Fcap. 8vo, cloth boards, 1s. 6d. each.

Old Maid's Sweetheart. By A. ST. AUBYN.
est Little Sara. By ALAN ST. AUBYN.
n Sleepers of Ephesus. M. E. COLERIDGE

Taken from the Enemy. By H. NEWBOLT.
A Lost Soul. By W L. ALDEN.
Dr. Palliser's Patient. By GRANT ALLEN.

Y LIBRARY. Printed on laid paper, post 8vo, half-Roxburghe, 2s. 6d. each.

tion and Examination of William Shakspeare
W. S. LANDOR.
Journal of Maurice de Guerin.

Christie Johnstone. By CHARLES READE.
Peg Woffington. By CHARLES READE.
The Dramatic Essays of Charles Lamb.

E POCKET LIBRARY. Post 8vo, printed on laid paper and hf.-bd., 2s. each.

Essays of Elia. By CHARLES LAMB.
Inson Crusoe. Illustrated by G. CRUIKSHANK.
ms and Oddities. By THOMAS HOOD. With Illustrations.
Barber's Chair. By DOUGLAS JERROLD.
ronomy. By BRILLAT-SAVARIN.
Epicurean, &c. By THOMAS MOORE.
h Hunt's Essays. Edited by E. OLLIER.

White's Natural History of Selborne.
Gulliver's Travels, &c. By Dean SWIFT.
Plays by RICHARD BRINSLEY SHERIDAN.
Anecdotes of the Clergy. By JACOB LARWOOD
Thomson's Seasons. Illustrated.
The Autocrat of the Breakfast-Table and The Professor at the Breakfast-Table. By OLIVER WENDELL HOLMES.

THE PICCADILLY NOVELS.

RARY EDITIONS OF NOVELS, many Illustrated, crown 8vo, cloth extra, 3s. 6d. each.

By F. M. ALLEN.
n as Grass.

By GRANT ALLEN.
Istis.
ylon.
nge Stories.
coning Hand.
ll Shades.
Tents of Shem.
Maimie's Sake,
Devil's Die.

This Mortal Coil.
The Great Taboo.
Dumaresq's Daughter.
Blood Royal.
Duchess of Powysland.
Ivan Greet's Masterpiece.
The Scallywag.

By EDWIN L. ARNOLD.
a the Phœnician.
Constable of St. Nicholas.

By ALAN ST. AUBYN.
ellow of Trinity.
Junior Dean.
ter of St. Benedict's.

To his Own Master.
In Face of the World.
Orchard Damerel.

y Rev. S. BARING GOULD.
Spider. | Eve.

By ROBERT BARR.
Steamer Chair. | From Whose Bourne.

By FRANK BARRETT.
Woman of the Iron Bracelets.

By "BELLE."
hti and Esther.

By W. BESANT & J. RICE.
Little Girl.
of Mr. Lucraft.
Son of Vulcan.
Golden Butterfly.
Celia's Arbour.
Monks of Thelema.
Seamy Side.

The Ten Years' Tenant.
Ready-Money Mortiboy.
With Harp and Crown.
'Twas in Trafalgar's Bay.
The Chaplain of the Fleet.

By WALTER BESANT.
Sorts and Conditions of Men.
Captains' Room.
In a Garden Fair.
r Panius.
Ivory Gate.
World Went Very Well Then.
Faith and Freedom.
Rebel Queen.
othy Forster.

Uncle Jack.
Children of Gibeon.
Bell of St. Paul's.
To Call Her Mine.
The Holy Rose.
Armorel of Lyonesse.
St. Katherine's by the Tower.
Verbena Camellia Stephanotis.

By ROBERT BUCHANAN.
dow of the Sword.
hild of Nature.
r of Linne.
  Martyrdom of Madeline.
and the Man.
e Me for Ever.

Annan Water.
Woman and the Man.
The New Abelard.
Foxglove Manor.
Master of the Mine.
Red and White Heather.
Matt. | Rachel Dene.

y J. MITCHELL CHAPPLE.
Minor Chord.

By HALL CAINE.
The Shadow of a Crime. | The Deemster.
A Son of Hagar.

By MACLAREN COBBAN.
The Red Sultan. | The Burden of Isabel.

MORT. & FRANCES COLLINS.
Transmigration. | From Midnight to Midnight.
Blacksmith & Scholar,
The Village Comedy. | You Play me False.

By WILKIE COLLINS.
Armadale.
After Dark.
No Name.
Antonina.
Basil.
Hide and Seek.
The Dead Secret.
Queen of Hearts.
My Miscellanies.
The Woman in White.
The Moonstone.
Man and Wife.
Poor Miss Finch.
Miss or Mrs.?
The New Magdalen.

The Frozen Deep.
The Two Destinies.
The Law and the Lady.
The Haunted Hotel.
The Fallen Leaves.
Jezebel's Daughter.
The Black Robe.
Heart and Science.
"I Say No."
Little Novels.
The Evil Genius.
The Legacy of Cain.
A Rogue's Life.
Blind Love.

By DUTTON COOK.
Paul Foster's Daughter.

By E. H. COOPER.
Geoffory Hamilton.

By V. CECIL COTES.
Two Girls on a Barge.

By C. EGBERT CRADDOCK.
His Vanished Star.

By H. N. CRELLIN.
Romances of the Old Seraglio.

By MATT CRIM.
Adventures of a Fair Rebel.

By B. M. CROKER.
Diana Barrington. | A Bird of Passage.
Proper Pride. | "To Let."
A Family Likeness. | Outcast of the People.
Pretty Miss Neville.

By WILLIAM CYPLES.
Hearts of Gold.

By ALPHONSE DAUDET.
The Evangelist; or, Port Salvation.

By H. COLEMAN DAVIDSON.
Mr. Sadler's Daughters.

By ERASMUS DAWSON.
The Fountain of Youth.

By JAMES DE MILLE.
A Castle in Spain.

By J. LEITH DERWENT.
Our Lady of Tears. | Circe's Lovers

THE PICCADILLY (3/6) NOVELS—*continued.*

By DICK DONOVAN.
Tracked to Doom. | Man from Manchester.

By A. CONAN DOYLE.
The Firm of Girdlestone.

S. JEANNETTE DUNCAN.
A Daughter of To-day. | Vernon's Aunt.

By Mrs. ANNIE EDWARDES.
Archie Lovell.

By G. MANVILLE FENN.
The New Mistress. | The Tiger Lily.
Witness to the Deed. | The White Virgin.

By PERCY FITZGERALD.
Fatal Zero.

By R. E. FRANCILLON.
One by One. | King or Knave?
A Dog and his Shadow. | Ropes of Sand.
A Real Queen. | Jack Doyle's Daughter.

Pref. by Sir BARTLE FRERE.
Pandurang Hari.

By EDWARD GARRETT.
The Capel Girls.

By PAUL GAULOT.
The Red Shirts.

By CHARLES GIBBON.
Robin Gray. | The Golden Shaft.
Loving a Dream. | Of High Degree.

By E. GLANVILLE.
The Lost Heiress. | The Fossicker.
A Fair Colonist.

By E. J. GOODMAN.
The Fate of Herbert Wayne.

By CECIL GRIFFITH.
Corinthia Marazion.

By SYDNEY GRUNDY.
The Days of his Vanity.

By THOMAS HARDY.
Under the Greenwood Tree.

By BRET HARTE.
A Waif of the Plains. | Susy.
A Ward of the Golden | Sally Dows.
Gate. | A Protegée of Jack
A Sappho of Green | Hamlin's.
Springs. | Bell-Ringer of Angel's
Col. Starbottle's Client. | Clarence.

By JULIAN HAWTHORNE.
Garth. | Beatrix Randolph.
Ellice Quentin. | David Poindexter's Dis-
Sebastian Strome. | appearance.
Dust. | The Spectre of the
Fortune's Fool. | Camera.

By Sir A. HELPS.
Ivan de Biron.

By I. HENDERSON.
Agatha Page.

By G. A. HENTY.
Rujub the Juggler. | Dorothy's Double.

By JOHN HILL.
The Common Ancestor.

By Mrs. HUNGERFORD.
Lady Verner's Flight. | The Red-House Mystery.

By Mrs. ALFRED HUNT.
The Leaden Casket. | Self-Condemned.
That Other Person. | Mrs. Juliet.

By CUTCLIFFE HYNE.
Honour of Thieves.

By R. ASHE KING.
A Drawn Game.
The Wearing of the Green.

THE PICCADILLY (3/

By EDMOND L
Madame Sans-Gene.

By HARRY
Rhoda Roberts.

By E. LYN
Patricia Kemball.
Under which Lord?
"My Love!"
Ione.
Paston Carew.

By H. V
Gideon Fleyce.

By JUSTIN
A Fair Saxon.
Linley Rochford.
Miss Misanthrope.
Donna Quixote.
Maid of Athens.
Camiola.

By GEORGE
Heather and Snow.

By L. T.
A Soldier of Fortune.

By BERTRA
The Gun-Runner.
The Luck of Gerard
Ridgeley.

By J. E.
Maid Marian and Rob

By D. CHRIS
A Life's Atonement.
Joseph's Coat.
Coals of Fire.
Old Blazer's Hero.
Val Strange. | Hearts
A Model Father.
By the Gate of the Sea
A Bit of Human Nature

By MURRAY
The Bishops' Bible.
One Traveller Returns

By HUM
"Bail Up!"

By W. E
Saint Ann's.

By G.
A Weird Gift.

By C
Held in Bondage.
Strathmore.
Chandos.
Under Two Flags.
Idalia.
Cecil Castlemaine's
Gage.
Tricotrin.
Puck.
Folle Farine.
A Dog of Flanders.
Pascarel.
Signa.
Princess Napraxine.
Ariadne.

By MARGA
Gentle and Simple.

By JAM
Lost Sir Massingberd.
Less Black than We'r
Painted.
A Confidential Agent.
A Grape from a Thorn
In Peril and Privation
The Mystery of Mi
bridge.
The Canon's Ward.
Walter's Word.
By Proxy.

CHATTO & WINDUS, PUBLISHERS, PICCADILLY.   29

THE PICCADILLY (3/6) NOVELS—*continued*.

By Mrs. CAMPBELL PRAED.
Outlaw and Lawmaker. | Christina Chard.

By E. C. PRICE.
Valentina. | Mrs. Lancaster's Rival.
The Foreigners. |

By RICHARD PRYCE.
Miss Maxwell's Affections.

By CHARLES READE.
It is Never Too Late to | Singleheart and Double-
 Mend. | face.
The Double Marriage. | Good Stories of Men
Love Me Little, Love | and other Animals.
 Me Long. | Hard Cash.
The Cloister and the | Peg Woffington.
 Hearth. | Christie Johnstone.
The Course of True | Griffith Gaunt.
 Love. | Foul Play.
The Autobiography of | The Wandering Heir.
 a Thief. | A Woman-Hater.
Put Yourself in His | A Simpleton.
 Place. | A Perilous Secret.
A Terrible Temptation. | Readiana.
The Jilt. |

By Mrs. J. H. RIDDELL.
Weird Stories.

By AMELIE RIVES.
Barbara Dering.

By F. W. ROBINSON.
The Hands of Justice.

By DORA RUSSELL.
A Country Sweetheart.

By W. CLARK RUSSELL.
Ocean Tragedy. | Alone on Wide Wide Sea.
My Shipmate Louise. | The Phantom Death.

By JOHN SAUNDERS.
Guy Waterman. | The Two Dreamers.
Bound to the Wheel. | The Lion in the Path.

By KATHARINE SAUNDERS.
Margaret and Elizabeth | Heart Salvage.
Gideon's Rock. | Sebastian.
The High Mills. |

THE PICCADILLY (3/6) NOVELS—*continued*.

By HAWLEY SMART.
Without Love or Licence.

By T. W. SPEIGHT.
A Secret of the Sea.

By R. A. STERNDALE.
The Afghan Knife.

By BERTHA THOMAS.
Proud Maisie. | The Violin-Player.

By ANTHONY TROLLOPE.
The Way we Live Now. | Scarborough's Family.
Frau Frohmann. | The Land-Leaguers.

By FRANCES E. TROLLOPE.
Like Ships upon the | Anne Furness.
 Sea. | Mabel's Progress.

By IVAN TURGENIEFF, &c.
Stories from Foreign Novelists.

By MARK TWAIN.
The American Claimant. | Tom Sawyer Abroad.
The £1,000,000 Bank-note. | Pudd'nhead Wilson.

By C. C. FRASER-TYTLER.
Mistress Judith.

By SARAH TYTLER.
Lady Bell. | The Blackhall Ghosts.
The Bride's Pass. | The Macdonald Lass.
Buried Diamonds. |

By ALLEN UPWARD.
The Queen against Owen.
The Prince of Balkistan.

By E. A. VIZETELLY.
The Scorpion: A Romance of Spain.

By J. S. WINTER.
A Soldier's Children.

By MARGARET WYNMAN.
My Flirtations.

By E. ZOLA.
The Downfall. | Dr. Pascal.
The Dream. | Money. | Lourdes.

CHEAP EDITIONS OF POPULAR NOVELS.
Post 8vo, Illustrated boards, 2s. each.

By ARTEMUS WARD.
Artemus Ward Complete.

By EDMOND ABOUT.
The Fellah.

By HAMILTON AIDE.
Carr of Carrlyon. | Confidences.

By MARY ALBERT.
Brooke Finchley's Daughter.

By Mrs. ALEXANDER.
Maid, Wife or Widow? | Valerie's Fate.

By GRANT ALLEN.
Strange Stories. | For Maimie's Sake.
Philistia. | The Tents of Shem.
Babylon. | The Great Taboo.
The Devil's Die. | Dumaresq's Daughter.
This Mortal Coil. | The Duchess of Powys-
In all Shades. | land.
The Beckoning Hand. | Ivan Greet's Masterpiece.
Blood Royal. | The Scallywag.

By E. LESTER ARNOLD.
Phra the Phœnician.

By ALAN ST. AUBYN.
A Fellow of Trinity. | Master of St. Benedict's.
The Junior Dean. | To His Own Master.

By Rev. S. BARING GOULD.
Red Spider. | Eve.

By FRANK BARRETT.
Fettered for Life. | Honest Davie.
Little Lady Linton. | A Prodigal's Progress.
Between Life & Death. | Found Guilty.
The Sin of Olga Zassou- | A Recoiling Vengeance.
 lich. | For Love and Honour.
Folly Morrison. | John Ford; and His
Lieut. Barnabas | Helpmate.

SHELSLEY BEAUCHAMP.
Grantley Grange.

By WALTER BESANT.
Dorothy Forster. | For Faith and Freedom.
Children of Gibeon. | To Call Her Mine.
Uncle Jack. | The Bell of St. Paul's.
Herr Paulus. | Armorel of Lyonesse.
All Sorts and Condi- | The Holy Rose.
 tions of Men. | The Ivory Gate.
The Captains' Room. | St. Katherine's by the
All in a Garden Fair. | Tower.
The World Went Very | Verbena Camellia.
 Well Then. | The Rebel Queen.

By W. BESANT & J. RICE.
This Son of Vulcan. | The Ten Years' Tenant.
My Little Girl. | Ready-Money Mortiboy
The Case of Mr. Lucraft. | With Harp and Crown.
The Golden Butterfly. | 'Twas in Trafalgar's
By Celia's Arbour. | Bay.
The Monks of Thelema. | The Chaplain of the
The Seamy Side. | Fleet.

TWO-SHILLING NOVELS—*continued.*

By AMBROSE BIERCE.
In the Midst of Life.

By FREDERICK BOYLE.
Camp Notes. | Chronicles of No-man's
Savage Life. | Land.

By BRET HARTE.
Californian Stories. | Flip. | Maruja.
Gabriel Conroy. | A Phyllis of the Sierras.
The Luck of Roaring | A Waif of the Plains.
Camp. | A Ward of the Golden
An Heiress of Red Dog. | Gate.

By HAROLD BRYDGES.
Uncle Sam at Home.

By ROBERT BUCHANAN.
Shadow of the Sword. | The Martyrdom of Ma-
A Child of Nature. | deline.
God and the Man. | Annan Water.
Love Me for Ever. | The New Abelard.
Foxglove Manor. | Matt.
The Master of the Mine | The Heir of Linne.

By HALL CAINE.
The Shadow of a Crime. | The Deemster.
A Son of Hagar.

By Commander CAMERON.
The Cruise of the "Black Prince."

By Mrs. LOVETT CAMERON.
Deceivers Ever. | Juliet's Guardian.

By AUSTIN CLARE.
For the Love of a Lass.

By Mrs. ARCHER CLIVE.
Paul Ferroll.
Why Paul Ferroll Killed his Wife.

By MACLAREN COBBAN.
The Cure of Souls. | The Red Sultan.

By C. ALLSTON COLLINS.
The Bar Sinister.

MORT. & FRANCES COLLINS.
Sweet Anne Page. | Sweet and Twenty.
Transmigration. | The Village Comedy.
From Midnight to Mid- | You Play me False.
night. | Blacksmith and Scholar
A Fight with Fortune. | Frances.

By WILKIE COLLINS.
Armadale. | My Miscellanies.
After Dark. | The Woman in White.
No Name. | The Moonstone.
Antonina. | Man and Wife.
Basil. | Poor Miss Finch.
Hide and Seek. | The Fallen Leaves.
The Dead Secret. | Jezebel's Daughter
Queen of Hearts. | The Black Robe.
Miss or Mrs.? | Heart and Science.
The New Magdalen. | "I Say No!"
The Frozen Deep. | The Evil Genius.
The Law and the Lady. | Little Novels.
The Two Destinies. | Legacy of Cain.
The Haunted Hotel. | Blind Love.
A Rogue's Life.

By M. J. COLQUHOUN.
Every Inch a Soldier.

By DUTTON COOK.
Leo. | Paul Foster's Daughter.

By C. EGBERT CRADDOCK.
The Prophet of the Great Smoky Mountains.

By MATT CRIM.
Adventures of a Fair Rebel.

By B. M. CROKER.
Pretty Miss Nevill. | Bird of Passage.
Diana Barrington. | Proper Pride.
"To Let." | A Family Likeness.

By W. CYPLES.
Hearts of Gold.

By ALPHONSE DAUDET.
The Evangelist; or, Port Salvation.

By ERASMUS DAWSON.
The Fountain of Youth.

TWO-SHILLING N

By JAME
A Castle in Spain.

By J. LEI
Our Lady of Tears.

By CHAR
Sketches by Boz.
Oliver Twist.

By DIC
The Man-Hunter.
Tracked and Taken.
Caught at Last!
Wanted!
Who Poisoned He
Duncan?
Man from Manchest
A Detective's Triump
In the Grip of the L

By Mrs. ANN
A Point of Honour.

By M. BETI
Felicia.

By EDW.
Roxy.

By G. MA
The New Mistress.

By PERCY
Bella Donna.
Never Forgotten.
Polly.
Fatal Zero.

By P. FITZC
Strange Secrets.

ALBANY D
Filthy Lucre.

By R. E.
Olympia.
One by One.
A Real Queen.
Queen Cophetua.

By HAROL
Seth's Brother's Wi
Pref. by Sir I
Pandurang Hari.

By HAIN
One of Two.

By EDWA
The Capel Girls.

By GILI
A Strange Manuscr

By CHAR
Robin Gray.
Fancy Free.
For Lack of Gold.
What will the Wo
Say?
In Love and War.
For the King.
In Pastures Green.
Queen of the Meado
A Heart's Problem.
The Dead Heart.

By WILLI
Dr. Austin's Guests.
James Duke.

By ERNES
The Lost Heiress.
A Fair Colonist.

By HENR
A Noble Woman.

By CECI
Corinthia Marazion.

By SYDN
The Days of his Van

By JOHN
Brueton's Bayou

By ANDRE
Every-day Papers.

By Lady DI
Paul Wynter's Sacri

& WINDUS, PUBLISHERS, PICCADILLY.   31

s—continued.
HARDY.
16.

HARWOOD.

HAWTHORNE.
Beatrix Randolph.
Love—or a Name.
David Poindexter's Disappearance.
The Spectre of the Camera.

SIR HELPS.

HERMAN.

HILL.

HILL.

[EL HOEY.

E HOOPER.

HOPKINS.

GERFORD.
A Mental Struggle.
A Modern Circe.
Lady Verner's Flight.
RED HUNT.
Self-Condemned.
The Leaden Casket.
NGELOW.

AMESON.

CTT JAY.
Queen of Connaught.
KERSHAW.
ns.
E KING.
Passion's Slave
Bell Barry.

LEYS.

LINTON.
The Atonement of Leam Dundas.
With a Silken Thread.
The Rebel of the Family.
Sowing the Wind.

W. LUCY.

McCARTHY.
Camiola.
Donna Quixote.
Maid of Athens.
The Comet of a Season.
The Dictator.
Red Diamonds.
IACCOLL.
icket.
ACDONELL.

MACQUOID.
Lost Rose.

ALLOCK.
The New Republic.

Two-Shilling Novels—continued.
By FLORENCE MARRYAT.
Open ! Sesame ! | A Harvest of Wild Oats.
Fighting the Air. | Written in Fire.
By J. MASTERMAN.
Half-a-dozen Daughters.
By BRANDER MATTHEWS.
A Secret of the Sea.
By LEONARD MERRICK.
The Man who was Good.
By JEAN MIDDLEMASS.
Touch and Go. | Mr. Dorillion.
By Mrs. MOLESWORTH.
Hathercourt Rectory.
By J. E. MUDDOCK.
Stories Weird and Wonderful. | From the Bosom of the Deep.
The Dead Man's Secret.
By MURRAY and HERMAN.
One Traveller Returns. | The Bishops' Bible.
Paul Jones's Alias.
By D. CHRISTIE MURRAY.
A Model Father. | A Life's Atonement.
Joseph's Coat. | By the Gate of the Sea.
Coals of Fire. | A Bit of Human Nature.
Val Strange. | First Person Singular.
Old Blazer's Hero. | Bob Martin's Little
Hearts. | Girl.
The Way of the World. | Time's Revenges.
Cynic Fortune. | A Wasted Crime.
By HENRY MURRAY.
A Game of Bluff. | A Song of Sixpence.
By HUME NISBET.
"Bail Up ! " | Dr. Bernard St. Vincent.
By ALICE O'HANLON.
The Unforeseen. | Chance ? or Fate ?
By GEORGES OHNET.
Dr. Rameau. | A Weird Gift.
A Last Love.
By Mrs. OLIPHANT.
Whiteladies. | The Greatest Heiress in
The Primrose Path. | England.
By Mrs. ROBERT O'REILLY.
Phoebe's Fortunes.
By OUIDA.
Held in Bondage. | Two Little Wooden
Strathmore. | Shoes.
Chandos. | Moths.
Idalia. | Bimbi.
Under Two Flags. | Pipistrello.
Cecil Castlemaine's Gage | A Village Commune.
Tricotrin. | Wanda.
Puck. | Othmar.
Folle Farine. | Frescoes.
A Dog of Flanders. | In Maremma.
Pascarel. | Guilderoy.
Signa. | Ruffino.
Princess Napraxine. | Syrlin.
In a Winter City. | Santa Barbara.
Ariadne. | Ouida's Wisdom, Wit,
Friendship. | and Pathos.
MARGARET AGNES PAUL.
Gentle and Simple.
By C. L. PIRKIS.
Lady Lovelace.
By EDGAR A. POE.
The Mystery of Marie Roget.
By Mrs. CAMPBELL PRAED.
The Romance of a Station.
The Soul of Countess Adrian.
Outlaw and Lawmaker.
By E. C. PRICE.
Valentina. | Mrs. Lancaster's Rival.
The Foreigners. | Gerald.
By RICHARD PRYCE.
Miss Maxwell's Affections.

Found Dead.
The Best of Husbands.
Walter's Word.
Halves.
Fallen Fortunes.
Humorous Stories.
£200 Reward.
A Marine Residence.
Mirk Abbey.
By Proxy.
Under One Roof.
High Spirits.
Carlyon's Year.
From Exile.
For Cash Only.
Kit.
The Canon's Ward.
Sunny Stories.
Lost Sir Massingberd.
A Woman's Vengeance.
The Family Scapegrace.
Gwendoline's Harvest.
Like Father, Like Son.
Married Beneath Him.
Not Wooed, but Won.
Less Black than We're Painted.
Some Private Views.
A Grape from a Thorn.
The Mystery of Mirbridge.
The Word and the Will.
A Prince of the Blood.
A Trying Patient.

By CHARLES READE.
It is Never Too Late to Mend.
Christie Johnstone.
The Double Marriage.
Put Yourself in His Place.
Love Me Little, Love Me Long.
The Cloister and the Hearth.
The Course of True Love.
The Jilt.
The Autobiography of a Thief.
A Terrible Temptation.
Foul Play.
The Wandering Heir.
Hard Cash.
Singleheart and Doubleface.
Good Stories of Men and other Animals.
Peg Woffington.
Griffith Gaunt.
A Perilous Secret.
A Simpleton.
Readiana.
A Woman-Hater.

By Mrs. J. H. RIDDELL.
Weird Stories.
Fairy Water.
Her Mother's Darling.
The Prince of Wales's Garden Party.
The Uninhabited House.
The Mystery in Palace Gardens.
The Nun's Curse.
Idle Tales.

By AMELIE RIVES.
Barbara Dering.

By F. W. ROBINSON.
Women are Strange. | The Hands of Justice.

By JAMES RUNCIMAN.
Skippers and Shellbacks.
Grace Balmaign's Sweetheart.
Schools and Scholars.

By W. CLARK RUSSELL.
Round the Galley Fire.
On the Fo'k'sle Head.
In the Middle Watch.
A Voyage to the Cape.
A Book for the Hammock.
The Mystery of the "Ocean Star."
The Romance of Jenny Harlowe.
An Ocean Tragedy.
My Shipmate Louise.
Alone on a Wide Wide Sea.

GEORGE AUGUSTUS SALA.
Gaslight and Daylight.

By JOHN SAUNDERS.
Guy Waterman. | The Lion in the Path.

The Golden Hoop.
Hoodwinked.
By Devious Ways.
Burgo's Romance.
Quittance in Full.

By R. A. STERNDALE.
The Afghan Knife.

By R. LOUIS STEVENSON.
New Arabian Nights. | Prince Otto.

By BERTHA THOMAS.
Cressida.
Proud Maisie.
The Violin-Player.

By WALTER THORNBURY.
Tales for the Marines. | Old Stories Retold.

T. ADOLPHUS TROLLOPE.
Diamond Cut Diamond.

By F. ELEANOR TROLLOPE.
Like Ships upon the Sea.
Anne Furness.
Mabel's Progress.

By ANTHONY TROLLOPE.
Frau Frohmann.
Marion Fay.
Kept in the Dark.
John Caldigate.
The Way We Live Now.
The Land-Leaguers.
The American Senator.
Mr. Scarborough's Family.
The Golden Lion of Granpere.

By J. T. TROWBRIDGE.
Farnell's Folly.

By IVAN TURGENIEFF, &c.
Stories from Foreign Novelists.

By MARK TWAIN.
A Pleasure Trip on the Continent.
The Gilded Age.
Huckleberry Finn.
Mark Twain's Sketches.
Tom Sawyer.
A Tramp Abroad.
Stolen White Elephant.
Life on the Mississippi.
The Prince and the Pauper.
A Yankee at the Court of King Arthur.
The £1,000,000 Bank-Note.

By C. C. FRASER-TYTLER.
Mistress Judith.

By SARAH TYTLER.
The Bride's Pass.
Buried Diamonds.
St. Mungo's City.
Lady Bell.
Noblesse Oblige.
Disappeared.
The Huguenot Family.
The Blackhall Ghosts.
What She Came Through.
Beauty and the Beast.
Citoyenne Jaqueline.

By ALLEN UPWARD.
The Queen against Owen.

By AARON WATSON and LILLIAS WASSERMANN.
The Marquis of Carabas.

By WILLIAM WESTALL.
Trust-Money.

By Mrs. F. H. WILLIAMSON.
A Child Widow.

By J. S. WINTER.
Cavalry Life. | Regimental Legends.

ESTABLISHED 1851.
BIRKBECK BANK,
Southampton Buildings, Chancery Lane, London.

TWO-AND-A-HALF per CENT. INTEREST allowed on DEPOSITS, repayable on demand.

TWO per CENT. on CURRENT ACCOUNTS, on the minimum monthly balances, when not drawn below £100.

STOCKS, SHARES, and ANNUITIES purchased and sold.

SAVINGS DEPARTMENT.
For the encouragement of Thrift, the Bank receives small sums on deposit, and allows Interest monthly on each completed £1.

BIRKBECK BUILDING SOCIETY.
HOW TO PURCHASE A HOUSE for Two Guineas per Month.

BIRKBECK FREEHOLD LAND SOCIETY.
HOW TO PURCHASE A PLOT OF LAND for Five Shillings per Month.

The BIRKBECK ALMANACK, with full particulars, post free.

FRANCIS RAVENSCROFT, Manager.

OSBORNE, BAUER and CHEESEMAN'S
CELEBRATED SPECIALTIES.

IT SOFTENS & IMPROVES THE HANDS, FACE AND SKIN GENERALLY.

Sold by all Chemists and Stores, in Metallic Tubes, 6d. and 1s. Sample, post free, for 6 or 12 Stamps from the Sole Manufacturers.

Prevent CHAPS and Roughness of the Skin by using

"GLYMIEL SOAP."
(Registered.)

A refined and delicately perfumed Toilet Soap, possessing all the properties of the world renowned and celebrated "Glycerine and Honey Jelly." Admitted to be the leading preparation for softening and improving the Skin of old and young. Useful in all seasons.

Price 6d. per Tablet, or Three Tablets in Box, 1s. 6d., post free on receipt of stamps.

Sold by all Chemists, Perfumers and Stores. Prepared only by

OSBORNE, BAUER & CHEESEMAN, Perfumers to the Queen,

Sole Proprietors of "The Incomparable Smelling Salts" (*as supplied to the Queen*), "Baby's Soap," specially prepared for Children or Adults with Tender Skin, 6d., "Bauer's Head (and Bath) Soap," "Nafatha Soap" for Tender Feet, &c.

19, GOLDEN SQUARE, REGENT STREET, LONDON, W.

Awarded Six Gold and Prize Medals, 1884, the only Year we have Exhibited.

LORIMER'S

LORIMER'S COCA WINE.

For Drowsiness, Hunger, Fatigue, Exhaustion, Nervous Disorders, Indigestion, Debility, and all who feel below par.

A **Retired Aged Gentleman** writes—" I was led to try Lorimer's Coca Wine, and the effect was simply marvellous. My pulse rose to its old rate of 64, in a few days my appetite returned, and I have not known fatigue since, though out in my garden seven or eight hours every day. In fact, I am stronger now than I have been during the past five years, and the blessing I feel it, . . . no tongue can tell. My whole frame thrills with gratitude."*

*The original letter may be seen at our office, but we are not at liberty to publish the writer's name.

Invaluable, alike for the Robust or Invalids.

HOUSEHOLD

PARRISH'S
GOLD MEDAL CHEMICAL FOOD.

CAUTION.—The only Chemical Food officially recognised as "Parrish's" by a jury of Medical Experts is "Parrish's GOLD MEDAL Chemical Food." The proprietors would respectfully ask the public to refuse all substitutes and highly-injurious imitations, and to see their name is on the label.

COMFORTS

LORIMER'S
COMPOUND SYRUP OF THE HYPOPHOSPHITES.

Recommended by the Medical Profession throughout the World for its Vitalising and Strengthening Powers.

"NEWCASTLE-ON-TYNE, February 26th, 1897.

"For two months I have been suffering from SCIATICA, the result of overwork, over worry and exposure, and for some time was so bad as to be unable to put foot to ground. . . . I consider myself almost entirely indebted to your Syr. Hypophosph. Co. for the rapidity of my convalescence. Yours faithfully,
———, M.B., C.M."

SOLD EVERYWHERE.

Sole Proprietors and Manufacturers :—

LORIMER & CO., Britannia Row, London, N.

www.ingramcontent.com/pod-product-compliance
Lightning Source LLC
Chambersburg PA
CBHW032101220426
43664CB00008B/1096